BERTRAND RUSSELL'S THEORY OF KNOWLEDGE

BERTRAND RUSSELL'S THEORY OF KNOWLEDGE

by

ELIZABETH R. EAMES, Ph.D.

Southern Illinois University

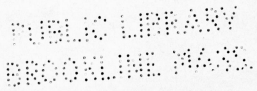
GEORGE BRAZILLER

NEW YORK

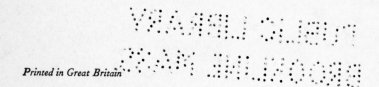

Printed in Great Britain

To My Parents

Vera and Frank Ramsden

PREFACE

In June of 1964 in London I had the privilege of meeting Bertrand Russell and of talking with him about some of the questions discussed in this book. Subsequently, in response to some articles I had written on his theory of knowledge, he wrote to me in a way which was both helpful and encouraging. For these kindnesses I wish to thank him.

I began my study of Russell's philosophy as a student at the University of Toronto and at Bryn Mawr College. Professors Isabel S. Stearns and Milton C. Nahm were particularly helpful when I was writing a dissertation on the controversy between John Dewey and Bertrand Russell in theory of knowledge. Of the colleagues and friends with whom I share an interest in Russell's philosophy, Professors A. C. Benjamin and Zora Lasch require special acknowledgment. In addition, the students in seminars on Russell's philosophy which I taught at Washington University and at Southern Illinois University provided the stimulus for the clarification of the views expressed here.

I wish to thank Southern Illinois University for the research grant with which this work was supported. The staff of Morris Library, particularly Professors Alan Cohn and Kathleen Eads, were of great assistance to me. I very much appreciate the translations done by Professor Paula Parish from Italian, and by Professor Cho Yee To from Chinese. For the typing of early drafts of the manuscript I wish to thank Miss Susan Brown and Mr Darryl Brown. I am especially grateful to Miss Pamela Seats for her typing and editing of the entire typescript. I appreciate the care and attention given this work by the late Sir Stanley Unwin and his staff.

For their understanding and cooperation during the writing of the book, I wish to express appreciation to Anne and to her grandparents, to whom the book is dedicated. I am most indebted to my philosophical partner and husband, S. Morris Eames.

ELIZABETH RAMSDEN EAMES

Acknowledgment is made to the following sources for permission to use material previously published:

Gerald Duckworth and Co., Ltd., London, and to Basic Books, Inc., New York: John Passmore, *A Hundred Years of Philosophy*, 1957.

The Library of Living Philosophers, Paul Arthur Schilpp, Editor. Vol. V, Northwestern University Press, Evanston, 1944.

The Journal of Philosophy: W. V. Quine, 'Russell's Ontological Development', Vol. 53, No. 20, November 10, 1966.

The Monist: Eugene Freeman, Editor. The Open Court Publishing Co. Lasalle, Illinois, Vol. 25, No. 2, 1915.

Proceedings of the Aristotelian Society, Vol. 36, 1936.

The Bertrand Russell Archives of McMaster University, Hamilton, Ontario, Canada, and Bertrand Russell for use of correspondence.

CONTENTS

CHAPTER I

INTRODUCTION

In 1972 a hundred years will have passed since the birth of Bertrand Russell, and in his long career he has published over ninety books on topics ranging from mathematics to world affairs. His name and his ideas are known to a wide audience, and his philosophy is recognized as one of the most significant of the century by academic philosophers. Few in the English-speaking world would deny that Russell is a major figure in the philosophy of the twentieth century.[1] In spite of this, Russell's philosophical work suffers from neglect and misunderstanding. The neglect is evident in the few full-length studies of his work which have been undertaken, and in the cursory treatment which is given of his thought in historical surveys of our century. The misunderstanding and misinterpretation of his philosophy can be seen in those shorter papers and articles which take some aspect of Russell's thought as their special target of criticism. For instance, in *The Philosophy of Bertrand Russell*,[2] 'The Library of Living Philosophers' volume devoted to his thought, the most striking feature of the book is the number of misinterpretations requiring correction by Russell in his reply to his critics. Morris Weitz and Roderick M. Chisholm, whose analyses are generally commended, have misinterpreted Russell's view of qualities such as 'red' as universals, whereas for him they are particulars.[3] James Feibleman has misunderstood Russell's view of relations and confused relations with logical connectives, and hence has failed to understand Russell's 'logical realism'.[4] Max Black's essay on Russell's theory of language is said, by Russell, to rest on a number of misunderstandings, that the ideal language must consist only of proper names, that one cannot be acquainted with relations, that a universal word can be uttered only in the presence of an instance of it.[5] Ernest Nagel has misunderstood his theory of matter.[6] W. T. Stace has interpreted neutral monism as equivalent to phenomenalism and missed the continuity of ideas from *The Analysis of Mind* to *The Analysis of Matter*.[7] There are other misunderstandings as well.[8]

Other treatments of Russell's philosophy have committed similar errors. Albert William Levi in *Philosophy and the Modern World*, although he works carefully through some of Russell's writings, presents Russell as, with Rudolf Carnap, exemplifications of the position of logical empiricism. To two of the six 'doctrinal theses of logical empiricism' set forth by Levi, Russell does not adhere, that is, the rejection of all metaphysical assertions and the principle of verifiability.[9] This latter principle is the basis of Russell's rejection of logical positivism as expressed with definite emphasis in two important works.[10] However, although Levi notes that Russell was sometimes critical of logical positivism he is mistaken in presenting him as a 'case study' in positivism, as well as attributing phenomenalism 'with a vengeance' to him.[11] In a paper tracing Russell's ontology, W. V. Quine also attributed phenomenalism to Russell, missing the tentative nature of the hypothesis of logical constructs in *Our Knowledge of the External World*.[12] Like Stace, Quine failed to see the significance of the causal theory of perception which is part of Russell's 'neutral monism'.[13]

Although misunderstandings of the works of philosophers are by no means uncommon, in this case there seems to be a common element in misinterpretations of Russell's work. One might call this 'the error of historical perspective'. Russell's work in mathematical logic of the first two decades of this century, *The Principles of Mathematics, Principia Mathematica*, and *The Introduction to Mathematical Philosophy*,[14] was of revolutionary importance and had an impact on many contemporary philosophers. The development of the new techniques of mathematical logic and the application of these techniques to epistemological problems, in *The Problems of Philosophy, Our Knowledge of the External World, Mysticism and Logic*, and *The Philosophy of Logical Atomism*,[15]

14

were strongly influential on the emerging Vienna Circle, and through them on later generations of logical positivists or logical empiricists. In this sense Russell might be called a 'father' of logical positivism; he is widely recognized as contributing to this movement,[16] and acknowledges himself to be sympathetic with it.[17] For this reason, Russell's later carefully reasoned criticisms of logical positivists, and the important respects in which his mature philosophy differs from theirs have tended to be forgotten or ignored. Both the logical empiricists themselves, and the critics of logical empiricism, have come to class Russell as himself a logical empiricist. In one case he is accepted, in the other he is rejected; but in both contexts his own contributions to philosophy, and, especially, the work he had done since the 1920s have been neglected. For instance, in *Logical Positivism*, the first essay A. J. Ayer includes is Russell's 'Logical Atomism', which is dated 1924.[18] In the collection of essays edited by Robert Charles Marsh, *Logic and Knowledge: Essays 1901–1950*,[19] eight of the ten essays pre-date 1930, and the collection includes 'Logical Atomism' of 1924 and 'The Philosophy of Logical Atomism' of 1919. In both collections of essays the interest is historical rather than analytic, and it is not maintained that a historical interest in the work of Russell is not legitimate or important. However, if the interest in a philosopher is biased towards the historical, the effect may be to distort the nature of his philosophy. The distortion involved is even more evident in the work of another group of philosophers for whom Russell is an important progenitor, that of contemporary British language analysts.

In the case of the treatment of Russell's thought by the followers of Wittgenstein II (as Russell labelled the Wittgenstein of *Philosophical Investigations*[20]), there is also a tendency to treat Russell historically. The interest here is centered on two aspects of Russell's thought. One is the period in which he and Wittgenstein agreed, ending with the publication of the *Tractatus Logico-Philosophicus*,[21] and with Russell's *Philosophy of Logical Atomism*.[22] Hence G. J. Warnock in *English Philosophy since 1900* concentrates on this period in Russell's development, although he enters a qualification to the effect that he has purposively ignored other and important aspects of Russell's thought.[23] John Passmore's book, *A Hundred Years of Philosophy*, devotes a chapter to G. E. Moore and Russell.[24] He notes the tendency of recent philosophers to overlook Russell's later work, but he attributes this to the contemporary distaste for large-scale philosophical 'murals' such as those of *History of Western Philosophy* and *Human Knowledge*.[25] It is interesting that of the twenty-six pages Passmore himself spends on Russell only two deal with work after *The Analysis of Matter*.[26]

The other aspect of Russell's work that interests the language analysts is what they regard as the inimical influence of Russell's view of language, of logic, and of the business of philosophy. Some have turned with particular intentness to reject and criticize Russell's work because of its influence on contemporary thought, an influence they regard as one that must be undone before sound philosophizing can begin. In an essay on 'Theory of Meaning', Gilbert Ryle traces the pathology of the misleading error of the denotative or name theory of meaning.[27] Although he credits Russell with some intermittent or dim insight into the weakness of treating all words as names, the main tenor of his argument is critical of Russell, and commendatory of the later Wittgenstein. In other cases there are attacks on Russell directly, by J. O. Urmson on his concept of philosophical analysis,[28] by P. F. Strawson on his theory of descriptions,[29] and by Paul Edwards on his theory of induction.[30] Russell himself has answered the first two attacks on his position and has commented on the prevalent neglect of his own later writings.[31] In the case of the article by Edwards, 'Bertrand Russell's Doubts about Induction', what is particularly striking is that, although this article was first printed in 1949, it refers almost exclusively to *The Problems of Philosophy* (with the exception of one reference to the treatment of Hume in *History of Western Philosophy*), and makes no mention of the major work *Human Knowledge: its Scope and Limits*, which had come out in 1948, and dealt mainly with the 'principles of non-demonstrative inference', the very problem of induction which

Edwards purported to discuss. Edwards is concerned in this
article to use Russell's early treatment of induction as an example
of the kind of error which philosophers of the past committed
through an insufficient analysis of concepts such as 'induction'.
However, this does not make his neglect of the later development
of Russell's thought excusable; it is an example of the distortion
of taking an exclusively historical view of Russell's thought. It is
interesting that, in criticizing the argument form used in Edwards'
article, Urmson defends the philosophical question of the kind of
the 'validity of induction' which Edwards had been attacking,
but makes no mention of the distortion of Russell involved in
it.[32]

The restriction of seeing Russell always in a historical context
which stresses his early work is perhaps understandable, although
unfortunate, when the context of the consideration of his philosophy is either to connect his early views with later developments
of them in logical empiricism, or to contrast these early views
with later rejections of them in linguistic analysis. But we find a
neglect of Russell's mature thought occurring also in contexts
which might be thought 'neutral', that is, in the context of the
presentation of a variety of alternative views on a given topic. In
a recent scholarly work, *Philosophical Problems of Space and
Time*,[33] Adolf Grünbaum analyses the philosophical consequences
of the scientific developments in the concept of space, time, and
cause, stressing particularly the developments of the last fifty
years. His references to contemporary philosophers who have
worked in this area are extensive; the work of A. N. Whitehead,
for instance, is discussed in two different chapters. Yet the only
references to the work of Russell occur in the context of the turn
of the century discussion of Poincaré and Russell.[34] In an extensive
bibliography of literature on the philosophical implications of the
concepts of space and time, Grünbaum's references to Russell's
works include only items which were originally published prior
to 1914. Yet Russell wrote extensively on this subject; following
the lead of Whitehead's method of extensive abstraction, he
employed his method of construction to all the basic concepts of

physics, notably in *The Analysis of Matter*, in a technical treatment of time of 1936,[35] and again in *Human Knowledge*.

The distorting effects of the contemporary context in which Russell's historical importance leads to the neglect of his mature philosophy can be summed up by saying that Russell is, in one sense, no longer a strictly contemporary philosopher. This is due not so much to the unusually long work span from 1895 to the present, but to the fact that in the last forty years the mainstream of development in Anglo-American philosophy has diverged from Russell. Present philosophers are close enough to feel Russell's influence as a pioneer of their own positions, or as a false prophet from which philosophy is still striving to be fully liberated. In neither case is the historical perspective long enough for justice to be done to Russell's position as a whole.

It is also true that the way Russell writes has had an effect on his philosophical reputation. Russell regards philosophy as akin to science in this respect, that it is improper to carry on one's inquiries with the consistency of dogma in mind.[36] To change one's mind, to correct earlier errors, is commendable, and no favoured status is attached to unchanging beliefs or philosophic systems. Accordingly, Russell has passed from the consideration of one problem to the consideration of a different problem; each book is an inquiry of its own. He did not attempt to employ the same terminology or to make any continuity between his present inquiry and what he had done before. Usually he did not stop to correct misunderstandings of his own philosophy, or to show any continuity in the development of his own work. In recent years there has been some change in this respect; the short history of his intellectual development in 'The Library of Living Philosophers' volume, and the systematic correction of his critics in the reply to that volume, are useful in helping the reader reconstruct elements of unity and consistency which had not been evident before.[37] The accident of the death of Alan Wood produced Russell's systematic reconstruction of his own intellectual career, when he completed Wood's uncompleted study in *My Philosophical Development*. Both of these works came after many philosophers' opinions of Russell had already been formulated, and they have had little observable effect in current discussion. It seems likely that future scholars will find it easier to come to the study of Russell with fewer presuppositions because of *My Philosophical Development*.

Other aspects of Russell's way of writing philosophy have contributed to the misunderstanding of his views. He has been generous about acknowledging the influence of the thoughts of others on his own development. He mentions explicitly the influence of A. N. Whitehead, for instance, in attributing to him the method of 'extensive abstraction'.[38] William James and American realists are acknowledged as helping to bring about his adoption of 'neutral monism'.[39] Russell's early acknowledgement of his debt to 'my friend and former pupil Ludwig Wittgenstein' was the first notice the English-speaking world had of the work of one who was to become a major figure.[40] In addition, Russell refers to the contributions in conversation of many minor figures, students, or friends with whom he discussed philosophical issues. This punctiliousness in giving credit wherever any other person has had a share in the forming of his views is in line with the view of scientific inquiry as a co-operative venture, but in the eyes of Russell's philosophical critics it has seemed an evidence of fickleness and instability in one who is influenced by each new wind of doctrine.[41]

Another habit of Russell's writing has had a share in producing an impression of numerous changes in thought. Russell is always careful to note where his opinions have changed, and where a formerly held opinion is no longer regarded as tenable. He is not only willing to change his mind, but scrupulous about warning his readers against his own former errors. Neither of these habits is common among philosophical writers, and they have increased the conviction of Russell's philosophical instability. As a matter of fact, most of the changes in Russell's thought have been on relatively less important aspects of his philosophy, and they have come about through the more rigorous application of a consistent method.[42] But this has not been clear to readers. It is understandable that A. N. Whitehead should be led to call Russell 'a Platonic dialogue in himself',[43] and that C. D. Broad should have made his famous remark that Bertrand Russell produces a new system of philosophy every few years.[44] The general impression of numerous changes in Russell's thought has produced a tendency among his critics to overlook the very many respects in which there has been a steady purpose, repeated work on the same set of problems, and continuity in the changes that have occurred through the use of a consistent method.[45]

Russell's philosophy has had its share of commentary and analysis in professional journals and reviews. However, there have been few large scale or comprehensive studies of his philosophy. The best published book in English on Russell's philosophy known to me is that of Charles A. Fritz, Jr., *Bertrand Russell's Construction of the External World*.[46] This is a careful and extended treatment of the method of construction as employed in Russell's philosophy. It is limited in that Fritz has restricted his consideration of analytic method to the method of construction as exemplified in the construction of the external world, of material objects, and of the entities of physics. The excellent study of Erik Götlind, *Bertrand Russell's Theories of Causation* follows the modifications made by Russell in response to new developments in physics in his concept of cause and causal laws.[47] It is of restricted scope, but of careful scholarship.

The essay of Morris Weitz in *The Philosophy of Bertrand Russell*, 'Analysis and the Unity of Russell's Philosophy', is a particularly valuable contribution to the understanding of Russell's method of analysis. This essay was highly commended by Russell himself, who found only 'a few misunderstandings' in it.[48] This essay is an abbreviated version of Weitz' doctoral dissertation, which has not been published, but which is a thorough study of the method of analysis.[49] Another careful study of Russell's logical atomism is that of the unpublished doctoral dissertation of A. C. Benjamin,[50] a former colleague from whom I learned much of Russell's early philosophy. Other books on Bertrand Russell's philosophy of interest are: Alan Dorward, *Bertrand*

Russell: A Short Guide to His Philosophy,[51] and R. Thalheimer, *A Critical Exposition of the Epistemology and Psycho-Physical Doctrines of Bertrand Russell*.[52] The first of these is a sketch which might serve as an introduction to the study of Russell for someone without philosophical training. The second is an earlier study and adds little to the understanding of Russell's mature philosophy.

In a recent work, *Bertrand Russell and the British Tradition in Philosophy*,[53] D. F. Pears analyses Russell's ideas in theory of knowledge during the period 1905 to 1919, especially in relation to Hume and Wittgenstein. The limitation of the topic restricts the significance of the work for Russell's thought as a whole. A book of essays, *Bertrand Russell: Philosopher of the Century*, edited by Ralph Schoenman,[54] contains much of interest to students of Russell. One group of these essays contains personal memories of Russell's life, another group concerns Russell's public life, a third group contains current work in mathematical logic in the tradition of *Principia Mathematica*. Two essays are of particular relevance to the work undertaken here: 'An Appraisal of Bertrand Russell's Philosophy' by A. J. Ayer, and 'Russell's Concept of Philosophy' by Werner Bloch.

The preliminary essay with which Alan Wood began what was to have been a full-length study of Russell's philosophy is suggestive and promising. The clear writing and careful scholarship, in addition to the advantage of personal friendship with Russell, all of which are evident in Wood's biography of Russell, *The Passionate Sceptic*,[55] would have made his study of Russell's philosophy extremely important and valuable. It is unfortunate that his death prevented the completion of his work; however, we are fortunate to have his work, completed by Russell himself in the book, *My Philosophical Development*. Bertrand Russell is still the best guide to Bertrand Russell, and his book traces the chronological development of his thought, his changing interests, the reasons for the rejection of some of his earlier views, the other philosophers who influenced and interested him, and his present philosophical view of the world.

The present study is intended to fill a gap which these earlier and excellent studies have left vacant. Where *My Philosophical Development* is presented chronologically, and is expository and summarizing in purpose, this study will be analytic and critical in purpose; that is, the intent of the study is to examine certain central themes in the philosophy of Bertrand Russell, to trace the way these themes have worked out in his mature philosophy, and to raise questions concerning their outcome and their compatibility with one another. In the course of doing this, consideration will be given to some of the chief criticisms and interpretations which have been presented by Russell's critics. In contrast to the studies of Fritz, Götlind, and Weitz, the intent is to make this study more extensive in that it will deal with all aspects of Russell's theory of knowledge, rather that with only the construction of the external world, or the treatment of causation, or the method of analysis. While I am indebted to the careful and detailed studies of these authors, it seems that it is now time to look back over a long lifetime of philosophical activity on the part of one of our foremost philosophers and ask what it all amounts to and what can be learned from it.

A question might be raised about the description of the scope of this study since it has been indicated that it is intended to be comprehensive and raise issues of central importance to Bertrand Russell's philosophy, yet, at the same time, it is restricted to Russell's theory of knowledge. It might be asked, can this be considered a comprehensive treatment of Russell's thought when it leaves out the extensive literature of Russell's writings on world affairs, on politics, on social questions, on education, and on ethics? For instance, *The Philosophy of Bertrand Russell* is more comprehensive in that it includes essays on his mathematical logic, his psychology, his metaphysics, his principles of ethics, his philosophy of religion, his social philosophy, his political and economic philosophy, his educational philosophy, and his philosophy of history.[56] None of these will be central themes in this work, and most of them will be excluded completely. I have sought to avoid direct confrontation with the difficult question of deciding which of Russell's ninety books and numerous articles are philosophy and which are not, by describing my task as the analysis of Russell's theory of knowledge, without specifying how this is related to any other division of his philosophy. However, I believe certain observations may be made here.

In the first place, Russell has said repeatedly that he did not always write as a professional philosopher, but was often writing for a different audience with a different purpose. He saw no reason for a professional philosopher not being allowed to have his opinions and passionate convictions, on political and other matters, and if he has them, why should he not voice them? But when he does so, his words are not intended to be taken as part of his philosophy.[57] In his reply to the essays of 'The Library of Living Philosophers' volume, he sets aside some of the essays as being from a different area of philosophy:

'I come now to what is, for me, an essentially different department of philosophy—I mean the part that depends upon ethical considerations. I should like to exclude all value judgments from philosophy, except that this would be too violent a breach with usage. The only matter concerned with ethics that I can regard as properly belonging to philosophy is the argument that ethical propositions should be expressed in the optative mood, not in the indicative.'[58]

The decision as to whether to include at least part of ethics in philosophy or not has never been entirely settled by Russell. In the introduction to *Human Society in Ethics and Politics*, he commented that he had originally intended to include the discussion of ethics in his book on 'Human Knowledge', but that he decided not to do so because he was uncertain 'as to the sense in which ethics can be regarded as "knowledge"'.[59] He is even more definite about excluding political and economic theories from the scope of philosophy.[60] 'Philosophy of history' he regards as a mistake.[61] He does not, in 'The Library of Living Philosophers' volume, exclude mathematical logic, or metaphysics, or psychology from the scope of philosophy. It seems clear from other evidence that mathematical logic has philosophical aspects, although Russell distinguishes between logic and philosophy.[62] As to psychology, Russell has often attempted to use evidence and hypotheses from psychology in his theory of knowledge. In this he treats psychology as he does physics; it provides data for the kinds of philosophical problems with which he is concerned.[63] Metaphysics is a different matter. Some metaphysics is criticized by Russell for being speculative and imaginative rather than controlled and logical,[64] but this does not mean that metaphysical questions are to be excluded from the scope of philosophy, or that he does not himself sometimes deal with 'what there is'.[65]

At a later point the relations between logic, philosophy, and science in Russell's conception of philosophy will be discussed. It is sufficient for introductory purposes to observe that Russell did not intend his use of the term philosophy to conflict with traditional meanings of the term. He did feel, however, that much that philosophers of the past had claimed to know including the answers to such questions as, Does the soul survive death?, Is the will free?, What is the essence of God?, and What is the ultimate nature of the universe? are, in fact, beyond the reach of our knowledge. As a corrective for the presumptuous claims of such philosophy he proposed a certain kind of philosophic method.[66] However, the wonderings of men which go beyond the present scope of our science are to be respected; from them come suggestions which may later bear important philosophic and scientific truth. One cannot be unduly restrictive about the kinds of questions that can be asked. In this sense, philosophy may include many kinds of subject matters.

However, when it is a matter of the kinds of philosophical questions which Bertrand Russell himself regards as important and which form the subjects of his inquiries, these are mainly epistemological. He has written over his long life on the relation of experience to the results of scientific inquiry, of the relation of common sense knowledge to experience, and of the relation of language to what language is about. In this sense, theory of knowledge has been a central concern of Russell's philosophizing. He commented on his own work:

My philosophical development may be divided into various stages according to the problems with which I have been concerned and the men whose work has influenced me. There is only one constant preoccupation: I have throughout been anxious to discover how much we can be said to know and with what degree of certainty or doubtfulness.'[67]

For these reasons, taking Bertrand Russell's theory of knowledge as a central theme of his philosophizing seems justified.

In the ensuing chapters I will analyse Bertrand Russell's views around four basic topics. In the second chapter the concept of the nature of philosophy will be discussed, emphasizing particularly Russell's way of distinguishing between logic and philosophy, and between science and philosophy. I will review the specific philosophic tasks which Russell set for himself in his different works, and the specific questions which were excluded from the scope of his work. The chapter will conclude with Russell's own summing up of his lifetime of philosophical activity, the degree to which he thought that he had been successful and the degree to which he thought that he had failed. Particular attention will be paid to the retrospective treatment of the 'prejudices' which have dominated his philosophizing, and which Russell set forth in *My Philosophical Development*.

In the third chapter the chief topic will be the method of analysis in philosophy, as Russell understood and practiced this method. The logical foundations of the analytic method will be discussed in the context of the philosophical applications of the work which Russell did in mathematics and mathematical logic. Then the use of the logical-analytic method in epistemology will be traced out in the programme of scrutiny and criticism which Russell proposed for theory of knowledge. Finally, particular attention will be paid to linguistic analysis as this was employed by Russell in the practice of epistemological analysis.

In the fourth chapter, the chief concern will be Russell's empiricism. The view of experience which Russell modelled on Hume will be described, and the kind of commitment to empirical method and empirical data which were constant factors in his philosophy will be traced out. Our second concern will be to trace in detail the changes which occurred in Russell's analysis of experience, in the treatment of sensation, the possibility of immediate knowledge, and the relation of perception to sensation. This will lead to a discussion of the two kinds of analysis by which Russell sought to support his changing views of perceptual knowledge—linguistic analysis and behavioural analysis. The chapter will conclude with a discussion of the epistemological problem of the analysis to data as this developed throughout Russell's empiricism. The outcome of his empiricism, as this is reflected in *Human Knowledge*, with the problems and limitations of his mature theory of knowledge will be the concluding topic of the fourth chapter.

It must be recognized that Russell has objected to the application of labels to philosophical positions, in particular to his own point of view, or to his opinions in one 'phase' or another. He feels that such labels are misleading, as the positions of individual philosophers are often not as far apart as the labels of 'schools' would indicate.[68] In this he is on sound historical and critical grounds, and here there has been an attempt to avoid such labels as 'logical atomism period' or 'nominalism'. It has been necessary, however, to point to certain persistent emphases in his theory of knowledge and to refer to these under some convenient terminology. For this reason, the terms 'analytic method', 'empiricism' and 'realism' have been chosen to refer to central themes in Russell's thought. But in using these terms, the intent is not to identify Russell with a specific school of British empiricism, for instance, but rather to use a term which can be given detailed meaning in the description of experience and use of the term 'experience' which Russell develops. In the case of 'realism', a particular caution is needed since this term has been applied so often to specific philosophic contexts, yet these different contexts have had little in common. The term here is given an extended explanation, and is chosen particularly in an effort to free Russell from what is regarded as opposed and distorting labels, those of 'phenomenalist' and 'positivist'.

The fifth chapter will be concerned with Russell's 'realism', both metaphysical and epistemological. It is maintained that, although important changes did occur in what may be called realism with respect to universals, that is, classes, relations, numbers, and abstract entities, there is a sense in which Russell always has been in some degree, however limited, a metaphysical realist. It is also maintained that from the time he abandoned idealism he was, and remained, a realist with respect to the independent existence of the object of knowledge, and that this is reflected in his treatment of belief, of proposition, of fact, of knowledge, and of truth. The common interpretation of Russell as at least a sometime phenomenalist is rejected. Accordingly, the problem of reference will be discussed in the different contexts of the reference of experience, of beliefs, of propositions, of sentences, of symbols, and of bodies of knowledge to what they are all about, or refer to. The topics of scientific realism, belief, truth, knowledge, probability, universals, and 'what may be' will provide the sequence of topics for the fifth chapter.

When the three central themes of Russell's epistemology, his analytic method, his empiricism, and his realism, are traced out, the continuity of Russell's thought becomes evident. The final task is to raise questions concerning the clarity, completeness, and consistency with which these concepts have been developed, and the success which they have had in solving the problems Russell set. First, I will consider the challenges offered to his analytic method by philosophical critics and the degree to which this criticism appears to be justified. Then I will discuss the problems connected with Russell's empiricism, both those raised by his critics, and the more serious ones he himself raised concerning it. Thirdly, I will deal with the critical analysis of the problems of his 'realism' as these are reflected in the misunderstandings and misgivings of his critics, and in the doubts of Russell himself.

Finally, the pervasive difficulties of the compatibility of these three different themes will be traced out and an evaluation of the remaining unsolved problems attempted.

NOTES TO CHAPTER I

1. Russell's importance in philosophy in this century is described in detail by W. V. Quine: 'Russell's books have run to forty, and his philosophical influence, direct and indirect, over this long period has been unequalled.' In 'Russell's Ontological Development', in 'Symposium: The Philosophy of Bertrand Russell'. This was held at the meeting of the American Philosophical Association, Philadelphia, Pennsylvania, December 29, 1966. Quine's paper is published in *The Journal of Philosophy*, Vol. LXIII, No. 21, November 10, 1966, 657.

2. *The Philosophy of Bertrand Russell*, 'The Library of Living Philosophers', Vol. V, edited by Paul Arthur Schilpp, The Northwestern University Press, Evanston and Chicago, 1944.

3. *Ibid.* Russell, 'Reply to Criticisms', p. 685, referring to Morris Weitz, 'Analysis and the Unity of Russell's Philosophy', pp. 55–122. 'Reply to Criticisms,' p. 714, referring to Roderick M. Chisholm, 'Russell on the Foundations of Empirical Knowledge', pp. 419–44.

4. *Ibid.* Russell, 'Reply to Criticisms', pp. 686–90, referring to James Feibleman, 'A Reply to Bertrand Russell's Introduction to the Second Edition of *The Principles of Mathematics*'. In spite of Russell's extensive rejection of Feibleman's interpretation of his views, Feibleman subsequently republished his essay without change, argument, or acknowledgement of Russell's comments. See James Feibleman, *The Revival of Realism*, The University of North Carolina Press, 1946; also, James Feibleman, *Inside the Great Mirror*, Martinus Nijhoff, The Hague, 1958.

5. Russell, 'Reply to Criticisms', pp. 691–5, referring to Max Black, 'Russell's Philosophy of Language', pp. 227–56, in *The Philosophy of Bertrand Russell*.

6. Russell, 'Reply to Criticisms', pp. 700–6, referring to Ernest Nagel, 'Russell's Philosophy of Science', *The Philosophy of Bertrand Russell*. It is interesting that in spite of the fact that Russell claimed that Nagel had misunderstood his view of matter, the Nagel essay was republished without change or comment in Ernest Nagel, *Sovereign Reason*, The Free Press, Glencoe, Illinois, 1954.

7. Russell, 'Reply to Criticisms', pp. 706–10, referring to W. T. Stace, 'Russell's Neutral Monism', pp. 351–84, in *The Philosophy of Bertrand Russell*.

8. *Ibid.* See the essays in the entire volume.

9. Albert William Levi, *Philosophy and the Modern World*, The University of Indiana Press, 1953, pp. 343–5.

10. Bertrand Russell, *An Inquiry into Meaning and Truth*, George Allen and Unwin, London, 1940, Chapters X, XI, and XII. Bertrand Russell, *Human Knowledge: Its Scope and Limits*, George Allen and Unwin, London, 1948, pp. 445–52.

11. Levi, *Philosophy and the Modern World*, p. 352.

12. Quine, 'Russell's Ontological Development', p. 667.

13. Stace, 'Russell's Neutral Monism', p. 707.

14. Bertrand Russell, *The Principles of Mathematics*, Cambridge University Press, 1903, George Allen and Unwin, London, 1950.
Alfred North Whitehead and Bertrand Russell, *Principia Mathematica*, Cambridge University Press, Vol. I, 1910, Vol. II, 1912, Vol. III, 1913.
Bertrand Russell, *Introduction to Mathematical Philosophy*, George Allen and Unwin, London, 1919.

15. Bertrand Russell, *The Problems of Philosophy*, Oxford University Press, 1912.
Bertrand Russell, *Our Knowledge of the External World*, First published by The Open Court Publishing Company, LaSalle, Illinois, 1914; revised ed., George Allen and Unwin, London, 1926.
Bertrand Russell, *Mysticism and Logic* (first published as *Philosophical Essays*, 1910); 2nd ed., George Allen and Unwin, London, 1917.
Bertrand Russell, 'The Philosophy of Logical Atomism', *The Monist*, Vol. 28, October, 1918, pp. 495–527. Lectures delivered in London, 1918. Reprinted in Bertrand Russell, *Logic and Knowledge: Essays 1901–1950*, ed. Robert C. Marsh, George Allen and Unwin, London, 1956, pp. 175–282.

16. Hans Reichenbach, 'Bertrand Russell's Logic', in *The Philosophy of Bertrand Russell*. Also, A. J. Ayer, 'Editor's Introduction', in *Logical Positivism*, ed. A. J. Ayer, The Free Press, Glencoe, Illinois, 1959.

17. Russell, *My Philosophical Development*, George Allen and Unwin, London, 1959, p. 216.

18. Ayer (ed.), *Logical Positivism*.

19. Russell, *Logic and Knowledge*.

20. Russell, *My Philosophical Development*, p. 216.

21. Ludwig Wittgenstein, *Tractatus Logico-Philosophicus*, Routledge and Kegan Paul, London, 1922.

22. Russell, 'The Philosophy of Logical Atomism', 1918.

23. G. J. Warnock, *English Philosophy since 1900*, Oxford University Press, London, 1958, p. 42.
24. John Passmore, *A Hundred Years of Philosophy*, Gerald Duckworth, London, 1957, pp. 215–41.
25. *Ibid.*, p. 215.
26. *Ibid.*, On the later Russell, see pp. 239–41.
27. Gilbert Ryle, 'Theory of Meaning', in *British Philosophy in Mid-Century*, ed. C. A. Mace, George Allen and Unwin, London, 1957.
28. J. O. Urmson, *Philosophical Analysis*, Oxford, at the Clarendon Press, 1956. See particularly Chapters 9 and 10.
29. P. F. Strawson, 'On Referring', *Mind*, Vol. LIX, 1950, pp. 320–44. Reprinted in *Essays in Conceptual Analysis*, ed. Antony Flew, Macmillan, London, 1956.
30. Paul Edwards, 'Russell's Doubts About Induction', *Mind*, Vol. LVIII, No. 23, April 1949. Reprinted in *Logic and Language* (First Series), ed. Antony Flew, Basil Blackwell, Oxford, 1951, pp. 55–79.
31. Russell, *My Philosophical Development*, Chapter XVIII. In referring to Urmson's arguments, Russell comments: 'And there is one important respect in which, from his own point of view, his book must be judged defective. He avowedly does not notice any writings of the schools which he is criticizing that have appeared during the last twenty years. The Logical Positivists and I have in various respects tried to remedy what seemed to us defects in our doctrines, but such attempts are not noticed by Mr Urmson. In this he is only following the practice of the whole school to which he belongs', p. 216. See also Russell's comments on p. 228.
32. J. O. Urmson, 'Some Questions Concerning Validity', *Essays in Conceptual Analysis*, pp. 120–33.
33. Adolf Grünbaum, *Philosophical Problems of Space and Time*, Alfred A. Knopf, New York, 1963.
34. *Ibid.*, pp. 44–8.
35. Bertrand Russell, 'On Order in Time', read to the Cambridge Philosophical Society in March of 1936, it first appeared in their *Proceedings*. It is reprinted in *Logic and Knowledge*, pp. 345–64.
36. Bertrand Russell, *Preface to Bertrand Russell's Dictionary of Mind, Matter and Morals*, ed., with an Introduction by Lester E. Dennon. Philosophical Library, New York, 1952. Russell says, 'But the kind of philosophy that I value and have endeavoured to pursue is scientific in the sense that there is some definite knowledge to be obtained and that new discoveries can make the admission of former error inevitable to any candid mind'.

37. Russell, 'My Mental Development', and 'Reply to Criticisms' in *The Philosophy of Bertrand Russell.*
38. Russell, *Our Knowledge of the External World*, p. 8, and p. 131. Russell, *My Philosophical Development*, p. 12; p. 103.
39. Russell, *My Philosophical Development*, p. 13; p. 135. Russell, *The Analysis of Mind*, George Allen and Unwin, London, 1921, pp. 23–6.
40. Russell, 'The Philosophy of Logical Atomism', the prefatory note, in Marsh, p. 177.
41. Passmore, *A Hundred Years of Philosophy*, p. 216. 'There is no trace of insularity in Russell; and he is always ready to admit, even at times to exaggerate, his indebtedness to his predecessors. His work displays, indeed, a quite unusual capacity for *learning* from his fellow-philosophers, even when they are foreigners, a capacity which has brought a certain amount of approbrium about his head and certainly complicates the task of a historian.' If the reader is puzzled about the reason for this lack of insularity complicating the historian's task, in view of the reference to Russell's habit of documenting his indebtedness, he is referred to page seven where Passmore admits or claims his history to be 'insular'. Alan Wood also comments on Russell's 'over-generosity in acknowledging his debts to others'. *My Philosophical Development*, p. 273.
42. In this I have the support of several able commentators on Russell. Weitz in 'Analysis and the Unity of Russell's Philosophy' in *The Philosophy of Bertrand Russell*, p. 58. Alan Wood in *My Philosophical Development*, p. 260.
43. Quoted by Alan Wood from a report to him of a conversation between Whitehead and Russell, *My Philosophical Development*, p. 260.
44. C. D. Broad, 'Critical and Speculative Philosophy', in *Contemporary British Philosophy*, First Series, ed. J. H. Muirhead, George Allen and Unwin, London, 1924.
45. This topic will be discussed at length below, in Chapter III.
46. Charles A. Fritz., *Bertrand Russell's Construction of the External World*, Routledge and Kegan Paul, London, 1952. A comprehensive study of the thought of Russell has appeared in Italian. See Emmanuel Riverso, *Il Pensiero di Bertrand Russell: Esposizione Storicocritica*, Instituto Editoriale del Mezzogiorno, Naples, 1958.
47. Erik Götlind, *Bertrand Russell's Theories of Causation*, Almqvist and Wiksells Boktryckeri AB, Uppsala, 1952.
48. Russell, 'Reply to Criticisms', *The Philosophy of Bertrand Russell*, pp. 684 *f.*
49. Morris Weitz, 'The Method of Analysis in the Philosophy of Bertrand

Russell' (unpublished doctoral dissertation). The University of Michigan, 1943.

50. A. C. Benjamin, 'The Logical Atomism of Bertrand Russell' (unpublished doctoral dissertation), The University of Michigan, 1924.

51. Alan Dorward, *Bertrand Russell: A Short Guide to His Philosophy*, published for the British Council, Longmans Green, London, 1951.

52. R. Thalheimer, *A Critical Exposition of the Epistemology and Psycho-Physical Doctrines of Bertrand Russell*, The Johns Hopkins Press, Baltimore, 1931. Although listed as a book in the catalogue of The Library of Congress, this is available only as a microfilm of an unpublished doctoral disseration.

53. D. F. Pears, *Bertrand Russell and the British Tradition in Philosophy*, Collins, London, 1967. See pages 207–8 below for further comments and evaluation of this book.

54. Ralph Schoenman, ed., *Bertrand Russell: Philosopher of the Century, Essays in his Honour*, George Allen and Unwin, London, 1967.

55. Alan Wood, *Bertrand Russell, The Passionate Sceptic: A Biography*, George Allen and Unwin, London, 1958.

56. For the complete list of authors and topics, see *The Philosophy of Bertrand Russell*.

57. *Ibid.*, pp. 720, 727.

58. *Ibid.*, p. 719.

59. Bertrand Russell, *Human Society in Ethics and Politics*, George Allen and Unwin, London, 1954, p. 7.

60. Russell, 'Reply to Criticisms', p. 729.

61. *Ibid.*, p. 734. Russell maintains that history is an art and may have some scientific aspects, but that it is a mistake to attempt to create a *philosophy* of history, in the sense of Hegel, Marx, or Spengler. He thus disclaims the description given in Sidney Hook's essay to his historical work, 'Bertrand Russell's Philosophy of History'.

62. Russell, *My Philosophical Development*, Chapters VI, VII, and VIII, entitled respectively, 'Logical Techniques in Mathematics', 'Principia Mathematica: Philosophical Aspects', and 'Principia Mathematica: Mathematical Aspects'. Russell comments in this book on the unfortunate consequences of logic being considered a branch of philosophy, and hence having been separated from mathematics, p. 65.

63. See specifically *The Analysis of Mind* and *An Inquiry into Meaning and Truth*. For a reference to his use of behaviouristic psychology, see pp. 128–30 of *My Philosophical Development*.

64. Russell, 'Mysticism and Logic', in *Mysticism and Logic and Other Essays*. Longmans Green, New York, Bombay, Calcutta, Madras, 1918, pp. 20–30; Russell, *Problems of Philosophy*, pp. 240–44.

65. Russell, *My Philosophical Development,* p. 217. Russell comments, 'In common with all philosophers before WII, [the later Wittgenstein] my fundamental aim has been to understand the world as well as may be, and to separate what may count as knowledge from what must be rejected as unfounded opinion'.

66. Russell, 'Logic as the Essence of Philosophy', in *Our Knowledge of the External World.*

67. Russell, *My Philosophical Development,* p. 11.

68. Bertrand Russell in a letter to the author, September 30, 1967. Commenting on my article 'The Consistency of Russell's Realism', in *Philosophy and Phenomenological Research,* Vol. XXVII, No. 4, June, 1967, Russell writes: 'The only point that I feel inclined to doubt in your interpretation of my philosophy is giving the name of this or that school of philosophy to my writing at various times. I do not much believe in current classifications and I think that the differences between philosophers of different schools are often very slight.'

CHAPTER II

THE NATURE OF PHILOSOPHY

Critics of Russell have been warned that it may be easy to find evidence of conflicting views on any one subject if one collects the different passages on this subject from a variety of Russell's writings.[1] The warning concerns an over-hasty conclusion that contradictions and inconsistencies occur in Russell's philosophy, a charge which would overlook the importance of two factors: the time at which the passage in question was written, and the particular context of the passage. If Russell changed his mind on an issue we should expect to find this change reflected in different statements, as, for instance, in the two editions of *The Principles of Mathematics*[2] on the treatment of universals. Further, any book or article is directed to a particular concern and for a particular audience. We should expect, therefore, that the explanation offered of the theory of descriptions in the context of the formal system of *Principia Mathematica*[3] would be different from the explanation of the same theory given as part of a brief chapter on the philosophy of logical analysis in *History of Western Philosophy*.[4]

Even with these warnings in mind, however, the welter of conflicting definitions, descriptions, criticisms, and commendations which are part of Russell's different discussions of the nature and function of philosophy might lead even the sympathetic critic to agree with Alan Wood that Russell has never made up his mind about what philosophy is.[5] Yet, one is struck by the fact that Russell seems to have had a clear idea about what he himself was trying to do, and some unequivocal judgments about what other philosophers have been doing. It is worth using the two interpretive principles of context and time to try to discover what philosophy is for Russell. This will

34

involve the questions of the relation of philosophy to religion, to science, and to logic.

In different descriptions, Russell associates philosophy in different ways with theology (or religion), with science, and with logic. In one passage he says that philosophy springs from an impulse of self-assertion, the desire to find in the world some pattern which answers to our wishes, and establishes man's importance.[6] In this respect philosophy would be closer to religion than to science or logic. In another place he rules from philosophy the desire to find answers which will support human purposes and identifies philosophy with science.[7] In still other passages he says that philosophy is halfway between religion and science, a 'No Man's Land'.[8] When he is speaking of philosophy as a science, Russell maintains that philosophy must have a province of its own, and must aim at results which other sciences can neither prove nor disprove.[9] In the same vein he describes a scientific philosophy as 'piecemeal, detailed, and verifiable'.[10] On the other hand, in other places he contrasts philosophy with science, not only in connecting philosophy with religion but in saying that 'science is what you know, philosophy what you don't know'.[11] In this sense philosophy deals with hypotheses, questions, and suggestions rather than with verifications and definite results.[12] With respect to the relation of philosophy to logic, the descriptions of their respective roles are equally conflicting; in more than one place Russell identifies philosophy with logic, claiming that philosophy is completely general, a priori, the science of the possible.[13] But in other places Russell contrasts logic with philosophy, stating that logic is no part of philosophy and that 'nine-tenths of what is regarded as philosophy is humbug. The only part that is at all definite is logic, and since it is logic, it is not philosophy'.[14]

In some passages the ethical neutrality of philosophy is stressed by Russell, and he says that he would exclude values from philosophy;[15] in other passages philosophy is said to be concerned with a 'way of life', with 'wisdom', and philosophy is said to have a moral purpose and moral value.[16] Perhaps the sharp contrasts in Russell's way of talking about philosophy could be best exemplified in two definitions which he offers of philosophy: 'an unusually ingenious attempt to think fallaciously',[17] and 'philosophy arises from an unusually obstinate attempt to arrive at real knowledge'.[18] The first definition reflects a frequent theme of Russell's, criticism of philosophers of the present and the past; the second expresses a different purpose, to promote the appreciation and understanding of philosophy.

In any attempt to make sense from the collection of apparently conflicting discussions of what philosophy is, what it does, and how it is related to science, religion, and logic, the first step is to make a distinction between Russell's description of what philosophy has been and is, that is, philosophy as practised by philosophers of the past and present other than Russell, and the description of what Russell believes philosophy ought to be, and what he tries to make it. When Russell identifies philosophy as itself a science, or, as itself logic, for instance, when he speaks of 'logic as the essence of philosophy', or of a 'scientific method in philosophy',[19] he is not speaking of what the history of philosophy shows, but of what he is recommending for philosophy. When he speaks of philosophy as piecemeal, detailed, verifiable, concerned with the science of the possible,[20] it is his own view of philosophy to which he is referring. On the other hand, when he describes philosophy as mid-way between science and religion, as embodying the impulses to understand the world and to find a way of life, as 'making greater claims and achieving fewer results' than any other branch of knowledge,[21] it is philosophy as it has been practised in the past to which he is referring. The distinction between what philosophy has been and what Russell wants it to be enables some of the apparent contradictions to be removed. However, some questions remain. What evaluation does Russell make of philosophy as it has been? As Russell would have it, is philosophy science, logic, or something else?

If we turn to the various descriptions which Russell has given of other philosophies we will find that, although he sometimes praises and sometimes criticizes these, he is consistent in selecting the characteristics for which he praises and for which he criticizes them. He also distinguishes between evaluating the work in the philosopher's own terms, and evaluating the philosophy in terms of what can be learned from it today. His historical interest in the philosophers of the past includes tracing the social and political context in which each philosopher worked in order to see the causes and the consequences of his holding and expounding his beliefs. These distinctions are evident in *History of Western Philosophy*, but they can be seen, as well, in earlier philosophical judgments, such as those of his Leibniz study.[22] In his judgments on historical figures Russell does not bring in his own contemporary judgment of what philosophy ought to be, but accepts the traditional concept of its nature and purpose. For instance, Spinoza is praised for his ethical insight, Leibniz for his logical analyses, although Russell himself excludes ethics from philosophy, and although modern mathematical logic goes far beyond Leibniz' foreshadowings.[23] Both Descartes and Leibniz are blamed for allowing their reasoning to be corrupted by the desire to find theological patterns in nature.[24] In Russell's view this might be called the besetting sin of philosophers, the reading of desired moral and religious patterns into the world they are trying to understand.[25] In addition to this weakness, philosophers have been arrogant and dogmatic in setting up comprehensive systems of belief which go far beyond any evidence and are not subject to correction as are the beliefs of science.[26] These two characteristics account for much of the negative comment of Russell on philosophy. It is not the questions which philosophers ask which are harmful; their wonderings, probings, doubtings, and asking of insoluble questions are appraised by Russell as valuable and proper.[27] It is in the giving of dogmatic, wholesale, monistic, and self-serving answers that they fail, and these answers may have harmful effects.

The value of the philosophy of the past is that it raises new questions, and keeps alive old questions during a period when they cannot be answered; this has a beneficial effect when the methods of science catch up with the questions. Even in the case of permanently unanswerable questions these have an effect of preventing a narrow parochialism, or a dull inactivity of mind in those who study philosophy.[28] Beyond that, philosophers, by trying to guess the answers to their own questions, often make suggestions for what turn out to be valuable scientific hypotheses.[29] Their efforts in working out the logical implications of ideas, and the science of logic itself, have the effect of liberating the imagination and broadening the vision. Accordingly, the effect of studing philosophy ought to be to decrease dogmatism, to widen the intellectual horizon, and to induce a certain caution in the habits of reasoning of its students. In this sense, philosophy has good and morally valuable effects, particularly if philosophy is itself ethically neutral. Although Russell seldom writes for a narrowly specialized academic audience, except in mathematics and in logic, the more popular presentations of what philosophy is and what it does are often in the contexts for the positive evaluation of philosophy. There Russell is trying to interest a wide public in the study of philosophy. Some of the most carefully reasoned criticisms of philosophers of the past are in the context of more technical discussion. However, Russell sometimes wishes to warn as well as entice his readers, and in popular contexts he may be guilty of the epigrammatic insult to philosophy. In any case, there seems no evidence of inconsistency or contradiction in what Russell says of philosophy in the context of his description of the work of other philosophers.

With respect to Russell's descriptions of his own philosophy, and of the way he believed philosophy should be related to logic, to science, and to other studies, a consistent view is less clear. It is evident that he wished to recommend that philosophy be closer to science and to logic than it has been in the past. The degree of the closeness or of the identity of philosophy to science and to logic, and the kind of results which we may expect to follow from the new practice of philosophy are less clear. A consideration of the sequence in time of Russell's different descriptions of what philosophy ought to be and what results it may hope to achieve may reveal whether the difficulties are due to a change in his position, or to some other historical factors.

In *The Problems of Philosophy* Russell offers a description of the value of the study of philosophy in terms of the educational effect of liberating the imagination by the consideration of intellectual alternatives, the pondering of difficult or unanswerable questions, and the pursuit of objective truth.[30] He claims that philosophy should be scientific in the sense that it strives to establish a truth unaffected by our desires, in the sense that it has no special source of wisdom available to it which is not accessible to science, and in the sense that it deludes itself if it believes that it has a special logic which reveals the structure of reality.[31] Unlike the special sciences, however, philosophy has the function of criticism, of subjecting the beliefs and methods of the scientist to a critical scrutiny to test their claims to credibility. In doing this the philosopher neither claims his own ground of unquestionable truth, nor sets himself up as a thorough-going sceptic. Rather, the philosopher assumes as generally true the beliefs of science and common sense, but inquires of each belief of its claim to acceptance.[32] The uncertainty of philosophical results is due in part to the fact that when any part of philosophical inquiry does achieve definite results it is no longer considered part of philosophy, but is a separate science, as the history of thought shows astronomy, physics, and psychology to have become.[33] The other reason for the uncertainty of philosophic truth lies in its historic concern with questions which have not, and probably never shall, admit of a scientific answer. Such questions as that of the immortality of the soul, for instance, seem likely never to receive a definite answer.[34]

In two works published in 1914, a new note was struck in Russell's description of philosophy and the method proper to it. In *Our Knowledge of the External World As a Field for Scientific Method in Philosophy* and in the essay 'On Scientific Method in Philosophy',[35] Russell announced the advent of a new method in philosophy. This method was said to be as revolutionary as the work of Galileo had been to modern science; it made philosophy capable of producing results as definite, verifiable, indisputable as those of science, of either deciding the eternal disputes of philosophy, indicating the direction in which a definite decision could be reached, or showing that no decision could be reached. In the preface to *Our Knowledge of the External World*, Russell writes:

'The following lectures are an attempt to show, by means of examples, the nature, capacity, and limitations of the logical-analytic method in philosophy. This method, of which the first complete example is to be found in the writings of Frege, has gradually, in the course of actual research, increasingly forced itself upon me as something perfectly definite, capable of embodiment in maxims, and adequate, in all branches of philosophy, to yield whatever objective scientific knowledge it is possible to obtain.'[36]

After referring to the contribution of Whitehead to the formation of the new method, Russell says of the new method:

'It will be seen that if his way of dealing with these topics is capable of being successfully carried through, a wholly new light is thrown on the time-honoured controversies of realists and idealists, and a method is obtained of solving all that is soluble in their problem.'[37]

The new method in philosophy for which these ambitious claims were made owed its origin to mathematical logic, as Russell's acknowledgments to mathematicians and logicians, and his reference to *Principia Mathematica* make clear. This method is the method of logic, not the logic of the Aristotelian tradition, nor the dialectical logic of idealism, nor even the inductive logic of the Mill and Bacon tradition, but the new logic of which he himself was a pioneer. It is the practice of this new logic which *is* the scientific method in philosophy. Russell in these works seems to identify philosophy, science, and logic. The problem for a modern reader is to understand how logic can be concerned with the 'knowledge of the external world' or any of the problems concerning sense data, concepts in physics, and common sense objects. Russell describes 'the province of philosophy' as consisting of those propositions which are 'general', 'applicable to everything that exists or may exist', '*a priori*', and ends by defining philosophy as 'the science of the possible'.[38] Thus, philosophy is defined as logic, but it is unclear how such a method can have any status other than that of a purely formal science, or how any problems but those of mathematical logic could be attacked by philosophy. How can philosophy, in the same essay, be defined in the following way?

'A scientific philosophy such as I wish to recommend will be piecemeal and tentative like other sciences; above all, it will be able to invent hypotheses which, even if they are not wholly true, will yet remain fruitful after the necessary corrections have been made. This possibility of successive approximations to the truth is, more than anything else, the source of the triumphs of science, and to transfer this possibility to philosophy is to ensure a progress in method whose importance it would be almost impossible to exaggerate.'[39]

The key to unravelling this mystery lies, I believe, partially in the conception of logic which Russell had at this time. He did not distinguish between logic and philosophy, but defined logic in a wider way than has since become customary. *Principia Mathematica* is said to be both mathematics and logic, mathematics being included as part of formal logic. The specifically philosophical aspects of this study can be distinguished only in that they are not concerned in the working out of the details of the systems of mathematics which are developed within the whole system of the *Principia*.

'Mathematical logic, even in its most modern form, is not

directly of philosophical importance except in its beginnings. After the beginnings, it belongs rather to mathematics than to philosophy. Of its beginnings, which are the only part of it that can properly be called *philosophical* logic, I shall speak shortly. But even the later developments, though not directly philosophical, will be found of great indirect use in philosophizing. They enable us to deal easily with more abstract conceptions than merely verbal reasoning can enumerate; they suggest fruitful hypotheses which otherwise could hardly be thought of; and they enable us to see quickly what is the smallest store of materials, with which a given logical or scientific edifice can be constructed. Not only Frege's theory of numbers, which we shall deal with in Lecture VII, but the whole theory of physical concepts which will be outlined in our next two lectures, is inspired by mathematical logic, and could never have been imagined without it.'[40]

With respect to the philosophical importance of the foundations of logic, Russell's analysis describes two aspects of logic as essential.

'The first part investigates what propositions are and what forms they may have; this part enumerates the different kinds of atomic propositions, of molecular propositions, of general propositions, and so on. The second part consists of certain supremely general propositions, which assert the truth of all propositions of certain forms. This second part merges into pure mathematics, whose propositions all turn out, on analysis, to be such general formal truths. The first part, which merely enumerates forms, is the more difficult, and philosophically the more important; and it is the recent progress in this first part, more than anything else, that has rendered a truly scientific discussion of many philosophical problems possible.'[41]

At this early stage, before the work of the *Principia* had come to be thought of as something having its own special subject matter, that is, mathematical logic, the only part of its programme that was excluded from philosophy was the technical mathematical development. The analysis of the forms of propositions was deemed close to the analysis of the forms of fact, as we shall see later in the programme of logical atomism, and hence both are both logical and scientific. As to the use of the methods of mathematical logic, this was to become the method of construction, a central technique of scientific philosophizing for Russell from that time up to its development as the search for minimum vocabularies in his later philosophy. This use of techniques developed within the *Principia* brought the new philosophical method to bear on the old philosophical problems concerning the inference from sensation to the things of common sense and the entities of physics, and to the 'construction of the external world' itself. Thus, the logical-analytic method which Russell proclaimed as *the* method of scientific philosophizing, was both formal and empirical. It was formal in dealing with the forms of propositions; empirical in using the distinctions developed in this formal analysis to analyse empirical propositions and empirical concepts. His method was both *a priori* and verifiable; both kinds of truths could be directly cognized as were, for instance, the truths of logic and sense data, respectively. His method was both analytic and constructive; analytic in its method of reducing complexes to units; constructive in reassembling these units according to a logical pattern and with a synthesizing intent. His early understanding of logical method permitted it to be concerned both with abstract forms of propositions and with 'the nature of the world'.

There were important changes in Russell's concept of the relation of philosophy to science and to logic as his thought developed. He came to see mathematical logic as a subject in itself which had 'philosophical aspects' and 'mathematical aspects' but which was a definite, scientifically progressive discipline. His own interest in this subject became less as it separated from philosophy proper,[42] as he acknowledged in his reference to Gödel's critique of the *Principia* in *The Philosophy of Bertrand Russell.* Russell's confidence in the completion of the programme outlined as the construction of the external world was considerably altered as difficulties in the analysis developed, and as his own analysis of the basic data of sensory experience changed.[43] The programme of logical atomism also required amendments partly for the same reasons, and partly because Russell came to realize the importance and complexity of the analysis of language assumed in it.[44] It seems to be the case, also, that after 1914, Wittgenstein's influence caused Russell to view mathematics and logic as tautological, and hence to alter his view of its philosophical implications.[45] These changes seemed to involve a sharper distinction between analytic and synthetic propositions than previously held, as is evident in the treatment of analytic propositions in *The Analysis of Matter*.[46] All these changes will be discussed later.

Whatever were the causes of the change in Russell's conception of philosophy as scientific and logical, they are reflected in his retrospective view of the progress of philosophy expressed in 1943.

'Many matters which, when I was young, baffled me by the vagueness of all that had been said about them, are now amenable to an exact technique, which makes possible the kind of progress that is customary in science. Where definite knowledge is unattainable, it is sometimees possible to prove that it is unattainable, and it is usually possible to formulate a variety of exact hypotheses all compatible with the existing evidence. Those philosophers who have adopted the methods derived from logical analysis can argue with each other, not in the old aimless way, but coöperatively, so that both sides can concur as to the outcome.'[47]

Russell now refers to his method as analytic, rather than as logical-analytic. Methods are said to be derived from logic, rather than to be identical with logic. He views philosophy as scientific in the sense of suggesting hypotheses for science proper. The claims of the new method are stated in more modest terms, as subsequent experience has modified Russell's earlier optimism. However, both the general conception of philosophy and the major points of its relation to logic and science have remained constant.

We might sum up the relation which Russell conceives should exist between logic and philosophy by making a distinction between 'logic proper' and the use of the word 'logical' in an adjectival sense. Logic proper, in the sense of a purely formal uninterpreted system of symbols intended to give an undergirding for mathematical and logical systems, is not itself philosophy nor part of philosophy but a technical study of its own. It is closer to science than to philosophy, and closer to mathematics than to any other discipline. However, the techniques of analysis which were originally developed in *Principia Mathematica* may be used in other inquiries. Specifically, the techniques such as the method of construction can be applied to philosophical problems of theory of knowledge and of the nature of the world. In addition the rigour of logical reasoning may serve as a model for philosophical inquiry. In this sense philosophy must be logical, and logic is still the essence of philosophy.

The relation of science to philosophy in Russell's view can be understood if an expanded interpretation is given of Russell's epigram, 'Science is what you know, philosophy is what you don't know'. One interpretation of this, likely to be given when it is quoted out of context, is a reflection on the comparative progress of science and philosophy. We have seen that Russell often did criticize philosophy for its looseness, lack of rigour, speculative overexpansion, claims to know more than it can know, and reading into nature of features satisfying to the philosopher's human and ethical desires. In this respect science has been superior in its limited inquiries, precise methods, modest tentativeness, and ethical neutrality. Another meaning of the epigram suggests a justification of the philosophizing of the past in terms of the history of thought. In this context Russell uses the examples of Democritus:[48] in his own time, on the basis of limited experience and with no experimental methods, he made an imaginative leap and a brilliant guess and invented the atomic hypothesis. In modern times, using the precise and experimental methods of modern science, physicists have verified the atomic hypothesis. In this way philosophy may serve as an inventor of hypotheses, ranging over wider areas of meaning than those which have become manageable by scientific techniques, and making guesses which serve to guide the work of later scientists. Philosophers may be pioneers in exploring new areas which have not yet come under scientific control. Later these same hypotheses and fields of inquiry may become part of science proper as they become the domain of 'what you know'. The work of suggesting hypotheses is still an important function of philosophers and one to which Russell himself has contributed, for instance in his analysis of the concepts of matter and mind, and of space and time.[49] In any event, the philosopher like the scientist is concerned with 'the theoretical understanding of the world'.

Science and philosophy are connected in another sense, in that Russell regards the connection between the conclusions of science and the data of perception as a vital philosophical problem. Both the data of perception and the conclusions of science are not to be questioned, but the philosopher's job is to build a bridge between them.[50] In the efforts of building this bridge, as in all of Russell's work in theory of knowledge, the results of science have contributed an important set of data; physics, psychology, and the other sciences are taken to be for the most part true, and whatever the picture we construct of the world and of the way we know the world, it must rely on and be consistent with these results. For this reason Russell continually modified his own work when new scientific theories seemed to require it, and for the same reason, he criticized contemporary Oxford philosophy for failing to recognize the importance of scientific knowledge for sound philosophizing.[51]

Philosophy, then, is identical neither with logic nor with science, but it has common grounds with both. Logic provides philosophy with a model of exact reasoning and careful analysis, and the tools and special techniques which were developed as part of logic itself. Science provides philosophy with the data of its inquiries, and the model of reliable knowledge; philosophy attempts to provide a theoretical analysis which will justify the results of science and suggestions which may ultimately become the hypotheses of the special sciences.

With regard to the history of philosophy Russell was willing to consider any problem within the traditional purview of philosophy as a genuine philosophical problem, whether it concerned the nature of God, the nature of the world, the nature of the soul, or the freedom of the will. But for his own philosophical work, it was concerned chiefly with certain recurring problems in the theory of knowledge. In *The Problems of Philosophy*, he raised the question of what we can know and with what degree of reliability, a problem which in one form or another remained a central concern throughout *Human Knowledge*. In *Our Knowledge of the External World*, Russell was particularly concerned with showing a logical connection between sense experience and physics, a problem approached again and again from different perspectives in his work. His theme of the relation of language and fact was an important part of the programme of inquiry into logical atomism as this appeared in 'The Philosophy of Logical Atomism'. *The Analysis of Mind* and *The Analysis of Matter* attempted to overcome the dualism of matter and mind by showing how the causal laws of psychology and the causal laws of physics could be constructed from the neutral particulars among which sensations were the empirical components. In *An Inquiry into Meaning and Truth* the problem of the scrutinizing of our beliefs, of both common sense and science, in order to display the degree of reliability which they possess and to order them as premises and as derived, was approached with particular emphasis on the 'relation between language and fact'. And finally in *Human Knowledge*, the epistemological scrutiny of beliefs is made particularly relevant to the problem of non-deductive inference, with a critical outcome in the evaluation of empiricism as a theory of knowledge.

In a chapter devoted to theory of knowledge in *My Philosophical Development*, Russell describes the way in which his interest turned to theory of knowledge after World War I.[52] He became convinced that he had paid insufficient attention to psychology and linguistics in his previous work on the subject, and accordingly, he set to work on the subject. The outcome of his work appears in *The Analysis of Mind* (1921), *An Inquiry into Meaning and Truth* (1940), and *Human Knowledge: Its Scope and Limits* (1948). He tells us that he began reading on the subject with a set of initial 'prejudices'. These appear to have been an important starting point for him, for none of the six prejudices which he describes have been abandoned since. In describing these beliefs as 'prejudices', Russell may be unfair to himself, for while he is thinking of them as prejudices in the sense of being prior to an investigation of their validity, they are not prejudices in the sense of their being immune to later criticism, emendation, or rejection, had the outcome of the investigation been to discredit them. The description which Russell gives of these six beliefs, or points of departure, provides important clues for understanding Russell's theory of knowledge. They fit in with the three main themes of analysis, empiricism, and realism which are taken as the basis for the analysis of Russell's thought in the present study. For this reason a review of Russell's reported 'prejudices', ordered around the three themes mentioned, provides a helpful introduction to the detailed treatment of Russell's theory of knowledge.

The initial prejudice which Russell regards as having the most important influence in his thinking is that in favour of a method of analysis. He reports that his method is to start from something which is vague but certain, indubitable but imprecise. A blurred belief carries conviction, but it is troubling in that no precise meaning can be given to it. In addition, there is no clear idea why it is believed. The process of analysis begins when attention is focused on these vague beliefs. Gradually, under prolonged scrutiny, the belief begins to reveal distinctions and divisions within it. Russell likens this to looking at something under a microscope and to watching something approaching through a fog. The distinctions which analysis reveals may be of different kinds, depending upon what is being analysed and for what purpose; it may be an analysis of various beliefs which together make up an observed complex. In any case, the method is that of analysis, which Russell defends as not a falsification, and as leading to knowledge. This is his 'strongest and most unshakeable prejudice as regards the methods of philosophical investigation'.[53]

Another prejudice with which this period of Russell's activity in theory of knowledge is said to begin is with the belief that 'meaning' and 'linguistic problems' were important in theory of knowledge. The method of analysis was to have as a primary target the various forms of speech and of discourse as these could be found to be related to what was non-linguistic. It was part of Russell's conviction concerning language that reference beyond language could not be left out of consideration. Both of these two forms of prejudice have to do with Russell's use of the method of analysis and will be discussed in the next chapter.

Two others of Russell's prejudices have to do with experience. On the one hand Russell maintains that insufficient attention has been given to the meaning of the term 'experience', which is a kind of catchword of contemporary philosophy. He believes that a careful analysis of what experience is, and what kind of knowledge it yields will reveal that much less can be known or inferred from experience than most empiricists believe. Accordingly, he has pointed out by means of a step-by-step analysis just how limited is the knowledge to be gained from experience; this is a main theme of the *Inquiry* and of *Human Knowledge*. On the other hand, and in the opposite direction, Russell also believes that all knowledge must have some basis in experience, that no *a priori* knowledge is possible. In this sense he may be called an empiricist who believes in the limitations of experience. The analysis by which Russell attempts to reveal the connections between the beliefs of science and common sense and their origin and partial validation in sensory experience, and the analysis of what constructions, inferences or postulates this analysis requires will be dealt with in Chapter IV.

A third set of Russell's prejudices concerns his view of nature. He tells us that he began with an emphasis on the 'continuity between animal and human minds'. The studies of the physiologists and psychologists are of importance in a theory of knowledge when they enable us to view our own minds and our own behaviour in the context of a world which we share with animals, and in which we exist as animals. Behaviourism appeals to Russell as a theory which can help him in a theory of knowledge. Although he goes along with it to see how far it can go, he retains a conviction that its application is limited.[54] The emphasis on behaviourism is noticeable in *The Analysis of Mind, An Inquiry into Meaning and Truth*, and *Human Knowledge*. It has the effect of preventing Russell from enclosing his concept of language within the study of language itself, or his analysis of knowledge, belief, and truth, within the scope of what is stated or made verbally explicit. All epistemological concepts are seen to depend upon pre-verbal modes of behaviour. I call this prejudice one aspect of Russell's realism.

Another prejudice which is also 'realistic' in its effect, is Russell's often expressed preference for the viewpoint of physics and astronomy, rather than that of the human, the subjective, and the psychological. Although he cannot hold that the vast impersonal universe is a locus of values, he still feels that man must see himself in the context of that universe if he is not to be parochial and morbid in his self-absorption. The conviction that all causal laws may eventually be reducible to those of physics is so beyond the reach of even approximate confirmation as to make this belief an article of faith, and as such, Russell confesses to it.[55]

For the fuller development of Russell's realism we need to consider the conclusion of his epistemological analyses in addition to their starting points. Yet I think the provisional acceptance of behaviouristic psychology and physics indicates a position which one might call 'scientific realism', a term appropriate to

Russell's philosophy. He himself says that he would be tempted to call himself a materialist were it not for the misleading implications of the concept of matter.[56] Accordingly, Russell's prejudices towards psychology and physics are taken as a clue to the more fully developed theory which will be treated as Russell's realism in Chapter V.

When we review the concept of the nature of philosophy, its past weaknesses and present possibilities, we find in Russell a combination of traditional goals for philosophy and new methods for achieving those goals. Some of the contemporary historians of this century have pointed out that Russell is a traditionalist in his concept of what philosophy is, and, in this respect, belongs on the far side of the current 'revolution' in philosophy.[57] Another way of commenting on Russell's position in comparison with that of contemporary logical positivists or language analysts, would be to say that Russell views their respective concepts of philosophy as indications of a new scholasticism.[58] He protests that the concept of knowledge of logical positivists like Otto Neurath restricts it to the scope of propositions and prohibits reference beyond propositions to what the propositions are about. On the other hand, analysts like Gilbert Ryle and J. O. Urmson exclude scientific knowledge and the techniques of logic from the scope of philosophy and restrict its methodology to what is said in 'silly ways by silly people'.[59] In both cases Russell stands in an older philosophical tradition for which the proper task of philosophy is to describe the nature of the world, and to ask how knowledge is possible, and how truth is to be attained.

The historical tradition in which Russell stands owes something to Descartes in the method of systematic doubt, the scrutiny of each idea, and the methods of analysis and synthesis. However, Russell rejects wholesale scepticism and does not deprecate knowledge gained from experience. With respect to Leibniz, Russell's theory of perspectives in the construction of spatial and temporal orders is modelled on that of Leibniz, while the *Principia* is the fulfilment of Leibniz' dream of the calculating philosophers with their 'universal characteristic'. However, Russell criticized Leibniz' theory of relations and his theology. The rationalists, Russell estimated, were right in that they emphasized the necessity of logical order, an order of evidence and of inferences, but they had an insufficient basis in experience. Russell is indebted to Hume for a concept of experience as consisting of discrete atoms of sensation and for a consistent questioning of the limits of what can be inferred from experience. Empiricism, according to Russell, was right in its emphasis on experience as providing the basis of our knowledge, but wrong in derogating the importance of logical order.

These judgments on his predecessors in philosophy foreshadow Russell's own view of what philosophy should be; it should provide an analysis of the experiential basis of our common sense and scientific knowledge in the tradition of Hume, and it should provide a systematic ordering of our beliefs and inferences governed by logical economy in the tradition of rationalism but with new logical methods.

When both empirical and logical methods are combined, in the context of what I call Russell's scientific realism, the outcome is a complex and comprehensive series of analyses. The disentangling of these various themes in Russell's theory of knowledge will be the task in the following chapters.

NOTES TO CHAPTER II

1. Russell, 'Preface' to *Bertrand Russell's Dictionary of Mind, Matter, and Morals*. Alan Wood, 'Cautionary Notes', in *My Philosophical Development*, p. 275.
2. Russell, *The Principles of Mathematics*, preface to the second edition. Here Russell refers to certain portions of the first edition which are superseded by the change in his views.
3. Russell and Whitehead, *Principia Mathematica*, Chapter III of the Introduction; also Part I, Section B, *14.

4. Russell, *History of Western Philosophy*, George Allen and Unwin, London, 1945, p. 831.
5. Alan Wood, 'Summary and Introduction', *My Philosophical Development*, p. 263, cf. footnote 1.
6. Bertrand Russell, 'Philosophy's Ulterior Motives', *Unpopular Essays*, George Allen and Unwin, London, 1950, pp. 56–7.
7. Russell, 'Mysticism and Logic', *Mysticism and Logic*, p. 32.
8. Russell, *History of Western Philosophy*, p. xiii.
9. Russell, *Our Knowledge of the External World*, p. 27.
10. *Ibid.*, p. 14.
11. Russell, 'Philosophy for Layman', *Unpopular Essays*, p. 24.
12. Russell, *History of Western Philosophy*, pp. xiii–xiv.
13. Russell, 'On Scientific Method in Philosophy', *Mysticism and Logic*, pp. 110–11.
14. The remark that logic is no part of philosophy occurs on p. v of the preface of *Human Knowledge*. The remark that nine-tenths of philosophy is humbug is quoted by Alan Wood without reference in *My Philosophical Development*, p. 276.
15. Russell, 'Reply to Criticisms', *The Philosophy of Bertrand Russell*, p. 719.
16. Russell, 'Philosophy for Laymen', *Unpopular Essays*, p. 22. See also, Bertrand Russell, *An Outline of Philosophy*, George Allen and Unwin, London, 1927; simultaneously published, W. W. Norton, New York, 1927; reprinted from the American edition as a Meridian Book, The World Publishing Co., New York, pp. 311–13.
17. Russell, 'Philosophy's Ulterior Motives', *Unpopular Essays*, p. 45.
18. Russell, *An Outline of Philosophy*, p. 1.
19. Russell, *Our Knowledge of the External World*, Preface, pp. 7–9. Lecture II, 'Logic as the Essence of Philosophy'.
20. Russell, 'On Scientific Method in Philosophy', *Mysticism and Logic*.
21. Russell, *Our Knowledge of the External World*, p. 13.
22. Bertrand Russell, *A Critical Exposition of the Philosophy of Leibniz*, 2nd ed., 1937; George Allen and Unwin, London, 1900.
23. Russell, *History of Western Philosophy*. For a discussion of Spinoza, see pp. 569 f; for a discussion of Leibniz, see pp. 581 f.
24. Russell, 'Philosophy's Ulterior Motives', *Unpopular Essays*, pp. 46–9.
25. Russell, 'Mysticism and Logic', *Mysticism and Logic*, pp. 6–7.
26. Russell, *The Problems of Philosophy*, Chapter XIV.
27. Russell, 'Philosophy for Laymen', *Unpopular Essays*, p. 26.
28. Russell, *The Problems of Philosophy*, Chapter XV.
29. Russell, 'Philosophy for Laymen', *Unpopular Essays*, p. 24.
30. Russell, *The Problems of Philosophy*, pp. 248–50.
31. *Ibid.*, pp. 220 f.

32. Russell, *The Problems of Philosophy*, pp. 234–6.
33. *Ibid.*, p. 240.
34. *Ibid.*, p. 241. Russell suggests elsewhere that if these questions do attain a definite answer it will be as part of science and not as part of philosophy. *Our Knowledge of the External World*, p. 27.
35. Bertrand Russell, 'On Scientific Method in Philosophy', was the Herbert Spencer Lecture at Oxford, 1914, and was published by the Clarendon Press, later reprinted in *Mysticism and Logic*, 1918.
36. Russell, *Our Knowledge of the External World*, p. 7.
37. *Ibid.*, p. 8.
38. Russell, 'On Scientific Method in Philosophy', *Mysticism and Logic*, pp. 110–11.
39. *Ibid.*, p. 113.
40. Russell, *Our Knowledge of the External World*, pp. 50–1.
41. *Ibid.*, p. 67.
42. Russell, 'Reply to Criticisms', *The Philosophy of Bertrand Russell*, p. 741. See also Russell, *My Philosophical Development*, p. 127. Here Russell comments: 'I have done no definitely logical work since the second edition of the *Principia* in 1925, except the discussion of the principles of extensionality and atomicity and excluded middle in the *Inquiry into Meaning and Truth*. Consequently, the later work on this subject has not affected my philosophical development and therefore lies outside the scope of the present volume.'
43. *Ibid.*, pp. 134–6.
44. *Ibid.*, pp. 145–55.
45. *Ibid.*, p. 119.
46. Russell, *The Analysis of Matter*, George Allen and Unwin, London, 1927. Reprinted with new introduction by Lester Dennon, Dover, New York, 1954, pp. 169–73.
47. Russell, *The Philosophy of Bertrand Russell*, p. 20.
48. Russell, 'Philosophy for Laymen', *Unpopular Essays*, pp. 24–5.
49. Russell, *My Philosophical Development*, 'I have found, to take an important example, that by analysing physics and perception the problem of the relation of mind and matter can be completely solved. It is true that nobody has accepted what seems to me the solution, but I believe and hope that this is only because my theory has not been understood', p. 15. With reference to the concepts of space and time, Russell says in the same work, 'I do not pretend that the above theory can be proved. What I contend is that, like the theories of physics, it cannot be disproved, and gives an answer to many problems which older theorists have found puzzling. I do not think that any prudent person will claim more than this for any theory', p. 27.

50. Russell, *My Philosophical Development*, p. 205.
51. *Ibid.*, p. 230.
52. *Ibid.*, Chapter XI.
53. *Ibid.*, p. 133.
54. *Ibid.*, p. 130.
55. *Ibid.*, p. 131.
56. Russell, *The Analysis of Mind*, preface, pp. 5–6.
57. Warnock, *English Philosophy Since 1900*, p. 29.
58. Russell, *My Philosophical Development*, pp. 217–18.
    Russell, *Inquiry*, pp. 442 f.
59. Russell, *My Philosophical Development*, p. 250, p. 230.

CHAPTER III

THE METHOD OF ANALYSIS

One aspect of Russell's philosophy upon which all commentators and critics are agreed is that it exemplifies and pioneered modern analytic philosophy. Russell himself recognizes the practice of analysis as the most persistent trait and the cardinal method of his thought.[1] Therefore, to understand fully the method of analysis as Russell employs it is to understand his philosophy. Accordingly, this will be a major part of the present study. A good place to begin is with Russell's own description of the general features of an analytic method. He describes the starting place of analysis as the holding of beliefs which are hazy or ambiguous, which are complex, and which are felt to be certain without one knowing what it is that one is certain about. The method of analysis proceeds by attention to component parts, by the tracing of connections, and by the ordering and organizing of the complex. It issues in a situation in which clarity and precision have replaced vagueness and fuzziness, in which simples have replaced complexes, and in which specific questions have replaced the large and indeterminate certainty of early belief. In 'The Philosophy of Logical Atomism', he uses the example of believing that there are people in the room where the lecture is being given:

'It is a rather curious fact in philosophy that the data which are undeniable to start with are always rather vague and ambiguous. You can, for instance, say: "There are a number of people in this room at this moment." That is obviously in some sense undeniable. But when you come to try and define what this room is, and what it is for a person to be in a room, and how you are going to distinguish one person from another, and so forth, you find that what you have said is most fearfully vague and that you really do

56

not know what you meant. That is a rather singular fact, that everything you are really sure of, right off is something that you do not know the meaning of, and the moment you get a precise statement you will not be sure whether it is true or false, at least right off. The process of sound philosophizing, to my mind, consists mainly in passing from those obvious, vague, ambiguous things, that we feel quite sure of, to something precise, clear, definite, which by reflection and analysis we find is involved in the vague thing that we start from, and is, so to speak, the real truth of which that vague thing is a sort of shadow.'[2]

In *My Philosophical Development* Russell stresses the importance of the method of analysis in his own philosophy. In addition to describing analysis on the analogy of seeing something through a microscope, of seeing something approaching through the fog, of replacing vague uncertainty with a clearer discernment of distinctions and complexities,[3] Russell defends his method of analysis against hostile criticisms:

'There have always been those who objected to analysis. They have been the same people as those who opposed every scientific advance. . . . All the advances of modern physics have consisted in a more and more minute analysis of the material world. . . . It is not only in relation to matter that analysis is the road to understanding. A person without musical training, if he hears a symphony, acquires a vague general impression of a whole, whereas the conductor, as you may see from his gestures, is hearing a total which he minutely analyses into its several parts. The merit of analysis is that it gives knowledge not otherwise obtainable. . . . To advance such considerations in defence of philosophical analysis is not, of course, to say that this or that philosopher has analysed rightly. It is only to say that he was right to attempt an analysis.'[4]

On his own use of analysis Russell comments that he has used a method of analysis since he abandoned the philosophy of Kant and Hegel and he believes that 'only by analysing is progress possible'.[5]

In the illuminating descriptions of the method of analysis, the images of the general view of the room which becomes specified, of the microscope and the water, and the object approaching through the fog, the stress is put on the discerning of distinctions or differentiations, the vague jumbled complexity becoming many clearly distinct components. These distinctions are found by attentiveness, analogous to visual alertness, accompanied by concentrated effort. But it is not only the identification of components which is the outcome of analysis, but the ordering of those components. Both the differentiation and the ordering are relevant to the purpose of the inquiry in question. The problems under investigation are not necessarily solved by being analysed, although they may be, but they are formulated in a way which facilitates further study, instead of remaining a vague puzzlement. When this general description of the method of analysis is applied to theory of knowledge, and to Russell's problems concerning the justification of scientific knowledge, we can see that the vague concept of scientific knowledge and the vague concept of empirical justification will have to be analysed into more simple, clear, and ordered concepts. This analysis will permit the problems under consideration to be reformulated as the specific questions of how to interpret perceptions, of how to formulate perceptual propositions, of how to state scientific hypotheses, of what specific assumptions must be made to support scientific generalizations, and so forth. The aim in view is an increase in clarity and a minimizing of the risk of error. For this reason, as we shall see, the ordering of beliefs which results from epistemological analysis is one of 'degrees of credibility',[6] and the analysis of scientific knowledge turns to a discussion of 'the minimum number of hypotheses from which a broad measure of truth will result'.[7]

Before specific tasks of Russell's method of analysis are discussed, some general aspects of the method must be described. Since the most usual term to describe this method is 'logical', our attention must first be directed to the sense in which Russell's method of analysis can be called 'logical'.

In the previous chapter it was noted that Russell distinguishes logic proper from philosophy while maintaining that the method of philosophy should be logical. This means that the techniques of logic proper are to be adapted to the formulation and analysis of philosophical problems. What are these techniques, and how are they adapted to philosophy? We may take *Principia Mathematica* as representing, for Russell, logic proper, and the questions may then be rephrased, What techniques of *Principia Mathematica* are used by Russell? and, How are these techniques adapted to philosophical analysis?

One of the most important techniques of *Principia Mathematica*, and one which is characteristic of all work in modern symbolic logic, is the use of an artificial language. The influence of the artificial language is important in Russell's philosophical analysis, as it has been in the work of logical empiricists. The construction and use of an artificial language has become, as well, a chief point of conflict between analysts of the logical and of the linguistic persuasions.[8]

An artificial language means the use of a symbolism different from that of ordinary or natural languages. The artificial language will include a special vocabulary in which symbols are created to fit the requirements of the logical or philosophical discourse. For example, when Whitehead coins the term 'prehension' he invents a new word to fit a specific need in his philosophy.[9] To that extent he is employing an artificial language, and in doing so, he is following a long philosophical tradition. In the case of symbolic logic, the vocabulary of the artificial language includes the use of Arabic and Greek letters, in both large and small case, to stand for the units of propositions, terms, and propositional functions which enter into the argument. The conventional nature of the symbols emphasizes the form of the argument, while showing the irrelevance of the content to a logical analysis. There are also special symbols invented to represent logical connectives, quantifiers, characteristics of relations, such symbols as the tilde and the horseshoe, for instance. In addition, a set of symbols is required for punctuation to aid in the representation of the syntax of the special language of logic. There must be, also, explicit rules formulated to specify the use of the symbols.[10]

Since the invention and use of the symbolism of modern logic have proved the power of this symbolism in logic proper, the relevance of its use to philosophy has been under debate. Some contemporary philosophers have thought an artificial language barbarous and beyond the proper scope of philosophical interest. They have insisted that the fascination of logicians with their 'made-up' language has caused them to overlook the richness of 'ordinary language' in flexibility, fruitful distinctions, and philosophical enlightenment. These critics claim that the neatness of the logical language oversimplifies, while its preciseness is actually much less than the distinctions of common speech which the attentive student of ordinary language can discern.[11] On the opposing side, Russell and the logical empiricists have found symbolic logic a potent weapon for avoiding metaphysical error and for achieving clarity.[12]

It should be noted that the defenders of the artificial language are not recommending that it should replace ordinary language. The latter has important advantages for most communications. Indeed, most of the philosophers who employ the language of mathematical logic do so only in limited contexts. Most of their books and articles are written in ordinary language, although they may insert specific formulations of arguments in a symbolized form. Russell seldom uses the artificial language for explanatory purposes, except as an addition to the language of ordinary usage. One reason for the limited use of the artificial language is that few people read it with any degree of ease, so that a philosopher who used it exclusively could be sure of a very select audience. Another reason is that the special symbolism may be used to clarify difficulties in particular cases, but may not be necessary in contexts where the normal language is clear enough for the kind of communication required. Another factor to be taken into account is that an author may keep the model of the artificial language in mind, writing in such a way that his argument *could* be formulated in symbolic terms, even though it is not. This is an important use of an artificial language and one that is common in Russell's writings, as one can see if a comparison is made between two presentations of the same material, one in symbolic and one in natural language. Even in *Principia Mathematica*, passages of ordinary explanation precede the explication of the formal argument in the artificial language.

Since the use of the artificial language is limited in philosophical discourse, is there any need of it at all in philosophy? What uses of it can be defended? The reasons advanced in *Principia* for its superiority suggest some uses for special symbolism in philosophy. In the *Principia* the first argument is that there are, in logic, ideas to be expressed which are different from those treated by the language of ordinary speech, and that, in order for them to be clearly and consistently expressed, it would be necessary either to give a special and limited meaning to some word of ordinary usage which is different from its common meaning, or it would be necessary to invent a new symbol. The first alternative is rejected as creating confusion between the special limited meaning required by logic. A similar argument would apply to the special needs of a philosophical vocabulary, and such an argument could be supported by instancing the notorious misunderstanding to which the philosophical adaptation of such ordinary words as 'idea' and 'object' have been subject.

A second reason for a special language for logic concerns the conventions governing the structure of propositions. Just as the vocabulary of ordinary language is inadequate to the needs of logic, so the grammatical structure of ordinary language is inadequate to the expression of the abstract kind of reasoning employed in logic. For this reason, although ordinary language can easily express complex ideas, for the expression of which it was developed, it is awkward to use it to express the simple ideas of logic and would require a long involved way of saying things. In symbolic logic, conventions of logical grammar are constructed in order to express its arguments with the greatest economy and clarity. If logic were required to use the somewhat arbitrary and accidental rules of the syntax of a natural language, its clarity and economy would suffer. To a somewhat lesser degree the same consideration would apply to the needs of philosophy.

A third reason for employing an artificial language for logic is that it produces a psychological advantage in freeing the understanding from its dependence on the imagination. The interest of the imagination in the content rather than the form of an argument is a disadvantage, particularly when the argument is abstract. This would also apply to the portions of philosophical discourse which are concerned with the forms of argument and with abstract concepts.

A fourth reason for preferring an artificial language is also psychological. When a complex argument, or a simple argument with complex terms, is presented in the more cumbersome language of ordinary speech, the very length of the argument makes it difficult to see its structure. When one is familiar with logical symbols, however, a long and complex argument can be expressed in a small compass, and this aids the intuition in seeing the structure of the argument. Obviously this advantage would accrue to philosophical discourse, but only to the degree to which an entire argument would be expressed in logical symbolism; and this is relatively rare, as is the ability to read the symbols with the required degree of ease.

A fifth advantage of the artificial language is that, since the purpose of a work on logic is to enumerate each step in reasoning, it must use a symbolism which is both terse and formal. Neither of these characteristics belong to ordinary language, but the language of symbolic logic is created intentionally to have these needed characteristics; it is 'made to order' for that task. It seems clear that, in some cases, the steps of philosophical reasoning also require clarification and that the model of the artificial language may help in this respect.

It is true that not all the requirements of philosophical problems are the same as those of formal logic; for instance, complete formality is not required in the formulation on most philosophical problems. However, as in logic proper, philosophical problems require abstract symbols, careful and consistent formulation, and more rigorous reasoning than can be provided by common language. Therefore, the claimed advantages can carry over where the artificial language functions not as the sole medium of expression but as a clarifier of difficulties and a model for an argument form which could be symbolized logically, even though it is not.

Two other philosophical implications of the use of a formal language are given by Russell:

'The purpose of the foregoing discussion of an ideal logical language (which would of course be wholly useless for daily life) is twofold: first, to prevent inferences from the nature of language to the nature of the world, which are fallacious because they depend upon the logical defects of language; secondly, to suggest, by inquiring what logic requires of a language which is to avoid contradiction, what sort of structure we may reasonably suppose the world to have.'[13]

The first advantage cited in this passage is perhaps the strongest and most common argument for the use of an artificial language; the second advantage is peculiar to Russell's own use of the language as a part of the method of analysis.

The justification of the use of an artificial language is based on its preciseness, clarity, and capacity for revealing the structure of an argument. The assumptions which are contained in the argument supporting the use of a constructed language are: that it is preferable for a language to be precise rather than vague or ambiguous, that the clarity of uniform meanings is to be sought in preference to the multiple and flexible meanings of ordinary language, and that the structure of discourse can and should be separated from its content. These assumptions, on which the claim to the usefulness of logical symbolism is based, are the target of contemporary criticism of Russell's method of analysis in particular and of the use of symbolic logic in general. Hence, the estimate of the success of Russell's analytic method depends, in part, on the degree to which the logical language and its assumptions can be accepted.

In addition to the symbolism of modern logic and the language of ordinary speech, there is the formulation of traditional Aristotelian logic which both models itself on and uses ordinary forms of speech and which, over the centuries, has itself influenced the forms of both speech and thought, including philosophical thought. Here Russell, as well as other philosophers, finds that the artificial language is a useful corrective.[14] The sources of error in traditional logic are both specific and general. One specific error is the confusion of propositions which imply the existence of the subject term, the particular affirmative and singular propositions of traditional logic, with those which state only the relation of properties without implying the existence of the terms related, the universal affirmative and universal negative propositions of traditional logic. By the distinction of proposition and propositional function and by the use of quantifier symbols, the new logic has overcome the traditional analysis of form which had obscured these differences and warned all users of language against the rash implication of existence to the terms of propositions. (It should be noted that the treatment of the existential import of propositions is a point on which contemporary critics such as P. F. Strawson have challenged the interpretation of Russell and of other modern symbolic logicians.)

The traditional analysis of propositions into subject and predicate classes, said to be included or excluded from one another, led many philosophers, including Aristotle, to attribute substantive reality to the classes, corresponding to the subject terms of the propositions. The natural 'metaphysics' of language was thus accentuated by the traditional logical formulations. The metaphysical snarls of substance, essence, and attribute may be said to be connected with the class analysis derived from grammar and traditional logic.

Another specific difficulty concerns the treatment of predicates in traditional logic. The syllogistic analysis did not differentiate between predicates related to other predicates and predicates related to subjects, as in the syllogism: 'All Greeks are human, Socrates is a Greek, therefore, Socrates is human.' In this syllogism, the predicate 'human' originally attributed to another predicate 'Greek' is transferred to a subject 'Socrates'. This syllogistic practice confuses and leads to error. Another error results from the confusion of identifying a class of one member with that member, a hurdle which had to be overcome before a satisfactory definition of the number 'one' could be achieved.

In cataloguing the errors of traditional logic, which the superior symbolism of modern logic had overcome, Russell stresses the poverty of the traditional restricted form of analysis. The categorical syllogism was the universal means of analysing arguments, and this overlooked other valid forms of deductive argumentation. For instance, when traditional class inclusion formulation is given to the proposition 'the book is to the right of the pen', it becomes 'All (the book) is (thing to the right of the pen)'. If one were to ask if the proposition 'the pen is to the right of the book' is consistent with the first proposition or not, traditional logic would have no way of treating the two propositions since the terms 'thing to the right of the book' and 'things to the right of the pen' are disparate. Yet common sense recognizes that if the first is true, the second must be false. Modern logic is able to deal with such inferences through its treatment of relations, as symmetrical, asymmetrical, or nonsymmetrical. Similarly, traditional logic could not cope with a syllogism in which it was stated that: 'since the book is to the right of the pen', and 'the pen is to the right of the newspaper', therefore, 'the book is to the right of the newspaper'. The formulation of an Aristotelian syllogism would fail to find three terms in this argument; but relational logic deals with this kind of inference by treating 'to the right of' as a transitive relation. This is one kind of deductive inference which is beyond the scope of the syllogism; it is particularly important because in order for a common set of logical symbols to be used for both logic and mathematics, these symbols must permit the elaboration of mathematical systems, and for this relational arguments are vital.[15] In general, the revision of traditional logic was needed not only to supply the glaring omissions of Aristotelian formulations, but to provide a basis for a system of logical primitives sufficiently rich and flexible that any form of deduction, mathematical as well as linguistic in form, could be analysed by means of them.[16]

One of the philosophical issues which was connected with the analysis of relational arguments was that of the philosophical concepts of internal and external relations. In his early study of Leibniz, Russell found that Leibniz was led to a doctrine of internal relations partially through his acceptance of the subject-predicate logic of Aristotle. If it was held that the predicate was contained analytically in the subject, as it was for Leibniz, then all the relations of a given subject term must be thought of as internal to that term. The metaphysical implications of this analysis of relations were evident, not only in Leibniz' monadology, but also in the absolute idealism of Bradley from which Russell (at this period) was engaged in liberating himself. He came to the conclusion that the doctrine of internal relations was wrong; and this was one more reason for welcoming the new logical symbolism which promised a better way of formulating relations.[17]

The new logic attempted to uncover the elements of form in inferences where these forms were obscured by irrelevancies of content, idioms of natural languages, traditional syllogistic forms, or formulations required for specific mathematical manipulations. Among the formal elements of major importance discriminated in the *Principia* are the above-mentioned kinds of propositional structure, especially the distinction of atomic and molecular propositions. This distinction of simple and complex propositions, although described in terms of the forms of propositions, had far-reaching epistemological and metaphysical consequences both in Russell's philosophy and in that of logical positivism.

The atomic proposition corresponds to the categorical proposition of Aristotelian logic which has a single subject and a single predicate. The atomic proposition is not further analysable into subsidiary forms but is analysable into its components. These components may be terms and a relation, or a term and a predicate.

The terms will vary in number according to whether the proposition contains a single term and a quality-word, which Russell for convenience refers to as a single-termed relation,[18] or a dyadic, triadic or other relation with the corresponding number of terms. Instances of atomic propositions would be 'Plato loves Socrates' and 'this pencil is red'. In these atomic propositions the terms such as 'Plato' and 'Socrates' and 'this pencil' name a particular, while words such as a relation word, 'love', or a predicate word, 'red', are understood only in the context of what is related, or of what the predicate is predicated of. In addition, the structure of the proposition itself is a component of the meaning, since 'Socrates loves Plato', and 'Plato loves Socrates' are different in meaning although made up of the same components. In this case the order of words gives the direction of the relation. The proposition is atomic in the sense that it is the smallest unit of assertion or statement; the components of the atomic proposition name, or apply to components named, but they do not assert.

It is in the relation of the atomic proposition to the fact asserted by it that the metaphysical and epistemological implications are evident. The clearest presentation of these implications is found in 'The Philosophy of Logical Atomism'. An atomic proposition is true if its components and its structure have a correspondence with the named elements and structure of the fact. Epistemologically, this means that each constituent of the proposition must be known directly by acquaintance; that is, each term of the proposition must be a 'proper name'. The example of 'Plato loves Socrates' would now fail to qualify since the grammatically proper names of this proposition are actually concealed descriptions.[19] Hence the atomic propositions would have to have terms which mean present nameable particulars, such as 'this pencil' in 'this pencil is red'. In addition to the proper names which name directly, the quality-words or relation-words would have to correspond with directly observable qualities or relations. And, in addition, the structure of the proposition would have to be seen to correspond point by point with the structure of the fact asserted. Only when these conditions are met can the structure of the proposition be said to correspond to the structure of the fact, and hence the atomic proposition can be said to be true. If one of the terms, relations, or predicates of the proposition lacks a correlate, or if the propositional structure does not parallel the factual structure, the proposition is false. Knowledge by acquaintance in the direct grasp of the terms, relations, and structure of the fact is assumed by the original programme of logical atomism. This view of acquaintance was later modified, as was the ideal of the complete isomorphism of the proposition and the fact. However, the epistemological importance of the role of 'logically proper names' and of basic propositions of atomic form has not changed[20] and has remained an important ingredient of Russell's empiricism. The connection between the basic atomic proposition and the derived and complex propositions required of science and common-sense knowledge has continued to be a central epistemological concern.

Each atomic proposition is independent of every other atomic proposition; the only way in which the atomic propositions can be linked is by the logical connectives of molecular propositions. The atomic propositions form the components of molecular propositions, and the truth of the molecular proposition is dependent on two factors, the truth-value of its component atomic propositions and the truth-functional definition of the logical connective which links those components. For instance, the molecular proposition 'it is raining and the wind is blowing' depends for its truth-value on whether, *in fact*, the atomic propositions 'it is raining' and 'the wind is blowing' are true; and, also on the meaning of 'and', that is, conjunction as a logical connective. 'And' means that the proposition containing 'and', or the conjunctive proposition, is true, if, and only if, all the conjuncts are true. Hence if, in fact, it is the case that it is raining and that the wind is blowing, then the molecular proposition 'it is raining and the wind is blowing' is true. The *Principia*, formulating the rules of the sentential calculus, showed how the truth-values of discourse involving molecular propositions could be built up by more complicated inferences from the truth-values of atomic propositions. This aspect of the analysis of the forms of propositions was the basis of the method of analysis which Russell proposed under the title 'logical atomism' and which Wittgenstein presented in *Tractatus Logico-Philosophicus*. It was a method by which statements remote from observation but claiming truth could be reduced to component propositions on which the truth claim of the original propositions could be shown to rest.[21] It was thus an epistemological method, and it carried certain metaphysical assumptions with it. The assumption that simples could be analysed out of facts as their constituents, as terms could be analysed out of propositions, seemed to say something about the correspondence of language to reality and about the nature of 'what there is'. Russell did not commit himself explicitly to 'ultimate simples'.[22] But his own shifting terminology in referring to simples sometimes as 'constituents of facts' and sometimes as 'constituents of propositions' lends itself to the interpretation of logical atomism as a comprehensive metaphysical and epistemological philosophy rather than as a tentative method of analysis.[23] He did realize that assumptions of the correspondence of reality to what can be said of reality were involved.

As will be discussed later, there were initial difficulties in logical atomism. The description of atomic propositions seemed to commit Russell to the existence of negative and general facts. At the same time the so-called 'non-truth-functional' propositions such as 'I believe that it is raining' appeared to resist truth-functional analysis since the truth of the component 'it is raining' seems to be unrelated to the truth of the whole proposition.[24] Later, when Russell changed his analysis of perception and gave up 'knowledge by acquaintance', further changes were required in his analysis. These and other reservations concerning logical atomism are discussed by Russell in *My Philosophical Development* and will be relevant in the present study in other contexts. However, it is clear that the distinction of atomic and molecular forms was and remains an important one in Russell's method of analysis.

In addition to the unfortunate consequences for philosophy of traditional logic and to its other restrictions, it was limited in that it overemphasized deductive inferences. Aristotelian logic was formed when the ideal of 'science' was one of classification and of the inference from one universal proposition to another. But in the modern world, with the presence of scientific methods of inquiry which depend upon techniques of observation, experimentation, and verification, the logic of Aristotle has no relevance to the most successful and progressive methods of knowing which man has been able to develop.[25] The early efforts of Bacon and Mill in the direction of a logic of induction were mere hints, and little systematic work has been done on the formulation of other than deductive forms of inference. The future of the use of the artificial language and the importance of logical analysis itself require a logic of non-demonstrative inference. This often acknowledged need Russell attempted to meet in *Human Knowledge*.[26]

One of the distinctive logical theories of *Principia Mathematica* is the theory of types. This theory was developed to resolve a set of contradictions which developed in the strictly logical and mathematical aspects of the theory. However, Russell's suggested solution to the problem posed by these contradictions had far-reaching consequences both in his own philosophy and in that of other contemporary philosophers.

Russell came upon the contradictions when, following his introduction to the work of Peano in 1900, he used the new notation to work out his fundamental ideas in the foundations of logic and mathematics. After an eighteen-month 'intellectual honeymoon' when every day saw new success for his method, Russell discovered the contradiction of classes which are not members of themselves.[27] The first form of the contradiction arose when he asked of this class, Is it a member of itself? If this class is a member of itself, it is a member of a class which is not a member of itself, and this is a contradiction. If the class is not a member of itself, then it belongs to the class of things which are not members of themselves, and thus, it is a member of itself. This is also a contradiction. This paradox proved recalcitrant to further analysis, and, on further investigation, Russell found that it was connected with a number of other contradictions, some of which had been discovered in mathematics, and some of which were old-fashioned puzzlers. To the first group belonged the contradiction of the greatest cardinal number, and to the second group belonged the classic paradox of Epimenides the Cretan who said that all Cretans are liars.

Eventually, Russell analysed these and a number of other contradictions which he showed could be generated in the same way, as arising when one tried to make a statement about a totality of propositions, when the statement itself was included in that totality. For a long time Russell had found no solution to the paradox, and in *The Principles of Mathematics*, published in 1903, he stated it as an unsolved problem.[28] However, some considerations concerning classes offered an unexpected key to the puzzle. He found that instead of treating numbers and classes as having some kind of undefinable reality, it is possible to treat both of them as propositional functions; that is, a class is the values that satisfy a given function. In this view a class is merely an expression rather than an independent reality, hence it is reasonable to put certain limits on the range of such an expression in the interests of its making sense. The theory of types distinguishes between a first-order and a second-order statement and specifies that when a statement is made about a totality of first-order statements, the statement concerning that totality is itself a second-order statement. We are prohibited from mixing the two different levels of statement. Hence when a statement is made concerning the class of things which are not members of themselves, that statement cannot itself be treated as a member of the class of statements to which it refers. There are two levels involved here and they must be kept separate. Similarly, when Epimenides made the statement that 'All Cretans are liars', this was a second-order statement concerning a number of first-order statements made by Cretans. His statement concerning the habits of Cretans could not itself be included in the totality of first-order statements to which he referred.[29]

Russell developed more than one version of the theory of types, and, as he points out, recent developments in mathematical logic have moved away from the technical statement of the ramified theory of types.[30] However, as Reichenbach observes,[31] all language systems in contemporary philosophy follow Russell in introducing rules concerning the levels of language in the syntax of their formal languages, both to avoid the contradictions discussed by Russell and to effect the clarification to be obtained by distinguishing a hierarchy of languages. The concept of levels of theory, of mathematics and meta-mathematics, of ethics and meta-ethics, in which the meta-study concerns an analysis of what is said in the study proper, derives from this insight of Russell. Thus, in spite of the fact that technical logic may, to solve the problem of the paradoxes discussed by Russell, develop techniques other than those of the ramified theory of types, the recognition of the paradox, and the recognition of the necessity of distinguishing levels of reference within the structure of a language remain important. The theory of types was developed to resolve the antinomies of classes which are members of themselves. However, this distinction gave rise to other distinctions, especially in the hands of Rudolf Carnap, of levels of language. Russell himself made use of this same idea of levels of language when, in his analysis of meaning in *Inquiry into Meaning and Truth*, he attempted to distinguish the object-language, the second level of propositions which have a certain relation to the object language in which 'logical words' occur, and succeeding levels of indirectness by which any statement can be seen to be certain degrees removed from the level of the object-language.[32] This will be discussed as part of the analysis of language.

Another technique developed by Russell to solve a problem in logical theory, incorporated into the formal system of *Principia Mathematica*, played an important philosophical role in Russell's theory of knowledge and in much contemporary analysis. This is what was called the theory of descriptions, the method of construction, or the resolution of incomplete symbols.[33] These terms refer to one technique; there are different contexts in which the technique is used and for which one term is more appropriate than another. In the original context in which Russell presented this theory, the stress was on logical theory, particularly on the problem of analysing the meaning of certain kinds of puzzling symbols and statements. The first statement occurred in an article, 'On Denoting', in *Mind* of 1905. In this article Russell pointed out that symbols like 'unicorn', 'round square', and 'golden mountain' present a problem in the analysis of meaning. These symbols seem to perform the same kind of role in sentences as are performed by symbols such as 'horse', 'isosceles triangle', and 'Matterhorn'. Yet, in the case of these peculiar symbols one cannot trace their meaning by pointing to their denotation, that is, to the objects to which they refer. Yet the puzzling symbols are not meaningless, nor are the propositions in which they occur nonsensical.

Russell earlier had followed Meinong, and, in the first flush of realism, had supposed that these symbols have referents; although the referents do not exist, they may be said to subsist. He now found this position to verge on contradiction and to be offensive to 'logical common sense'. On the other hand, Frege had proposed that, in the case of these symbols without referents, their meaning lay not in their denotation but in their connotation. This seemed unsatisfactory because, as Russell pointed out, it strains the imagination to believe that the meaning of a statement about the present president of the United States lies in the man, while the meaning of a statement about the present king of the United States lies in a complicated analysis of the conceptual meanings of the symbols used.[34]

What Russell proposed was a new analysis of such 'denoting phrases', as he called them. This analysis would show how words like 'unicorn' have meaning; it would show how some statements 'the present king of France is bald' and 'Scott is the author of Waverley' can be analysed. The assumption on which both the problem and the solution is based is that in the analysis of the meaning of a proposition one seeks to connect each component of the proposition with a constituent of experience, either directly or indirectly. Some place in the analysis of a proposition one must come to something with which one is acquainted, for which the component of the proposition is a name. The problem arises because these symbols in question do not refer to such components of experience. Russell says that 'denoting phrases' are 'incomplete symbols' which appear to be names but are actually symbols which have meaning only in the context of the proposition in which each occurs. He goes on to show how these apparent names can be replaced in their propositions so that the meaning is revealed, but the seeming-name-symbol drops out.

He applies this theory of denotation to the puzzle of 'the present king of France is bald'. This proposition seems to have meaning and to be false, yet it is not false in the sense that the king of France has hair. This puzzle is solved when we replace 'the present king of France is bald' with 'one and only one person is the present king of France, and that person is bald'. We then see that it is the first part of this conjunction which is false. It is not the case that there exists a person who is the present king of France, and this is what makes the whole proposition false.

Similarly, there is a puzzle about 'Scott is the author of Waverley'. It appears that 'the author of Waverley' is a name, just as 'Scott' is a name, and that the statement is one of identity, similar to 'Scott is Scott'. Yet, it seems that one could know who Scott is without knowing that he wrote Waverley, or know the author of Waverley without knowing his name. Hence, it cannot be a statement of identity, and the two symbols 'Scott' and 'the author of Waverley' are not two names for one referent. Russell, by his method, shows that 'the author of Waverley' is an incomplete symbol which can be analysed as 'one and only one person wrote Waverley, and that person is Scott'. Here the seeming-name-symbol drops out, but the meaning is retained.

Russell presents his theory as a more satisfactory analysis of the meaning of these troublesome symbols and propositions than had yet been put forth. From the beginning he intended the analysis to apply to all phrases of the form 'the such and such', which he called definite descriptions, and phrases of the form 'a such and such', which he called indefinite descriptions. These descriptive phrases, on analysis, could be shown not to name or to refer directly, but to have meaning only in the context of the proposition in which they occur and to be amenable to a re-statement in which the original symbols drop out.

Although this was first put forward as a theory designed to solve a problem in theory of meaning and to have a formulation and an application in the formal system of the *Principia*, it was connected with an epistemological conception which Russell held at this time, the distinction between knowledge by description and knowledge by acquaintance.[35] These two matters are connected because it was a rule for the analysis of the meaning of a proposi-that 'propositions which we can understand are composed of con-stituents with which we are acquainted'. These denotative ele-ments of meaning direct us to the search for those elements of our knowledge with which we have direct acquaintance. Russell explained that there is a direct two-term relation between subject and object in acquaintance in which an object is directly presented to the subject without formulation or risk of error. All com-ponents of propositions which cannot be brought back to this kind of confrontation must be known indirectly, that is, by des-cription. For instance, 'yellowness-here-now' would refer to something directly known by acquaintance, while 'the book', 'the table' would be a descriptive term, an incomplete symbol.[36] It could be given meaning only in terms of being brought back to items with which the knower is directly acquainted, through an analysis of the symbol in question.

There was a continuing search in Russell's theory of knowledge to find the components of propositions which directly refer to experience, that is, logically proper names, and then to show how other symbols can be analysed as descriptions, in terms of these names with direct denotations. At the early period in which he held the distinction between knowledge by acquaintance and knowledge by description, he found that most words which are considered proper names by grammar are actually descriptions.[37] Even in the case where the proper name refers to someone or something with which we have direct acquaintance, that acquaintance is partial. Proper names, like common nouns, are often terms used for convenience to refer to a class of 'appearances'. Later on in the development of Russell's philosophy, the problem was complicated by the relinquishing of the distinction between knowledge by acquaintance and knowledge by description. The direct two-term relation of acquaintance was given up, and this made the finding of logically proper names more difficult. The problem remains in the discussion of minimum vocabularies in *Human Knowledge* and of logically proper names in the *Inquiry* and in *My Philosophical Development*.[38]

In addition to the use of the method of the analysis of incomplete symbols and the analysis of descriptions, the same method had an important application under the title of 'the method of construction'. In *Principia Mathematica* Russell and Whitehead had effected a logical economy by replacing numbers and classes as undefined entities with propositional functions, thus eliminating the need for postulating them and satisfying the demands of Occam's razor. In a similar way, Whitehead had suggested that points and instants of physical space and time could be constructed; that is, they could be shown to be incomplete symbols whose complete explication would be in terms of the analysis of their meaning in a given context. Their meaning thus analysed, the symbols were used as a notational convenience without the necessity of inferring or postulating entities to which they refer.[39] Russell adopted this method and extended its use to deal with other concepts used in physics and with concepts used in common sense. This is the method of construction which is presented as the new scientific method of philosophizing in *Our Knowledge of the External World*.[40] In this work the units of sense-data are used as the basis of the constructions by which a bridge is built between perception and the entities of physical science. 'Matter', 'cause', and other concepts of physics are to be resolved by analysis into constructions from sense-data, thus eliminating the need to postulate a world of space, time, matter as real in order for the conclusions of science to be meaningful.

In a 1914 essay, 'The Relation of Sense Data to Physics', Russell prophesies:

'A complete application of the method which substitutes constructions for inferences would exhibit matter wholly in terms of sense-data, and even, we may add, of the sense-data of a single person, since the sense-data of others cannot be known without some element of inference.'[41]

Russell recognized that the realization of this ideal was far off, and, as a matter of fact, it failed to be realized at all. However, the method by which it was approached is of crucial importance in Russell's theory of knowledge.

The method of construction was used in constructing the objects of common sense as well as those of science. Sense data are again the units employed, and the analysis attempts to show how the object can be constructed as that symbol for which the class of sense data (what would ordinarily be called its 'appearances') would be the resolution of the object-name as an incomplete symbol. Russell shows how we can get along without the idea of a permanent substance or thing:

'We say, for example, that things change gradually—sometimes very quickly, but not without passing through a continuous series of intermediate states, or at least an approximately continuous series, if the discontinuities of the quantum theory should prove ultimate. What this means is that, given any sensible appearance, there will usually be, *if we watch*, a continuous series of appearances connected with the given one, leading on by imperceptible gradations to the new appearances which common sense regards as those of the same thing. Thus a thing may be defined as a certain series of appearances, connected with each other by continuity and by certain causal laws. In the case of slowly changing things, this is easily seen. Consider, say, a wall-paper which fades in the course of years. It is an effort not to conceive of it as one "thing" whose colour is slightly different at one time from what it is at another. But what do we really *know* about it? We know that under suitable circumstances—i.e. when we are, as is said, "in the room"—we perceive colours in a certain pattern: not always precisely the same colours, but sufficiently similar to feel familiar. If we can state the laws according to which the colour varies, we can state all that is empirically verifiable; the assumption that there is a constant entity, the wall-paper, which "has" these various colours at various times, is a piece of gratuitous metaphysics. We may, if we like, *define* the wall-paper as the series of its aspects. These are collected together by the same motives which led us to regard the wall-paper as one thing, namely a combination of sensible continuity and causal connection. More generally, a "thing" will be defined as a certain series of aspects, namely those which would commonly be said to be *of* the thing. . . . Everything will then proceed as before: whatever was verifiable is unchanged, but our language is so interpreted as to avoid an unnecessary metaphysical assumption of permanence.'[42]

After the adoption of neutral monism a further development of the method of construction enabled Russell to resolve the supposed difference between mind and matter to a difference in the method of constructing causal laws of physics and of psychology. The causal laws of physics are constructed by grouping the particulars which could be thought of as the 'appearances' of a thing from different simultaneous 'perspectives'. The laws of psychology result from the grouping of 'appearances' at succeeding times from one given spatial perspective. The method of construction is applied to a number of concepts of physics and of psychology in the two books, *The Analysis of Matter* and *The Analysis of Mind*.[43] Altogether, Weitz estimates that Russell worked out in detail the construction of 'about twenty constructions'. These include: in physics, 'space', 'time', 'thing', or 'matter', 'points', 'instants', 'qualitative series', 'space-time', 'interval', and 'quantity'; and, in psychology, 'instinct', 'habit', 'desire', 'feeling', 'perception', 'memory', 'conception', 'thought', 'belief', 'emotions', 'will', and 'consciousness'.[44]

A good example of Russell's use of the method of construction is the construction of instants of time, and time series, as these are described in *Our Knowledge of the External World*.[45] This example is particularly valuable for our purposes for several reasons. It occurs in the book in which Russell's intention is to explain and exemplify the method of construction, and for this reason explanatory comments accompany the example. The language employed is not so technical as to be incomprehensible to the reader who is untrained in mathematics and physics. In addition, the example concerns the treatment of time, a continuing concern of Russell's throughout his career and one judged by him to be of importance and value.[46]

He begins the analysis of time by describing the problem which the construction is designed to solve; that is, the problem of the gap between the unit of a time series required by science and the actual perception of temporality as this is given in human experience. Science requires instants of time, a compact series of infinitely divisible units of time with certain logical and mathematical properties. But time as experienced is always of events which last for some finite length of time however short. Events themselves may or may not be instantaneous; in any case, our sense data are not. Therefore, instants must be constructed. The material from which instants and time series are to be constructed is that of 'immediate experience'. Russell finds that what is given in immediate experience is a number of events in time relations of being simultaneous and earlier or later than one another. Events have durations of varying lengths so the simultaneity and succession may include overlapping events. For instance, one event may begin before another; then the second event may begin and the two events be simultaneous; then the first event may continue after the second event has ended, and thus the first may also be later than the second. The time relations of simultaneity and succession are part of the 'crude data', but this does not include any absolute dating, as it is merely relative order. Instants and an objective dating order must both be constructed.[47]

Russell begins his construction by postulating a number of

events simultaneous with one another. He proposes that we have an event A and an event B which partly overlap, but B ends before A ends. In that case, an event which is simultaneous with both A and B must exist during the time when A and B overlap. This third event may be called C and it may be considered to be dated by its simultaneity with A and B. However, there is still a time-span of its possible exact dates. This span may be narrowed by postulating a fourth event which is simultaneous with the overlapping of A and B and C. Each time the simultaneity of an additional event is added to the series the time spread of the overlapping of these events is narrowed. This leads to the following definition of an instant of time:

'Let us take a group of events of which any two overlap, so that there is some time, however short, when they all exist. If there is any other event which is simultaneous with all of these, let us add it to the group; let us go on until we have constructed a group such that no event outside the group is simultaneous with all of them, but all the events inside the group are simultaneous with each other. Let us define this whole group as an instant of time.'[48]

Russell then proceeds to show that an instant constructed in this way will have the properties required of an instant for the purposes of physics and the mathematical treatment of time. The required properties are said to be three: instants must form a series, each event must be 'at' a certain number of instants and the series of instants must be compact. The first requirement means that the relation of before and after must be asymmetrical and transitive; if one instant is before another, and that other is before a third, then the first is before the third. The second requirement means that events may be dated in terms of simultaneity and succession of instants. If a given event lasts for a certain number of instants, there will be an instant before the event-instants at which the event is not occurring, and an event occurring at the earlier instant is not simultaneous with the event occurring at the later instants. The third requirement means that, assuming some change to be always going on in some place during the time when an event persists, any two instants will have other instants between them.

Russell proceeds to demonstrate that instants constructed according to the suggested pattern will have the required characteristics. The demonstration of the satisfaction of the first requirement involves a definition of the relation of 'wholly precedes' to apply to events which are earlier than a given event and do not overlap it. Similarly, the demonstration given for the second requirement involves the definition of the 'initial contemporaries of an event', as the events which are simultaneous with a given event and do not begin later than the given event. This is the first instant at which the given event exists and allows us to have a satisfactory definition of the duration of an event in terms of instants. One problem is suggested by the third requirement; that is, an assumption is required about what is empirically true of the occurrence of events which are not observed. Accordingly, Russell sets forth in detail what the treatment of instants and time series assumes concerning time relations in experience:

'The assumptions made concerning time-relations in one experience in the above are as follows:

I. In order to secure that instants form a series, we assume:
    (a) No event wholly precedes itself. (An "event" is defined as whatever is simultaneous with something or other.)
    (b) If one event wholly precedes another, and the other wholly precedes a third, then the first wholly precedes the third.
    (c) If one event wholly precedes another, it is not simultaneous with it.
    (d) Of two events which are not simultaneous, one must wholly precede the other.
II. In order to secure that the initial contemporaries of a given event should form an instant, we assume:

(e) An event wholly after some contemporary of a given event is wholly after some *initial* contemporary of the given event.

III. In order to secure that the series of instants shall be compact, we assume:

(f) If one event wholly precedes another, there is an event wholly after the one and simultaneous with something wholly before the other.

'This assumption entails the consequence that if one event covers the whole of a stretch of time immediately preceding another event, then it must have at least one instant in common with the other event; i.e. it is impossible for one event to cease just before another begins. I do not know whether this should be regarded as inadmissible.'[49]

It seems that only assumption (f) requires anything more than a formal statement of what we have found the experience of time to be. This assumption, required if instants of time are to form a compact series, means that we must 'either bring in events wholly outside our experience, or assume that experienced events have parts which we do not experience, or postulate that we can experience an infinite number of events at once'.[50]

Russell does not regard the construction of instants and time-series contained in this passage as complete. It is incomplete in that explicit development of the construction in terms of the technical problems of physics is needed to amplify it. The construction is incomplete, also, in that no attention has been given to the problem of the correlation of the times of different 'private worlds'. But at least a framework of construction has been provided which will permit the further elaboration of the construction in physics. Russell concludes,

'The above brief outline must not be regarded as more than tentative and suggestive. It is intended merely to show the kind of way in which, given a world with the kind of properties that psychologists find in the world of sense, it may be possible, by means of purely logical constructions, to make it amenable to mathematical treatment by defining series or classes of sense-data which can be called respectively particles, points, and instants. If such constructions are possible, then mathematical physics is applicable to the real world, in spite of the fact that its particles, points, and instants are not to be found among actually existing entities.'[51]

We might sum up Russell's use of the method of construction according to the motives which made this method desirable and effective in his eyes. There is first of all the general motive of all analysis—clarification. The breaking up of vague complex notions or entities or things into components means an increase in precision and clarity of conception. Secondly, there is the consideration of attempting to build a bridge between the world of science and the world of sense and the justification of science in terms of some kind of inference from, or reduction to, the data of sense. In this sense, Wood says that it is characteristic of Russell's method to work backwards from conclusions to premises, asking what assumptions must be accepted, what steps of inference must be taken in order that the conclusion follow.[52] This is a long-term aspect of Russell's work, and it is present in the early efforts of the method of construction. These first two emphases in Russell's method of analysis in general, and the method of construction in particular, are referred to in the concluding lecture of *Our Knowledge of the External World*:

'The nature of philosophic analysis, as illustrated in our previous lectures, can now be stated in general terms. We start from a body of common knowledge, which constitutes our data. On examination, the data are found to be complex, rather vague, and largely interdependent logically. By analysis we reduce them to propositions which are as nearly as possible simple and precise, and we arrange them in deductive chains, in which a certain number of initial propositions form a logical guarantee for all the rest. These initial propositions are *premisses* for the body of knowledge in question. Premisses are thus quite different from data—they are simpler, more precise, and less infected with logical redundancy. If the work of analysis has been performed completely, they will be wholly free from logical redundancy, wholly precise, and as simple as is logically compatible with their leading to the given body of knowledge. The discovery of these premisses belongs to philosophy; but the work of deducing the body of common knowledge from them belongs to mathematics, if 'mathematics' is interpreted in a somewhat liberal sense.'[53]

This passage refers to the clarification and simplification, to the effort of using logical techniques to bridge the gap between the knowledge which is accepted and the premisses from which it must be shown to follow. This brings us to the particular use of the method of construction; in working back from conclusions to premisses any steps of valid inference are acceptable, but there is a difficulty in finding methods of inference which can effect this reduction. It is here that the method of construction comes in, as an application of the use of Occam's razor. Occam's razor advises the avoidance of unnecessary postulations, or of the multiplications of inferred entities, both because postulations and inferences involve a greater risk of error, and because the simpler and logically more economical system is to be preferred as a logical ideal here, as in 'mathematics' in the narrower sense. By making the symbols referring to 'things', 'entities', and so on, incomplete symbols, the resolution of which would show them to be constructions from uninferred units, particulars, or sense data, this scientific method of philosophizing clarifies, orders, and effects a logical economy. The other motive in the method of analysis which is particularly evident in the method of construction is the attempt to render scientific and common-sense knowledge *empirically* justified. It is for this reason that units of sense experience are specified as that which the construction is a construction of, or that for which the resolved symbols are shown to be symbols for. Whether these are termed sense data or sensed particulars, their status as basic in construction is due to their being experienced. The empiricist motive is evident, further, in the theory of descriptions, where the meaning of the symbol is given in terms of its sense-data equivalents, the descriptive term 'table' being equated with the 'class of what would ordinarily be called its appearances'. Here, the validation of descriptive knowledge by its analysis in terms of meanings given in knowledge by acquaintance, is the epistemological correlate of the logical treatment of 'incomplete symbols'. Accordingly, the epistemological, if not the logical force, of the theory of descriptions was weakened by the surrender of 'knowledge by acquaintance'. In a similar way, the meaning analysis which followed the dictum that 'every proposition which we can understand must be composed wholly of constituents with which we are acquainted' encountered analogous difficulties.[54] As we shall see, it was this empiricist aspect of the method of construction which ran into the greatest difficulty; the hope that all concepts and entities could be constructed from the sense data of a single person proved unfounded, and the original postulations, the unsensed particulars, the minds of others, and the causal theory of perception, instead of being reduced, required to be supplemented. This theme is to be expanded in a later chapter.

The method of construction itself was never actually abandoned by Russell, but it gradually played a less important role in his philosophy. The entities which he was able to show as constructions retained this status, but in other cases, he was not able to complete the required constructions. He became more and more aware of the gaps in the analysis and used other techniques in an attempt to construct a continuity between the premisses and the conclusion. However, Occam's razor remained a logical leading principle for him. After his exploration of language in the *Inquiry* and in *Human Knowledge*, the motive of logical economy showed itself more particularly in the search for a 'minimum vocabulary', for 'logically proper names'.[55]

The consideration of what is meant by the analytic method in Russell's philosophy might be concluded appropriately by indicating how the fulfillment of Russell's own programme for philosophizing, if it could be accomplished in the way he thought desirable, would end by transferring many topics which are now undecided and the subject of philosophical debate to the realm of science, where they would have answers which meet the requirements of scientific conclusions. A likely candidate for this successful treatment is the concept of time. Russell has indicated how the units of experience, sensed or psychological time, can be so ordered according to the concepts of overlapping presents, or specious presents, or events, that by means of the method of construction, the needed scientific concepts of continuity, of the space-time dimensions, can be constructed logically from them. If this analysis were carried out, the whole construction could be formulated in symbols. It would appear, in that case, as a hypothesis which could be employed by physics, and perhaps by psychology, in the formulations of those sciences. If this project could be carried out, the logical techniques we have discussed would be employed cooperatively and successfully to the solution of a philosophical problem. The difficulties to be overcome before any concepts would be ready for transference have to do with the supplementary postulates which Russell still regarded as necessary in order to make the argument rigorously derived from experience. Accordingly, we must turn our attention to the difficulties which Russell met in his use of experience and the means by which he attempted to overcome them.

NOTES TO CHAPTER III

1. Russell, *My Philosophical Development*, p. 133.
2. Russell, 'The Philosophy of Logical Atomism', *Logic and Knowledge*, pp. 179–80.
3. Russell, *My Philosophical Development*, p. 133.
4. *Ibid.*, pp. 229–30.
5. *Ibid.*, p. 14.
6. Russell, *Inquiry*, pp. 350 *ff*.

7. Russell, *My Philosophical Development*, p. 219.

8. For instance, Urmson, *Philosophical Analysis*, Chapters II and IX. For Russell's response, cf. *My Philosophical Development*, p. 224.

9. A. N. Whitehead, *Process and Reality*, Chapter II, Macmillan, New York, 1929.

10. Whitehead and Russell, *Principia Mathematica*, Introduction to first edition. The following arguments, one to five, are adapted from this introduction.

11. Ludwig Wittgenstein, *Philosophical Investigations*, translated by G. E. M. Anscombe, Basil Blackwell, Oxford, first edition, 1953, second edition, 1958, Part I, No. 81.

12. Rudolph Carnap, 'The Old and the New Logic', translated by Isaac Levi from 'Die alte und die neue Logik', *Erkenntnis*, Vol. I, No. 1, in *Logical Positivism*, pp. 136–7.

13. Russell, 'Logical Atomism', *Contemporary British Philosophy*, First Series, George Allen and Unwin, London, 1924, reprinted in *Logic and Knowledge*, p. 338.

14. Russell, *History of Western Philosophy*, Chapter XXII. This chapter contains a summary of the criticisms of Aristotelian logic.

15. Russell, *My Philosophical Development*, pp. 54–5.

16. *Ibid.*, pp. 65 *f.*

17. *Ibid.*, pp. 67 *f.*

18. Russell, *Logic and Knowledge*, p. 199.

19. *Ibid.*, p. 200.

20. Russell, *Inquiry*. For a discussion of atomic form, see pp. 44 *f.* For a discussion of proper names, see pp. 94 *f.*

21. Some historians trace important concepts of logical positivism to this distinction between atomic and molecular propositions. This distinction, especially as incorporated by Russell and Wittgenstein into their respective 'logical atomisms', led the emerging Vienna Circle to formulate the verifiability criterion of truth as a version of the comparison of the form of the fact with the form of the atomic proposition as described by Russell and Wittgenstein. This concept was also connected with the distinction of factual and syntactical propositions, the latter corresponding to the statement of the translation rules of the sentential calculus shown by Wittgenstein to be tautologous. See Rudolph Carnap, 'Intellectual Autobiography', in *The Philosophy of Rudolph Carnap*, 'The Library of Living Philosophers', edited by Paul Arthur Schilpp, The Open Court Publishing Co., Lasalle, Illinois, 1963, p. 57.

22. Russell, *Logic and Knowledge*, p. 337.

23. *Ibid.*, p. 248, This was pointed out by A. C. Benjamin, 'The Logical

Atomism of Bertrand Russell' (unpublished doctoral dissertation), The University of Michigan, 1924.

24. Russell, *Logic and Knowledge*, p. 216.

25. Russell, *History of Western Philosophy*, p. 199.

26. Russell, *Human Knowledge*, Part Six.
Russell, *My Philosophical Development*, Chapter XVI.

27. Russell, 'My Mental Development', *The Philosophy of Bertrand Russell*, pp. 12–13.
Russell, *My Philosophical Development*, Chapter VII.

28. Russell, *The Principles of Mathematics*, Chapter X

29. Whitehead and Russell, *Principia Mathematica*, Introduction, Chapter II.
Russell, *The Principles of Mathematics*, 2nd edition preface, pp. xii–xiv.

30. Russell, *My Philosophical Development*, p. 82.

31. Reichenbach, 'Bertrand Russell's Logic', *The Philosophy of Bertrand Russell*, pp. 37–9.

32. Russell, *Inquiry*, p. 19. See Chapters IV–VII.

33. Bertrand Russell, 'On Denoting', *Mind*, 1905, reprinted in *Logic and Knowledge*. This is the first statement. For the formal statement, see *Principia Mathematica*, Introduction, Chapter III. For more popular explanations, see Russell, *Our Knowledge of the External World*, pp. 94 *ff.*, and pp. 120 *ff.* Also see Russell, 'The Relations of Sense-Data to Physics', *Mysticism and Logic*, pp. 156 *ff.*

34. Russell, 'On Denoting', *Logic and Knowledge*, pp. 45–6.

35. Bertrand Russell, 'Knowledge by Acquaintance and Knowledge by Description', *Proceedings of the Aristotelian Society*, 1910–11, reprinted in *Mysticism and Logic*. Note that Russell warns against connecting this essay too closely with the theory of descriptions, for in the essay the distinction of acquaintance and descriptive knowledge is connected with the 'fundamental epistemological principle in the analysis of propositions containing descriptions is this: *Every proposition which we can understand must be composed wholly by constituents with which we are acquainted*' (p. 219). While it is true that the theory of descriptions was developed first to solve a problem in theory of meaning and in logic, yet the essay referred to gives abundant evidence of the application of the method of construction to the carrying out of the principle just stated as the references below show. Russell's caution is expressed in his 'Reply to Criticisms', *The Philosophy of Bertrand Russell*, p. 692.

36. Russell, 'Knowledge by Acquaintance and Knowledge by Description', *Mysticism and Logic*, pp. 212–13.

37. *Ibid.*, pp. 216 *ff.*

38. *Human Knowledge*, Part IV, Chapter II. *Inquiry*, Chapters IV–VII. Russell, *My Philosophical Development*, pp. 165–74.
39. Russell, *Our Knowledge of the External World*, pp. 119–21. Here Russell states Whitehead's use of the method, called by him the method of extensive abstraction.
40. Russell, *Our Knowledge of the External World*, p. 51.
41. Russell, 'The Relation of Sense-Data to Physics', *Mysticism and Logic*, p. 157.
42. Russell, *Our Knowledge of the External World*, pp. 111–12.
43. Russell, *The Analysis of Mind*, pp. 104–7.
44. Weitz, 'Analysis and the Unity of Russell's Philosophy', *The Philosophy of Bertrand Russell*, p. 108, also see footnote 76 on that page.
45. Russell, *Our Knowledge of the External World*, pp. 121–9.
46. Russell, 'My Present View of the World', in *My Philosophical Development*.
47. *Ibid.*, pp. 122–3.
48. *Ibid.*, p. 124.
49. *Ibid.*, Footnote 1, pp. 125–6.
50. *Ibid.*, pp. 126–7.
51. *Ibid.*, pp. 128–9.
52. Wood, 'Summary and Introduction', in *My Philosophical Development*, p. 265.
53. Russell, *Our Knowledge of the External World*, p. 214.
54. Russell, *Mysticism and Logic*, p. 219.
55. Russell, *Inquiry*, Chapters IV–VII, and *Human Knowledge*, Part IV, Chapter II.

CHAPTER IV

RUSSELL'S EMPIRICISM

From *The Problems of Philosophy*,[1] to *My Philosophical Development*[2] of 1959, Russell maintains that all knowledge of what exists must come directly or indirectly from experience. The question asked by the theory of knowledge—what beliefs can we find which are reliable?—directs us first of all to a consideration of experience and of the steps of analysis by which we may pass from what is presented in experience to the beliefs which may validly be derived from it. As we shall see, the language in which Russell describes presented experience, and his appraisal of the steps necessary to pass from it to a valid inference, change through the development of his philosophy. There are certain common elements, however.

One common aspect of Russell's description of experience is that it is close to that of Hume.[3] Experience consists of units of sensation; each unit is derived from one sense, colour and visual pattern, or texture and felt temperature, for instance. Each unit has its discreteness, its separateness from the rest of experience. This is true of the separation of a visual unit of sensation from a tactile unit of sensation, but it is also true of one visual unit of sensation from another visual unit of sensation. For instance, when we see a white field of snow in which a black dog is walking, the two parts of the visual field are sharply distinct.[4] This is not to say that an experience is always so marked by discreteness that one cannot avoid noticing it. Some experiences may be of complexes, and some of blended and fused complexes; in such cases attention is required in order to become aware of the separate components of the experience. For instance, this may often be the case when orchestral music is heard.[5] But whether the given experience is marked by contrasts so sharp as to be inescapable, or whether it requires concentrated attention in order to find the separate parts, for Russell experience is composed of atoms, noticeable, analysable, namable divisions within experience. In this way Russell contrasts someone looking at a two of clubs and someone looking at a ten of clubs. In the first case he would recognize the card immediately as a two of clubs, and even if he were unfamiliar with cards he would see that it has two black pippits on a white ground.[6] In the latter case it would require the effort of attention and actual counting to see the ten pippets, although someone familiar with the cards might be immediately aware of the card as the ten of clubs. In either case, and whether or not the recognition was verbalized, the point is that there are separations there *to be noticed.*

With regard to the relations which are given in the presented experience, Russell is close to Hume in restricting these relations to spatial and temporal orderings and similarities and differences of the given experience. That is, the visual experience, when it is seen, noticed, attended to, or stated in a judgment of perception, is ordered by up and down, right and left, by the juxtaposition and spatial arrangement of distinguishably different coloured parts of the visual field. This is evident in the discussion of the analysis of judgments of perception attempted in the chapter on 'Analysis' in the *Inquiry.* Here Russell attempts to construct the spatial relations usually referred to as right and left, up and down, above and below, from the naming of qualities distinguishable within a single, and then within overlapping visual fields.[7] In addition to these spatial relations, there are relations of 'inside of' such as might be referred to in judgments such as 'red inside blue' and of 'circle inside square'. There are also comparative relations, '*A* is more like *B* than *C*'.[8] The relation of similarity is also an irreducible part of the given experience, and judgments of identity and similarity are important aspects of the analysis of experience. In visual experience the judgments of similarity and the comparative judgments will concern the visual qualities of colour, shape, and position.[9]

Other areas of perception will yield different qualities and

BERTRAND RUSSELL'S THEORY OF KNOWLEDGE

different judgments of comparison, identity, and similarity. Hense, the sense of touch will allow analysis of 'this is hotter than that', and 'this smooth surface is contiguous with this rough surface'. Spatial relations are given by the sense of touch as well as by sight, shape as felt being an important example. Even the sense of hearing has some spatial relations implied in it, while similarities and comparisons of sounds (loudness, pitch, and so forth) can also be distinguished in judgments of analysis. The presented qualities of taste and smell may be less vital to man's knowledge of the world, but it seems clear that judgments of comparison and similarity are appropriate here as well.

In addition to the given relations of spatial ordering, and of comparison and similarity, there are given temporal relations. In fact the temporal relations of before and after, simultaneity, succession, are perhaps the most important of all given sensed relations. For these relations of earlier than, at the same time as, and later than, are characteristic of the perceptive experiences derived from all senses; that is, one smell precedes another, one sound is later than another, one visual pattern is simultaneous with another.[10] And the sensations derived from different senses are given in one temporal order, the relations of simultaneity holding between colours, sounds, and feelings of touch.[11] Temporal relations are the most pervasive forces of order given in experience.

Russell's early treatment of the experience of time began from the premise that the given sensation must be momentary.[12] The relation of acquaintance held between the subject and the presented objects of which the subject was immediately aware, and which could be named at any one moment of his experience. This was the relation of simultaneity and was the basic given relation of acquaintance; but in order for the relations of succession of 'this before that', of the memory of what had just occurred to be part of the present experience, the temporal span of experience must be longer. But moments of experience, although they provide simultaneity, have insufficient duration to allow any earlier or later within the moment. One moment after another cannot produce a relation of succession, and the analysis of time could proceed no further. Russell, accordingly, makes use of the concept of the 'specious present'. This concept had been employed by psychologists to designate the span of attention, and attempts had been made to measure the duration of the time within which subjects are immediately aware of successive experiences, such as the striking of a clock. William James adapted this concept in explaining the experience of time. In James' use, and in the later use of Russell and others, the 'specious present' functions as an expanded moment which contains within itself a past, a present, and a future emerging as a present. While we listen to a clock striking we are aware of the chimes already sounded, and still somehow present in our immediate experience. We are even able to count the chimes which are still part of our present experience although the sound has faded away. According to Russell, then, there is a spread of events, earlier and later within each 'specious present'.[13] The earlier occurrence is still within the specious present but is perceived *as* earlier. Thus, immediate memory refers to earlier events still perceived within the limits of the present experience. Since each specious present overlaps with succeeding specious presents, the given temporal relations can be ordered in time as the event which is wholly before the first specious present, the event which is simultaneous with the first event, but is in the same specious present with an event which is not simultaneous with the first event. An order of succession can be built up in this way.[14]

At a later point, Russell preferred to speak of the experienced whole of our present experience which is defined by the relation of compresence.[15] In any case, the treatment of time is not essentially different; experienced relations of simultaneity, before and after, earlier and later, this before that, are the basis of an analysis of perception which provides the basis for the order of both time and space relations, psychological, interpersonal, and physical.

In addition to units of visual, auditory, tactile, olfactory, and gustatory sensations, and to the relations of space and time with which these units of experience are ordered, are there any other elements of experience as Russell analyses it? Intimately associated with these sensations are sensations of pleasure and pain which are given. These also have elements of spatial and temporal order, as a pain is located somewhere in the body, and in a sequence of observed events which include before, during, and after pain. Such sensations as hunger, fear, anger, surprise would also appear to be part of experience. There are, as well, units called images of imagination. Russell argues that these are not immediately recognizable in experience as distinguishable from sensations by degree of vividness. On this point he expresses some doubt with respect to Hume, concluding that it is necessary to undertake a causal analysis in order to establish distinctions between 'ideas of sensation' and 'of imagination'.[16] Images have qualities and relations similar to those of sensations.

In the case of memory, the backward reference is already given in what he calls 'immediate memory', that part of a given experience which is felt to be just immediately past. In the case of memories of earlier events, these are largely inferred and constructed from the materials of the present and recent past experience.[17]

A question is raised at various times in Russell's analysis of experience as to whether there is such an experience as that of the self, or of one's own consciousness. At an early stage Russell felt that there was an experience which might be described as that of consciousness of the self.[18] However, the change in his conception of consciousness led him to speak rather of the experience of being aware that one is perceiving something, and to speak of introspection as yielding such data as the awareness of one's own pain, hunger, and fear.[19] He concludes that there are some kinds of experience which can be distinguished as private rather than as public. But this means that, while all experiences are in one sense private , that is, they are experiences of one's own, and through introspection one is aware of this, yet for most elements of experience, it is possible to set up correlations of one's own experiences with those of others.

Where such correlations are not possible, the experiences may be described as private data. This distinction is derived rather than given, as is the case with the distinction between sensations and images.

At an early stage in the development of Russell's philosophy he held that intuitive knowledge is possible, and that what is intuited includes sensations, knowledge of universals, and logical truths. This was asserted in *The Problems of Philosophy*.[20] In the essay, 'Knowledge by Acquaintance and Knowledge by Description', a similar claim was made for the immediate grasp of universals. In a paper of 1913 Russell argued that the philosophical implications of mathematical logic included the necessity of there being *a priori* and universal truths which are not known by the senses. 'We have immediate knowledge of an indefinite number of propositions about universals: this is an ultimate fact, as ultimate as sensation is.'[21] The subsequent development of Russell's thought made important changes in his treatment of the knowledge of universals and of logical truths. The latter came to be seen as tautologous, but as late as 1936, Russell still maintained a kind of immediate knowledge of some universals and relations.[22] The topic of Russell's treatment of universals and of logical truths will be discussed in a later chapter.

The foregoing outlines Russell's description of experience. Experience is made up of discrete atoms of sensation, derived from the five sense organs. In addition, units of what might be called interior sensations, such as those of pain, pleasure, emotion, are part of experience. The relations which experience itself gives, or which can be analysed out of experience most readily and immediately, are those of spatial order and of temporal order. Causal references are intimately connected with the perceptual experience, but these references are taken to be inferred, constructed, or postulated, rather than given.[23] This analysis of experience is close to that of Hume; it is in deliberate opposition to much contemporary empiricism which stresses the continuity, the fused quality of experience.[24] The range of relations given in experience is narrower than that of James' radical empiricism.

It has been indicated that, although the general Humean character of this description of experience has remained constant in Russell's philosophy, some modifications have occurred in the conception of the scope, the contents, and the directness of knowledge gained from experience. The following pages will trace the outlines of the significant changes which took place in Russell's conception of experience.

It has been suggested that while Russell's description of experience remained basically Humean throughout his work on theory of knowledge, there were important changes in his treatment of sensation and perception and in the way in which the knowledge acquired through experience was analysed and reconstructed. Russell tells us that the major change in his thinking regarding perception and sensation occurred in 1918 but that it was some time before all the problems and difficulties involved in this change were fully evident to him.[25] Accordingly, it seems fair to say that there were three periods in Russell's thought concerning these issues; the first could be taken to include *The Problems of Philosophy*, the essays included in *Mysticism and Logic*, and *Our Knowledge of the External World*; the second period was that of the change itself and would include *The Philosophy of Logical Atomism*, *The Analysis of Mind*, and *The Analysis of Matter*; the third period was that of the systematic working out of the full implications of the change and would include *An Inquiry into Meaning and Truth* and *Human Knowledge*. The separation of three periods by this analysis and Russell's own identification of a specific change in his views might be misleading if they were interpreted as sharp and sudden changes. For the early period is marked by some questions raised and not answered, some indications of a leaning toward the later view which prepared the way for the change. Contemporary influences, such as those of Wittgenstein, also had their effect, and it took some time for the various new influences to be absorbed and worked through Russell's empiricism.

The early period is marked by an analysis of sensation which assumes that there is a subject doing the sensing and that what are sensed are sense-data.[26] This is a direct two-term relation in which the subject is said to be acquainted with the sense data, or to know them immediately.[27] There is no possibility of error in this direct relationship, nor is there any judgment involved. Judgment and error enter when one passes from immediate acquaintance to knowledge by description where indirect, inferred, and derivative knowledge takes the form of propositions expressing beliefs.[28] However, we are warned that a much smaller percentage of our knowledge is immediate and direct than common sense supposes.[29] There are thus several problems facing the philosophical analysis of knowledge: One is the problem of just what elements of our knowledge are known directly and immediately,[30] and another is by what means the derived elements of our knowledge are inferred from the un-derived elements.[31] The most important questions are: What ought to be accepted as the premises of our knowledge?[32] and: What ought to be the steps by which the inferred or constructed beliefs can justifiably be inferred so that common sense and scientific beliefs may be validly derived from the material of sense data and other given elements of our knowledge?[33]

The discrepancy between what common sense believes our experience to show us of the nature of the world and what science reveals of the world's structure, the frequent occurrence of error in our common-sense beliefs, and the psychologist's conclusion as to the pervasive influence of memory and habit in the unconscious interpretation or distortion of our sensations leads the argument of *The Problems of Philosophy* into a certain tentativeness regarding the required steps of inference and the premises from which these follow.[34] In *Our Knowledge of the External World* this unsatisfactory state of epistemological analysis was remedied by the introduction of a distinction bet-ween 'hard' and 'soft' data, where the method of philosophical doubt was recommended to distinguish between seeming and genuine immediately given elements of our experience.[35] In addition, the use of the term 'knowledge by description' had already foreshadowed the new method of description by which

Russell sought to replace the tenuous inferences with rigorous constructions in passing from the data to 'objects' of common sense and to 'concepts' of science.[36]

However, certain problems in the treatment of data were taken note of, and these were problems which also foreshadowed the difficulties leading to the adoption of a different analysis of sensation. One of these difficulties had to do with the experience of temporal order. It seems that we have immediate knowledge of what has just happened, yet memory is notoriously fallible. If memory is put within the category of derived knowledge, however, it leaves the scope of what can be immediately sensed intolerably limited. Russell tried to meet this problem by distinguishing between immediate memory (part of the specious present) and more remote memory which involves description, or the relating of a present image to a past occurrence. Another problem concerns one's self-awareness; older empiricists had simple ideas of reflection, and experience does seem to show that there is some awareness of one's own hunger or pain, or one's awareness that one is seeing the sun. Is this introspective awareness to be classed with immediate knowledge and considered to be direct awareness of the sensing subject? Russell hesitates. On the one hand, it does seem to be part of one's immediate awareness to feel pain, but on the other hand, it seems doubtful that there is such a thing as an awareness of the 'sensing subject'. Russell tentatively concludes that if there is no awareness of the self as such, the 'I' could be defined as a term of a relation, that of sensing, in which the relation and what is related to it are objects of acquaintance, but the self is not directly sensed.[37]

The probem of self-awareness is connected with the general problem of awareness of, or acquaintance with, a complex. Russell thinks that awareness is often of a complex, such as 'this-before-that', but does not know if it is possible to be aware of a complex without being aware of the parts which make it up.[38] In another passage he classifies an 'observed complex fact' as a sense-datum, but asserts that there is a difference in logical structure between it and a simple sense-datum.

'Its *logical* structure is very different, however, from that of sense: *sense* gives acquaintance with particulars and is thus a two-term relation in which the object can be *named* but not *asserted*, and is inherently incapable of truth or falsehood, whereas the observation of a complex fact, which may be suitably called perception, is not a two-term relation, but involves the propositional form on the object-side, and gives knowledge of a truth, not acquaintance with a particular.'[39]

It seems that if awareness is of a complex, then it would always involve a 'propositional form on the object-side', as 'blue-to-the-right-of-green' or 'bell-before-knock'; but if awareness is restricted to acquaintance with simples, it would be so narrowly restricted that it is difficult to see how any knowledge could be derived from it. In the later development of his thought in the *Inquiry*, Russell was able to deal more successfully with this question, but only after the sharp distinction of acquaintance and description, sensation and perception, had been broken down.[40]

This period prior to the adoption of neutral monism was marked by a clear objective held to be capable of achievement in the course of patient analysis. The application of the methods of analysis of the new logic would yield a truly scientific philosophy.[41] The ambitious programme of construction embarked on in *Our Knowledge of the External World* was an illustration of the scientific method in philosophy. In this book Russell began by purifying the rough data from which the inquiry began by a kind of Cartesian scrutiny by which the 'hard' data which survived the scrutiny and the 'soft' data which seemed doubtful under analysis were distinguished. The 'hard' data were the particular facts of sense and the truths of logic. The problem was to use only these as starting points for logical constructions which would reconstitute the 'things' of common sense and the reliable portions of its beliefs, and the 'entities' of physics and the verifiable laws which compose it.[42] When this method of construction ran into obstacles, Russell added to his starting points,

as an hypothesis, such principles or entities as were minimally
necessary to support the required conclusions not open to any
disproof and commonly accepted by either common sense or
physics.[43] The plan was to reduce these temporary postulations
by further efforts of logical construction until the whole of
common sense and physics could be constructed from the material
of the sense-data of a single person.[44] Three major postulations
were required: the existence of other minds similar to our own
where we observe actions and reports of sense-data similar to
our own, thus validating the testimony of others for use as the
material of construction;[45] projected unsensed sense-data,
'sensibilia', to fill in the gaps between actually sensed sense-
data;[46] and the postulation of what science and common sense
accept, the existence of objects which are the causes of our
sense-data (that is, the causal theory of perception).[47]

In a critical essay of 1914, 'On the Nature of Acquaintance',[48]
Russell attempts to state and evaluate the position of neutral
monism which he was soon to adopt. The position of 'neutral
monism' was connected with the work of the American Philosophers, William James, E. B. Holt, and R. B. Perry. In particular,
James' articles, 'Does "Consciousness" Exist?' raised the question
of the reality of an entity which had been considered to be one
pole of the dualistic relation of knower and known, subject
and object, inner and outer. James' suggestion was to replace
these dualisms with a position in which there is one experience
which, taken one way, can be considered subjective, ideational,
and inner, but taken another way, it can be considered objective
and external. This new position is monistic in that it eliminates
the necessity for supposing two kinds of reality, and two different
kinds of terms in the knowledge relation. The new position is
neutral in that it is weighted neither toward idealism nor
materialism. Thus, neutral monism avoids the metaphysical
dualism of matter and mind, or body and mind, as it avoids the
epistemological dualism of subject and object. This position
was connected with radical empiricism in the work of James,
but in less specifically pragmatic terms, it became part of the

programme of the 'new realists'. It is in this form that Russell evaluated neutral monism in his essay. In its favour he found several factors, the first of which was the fact that this theory dispensed with the subject, thus removing the necessity of positing an unobservable entity. In removing the subject and supposing that particular existents could be directly experienced, the theory effected a logical simplification because it was no longer necessary to postulate two kinds of entities: objects belonging to the physical or material world and subjects belonging to the mental world. Occam's razor recommended this simplification to Russell and it was a major reason for his own later adoption of the position. Further, Russell approved of the criticism of idealism involved in neutral monism's refusal to consider that all knowledge and experience must be of 'ideas'. But there were also fatal difficulties with neutral monism which first caused him to reject it, and after he later accepted it, cost him much difficult analysis. Russell felt that neutral monism overlooked the importance of the immediate experience in which data were given directly. Having begun with a non-relational view of sensation the neutral monists went on to ignore the essential duality of belief. The result of this was an insufficient view of error, of memory, and of knowledge of non-temporal facts.

'. . . I conclude that neutral monism, though largely right in its polemic against previous theories, cannot be regarded as able to deal with all the facts, and must be replaced by a theory in which the difference between what is experienced and what is not experienced by a given subject at a given moment is made simpler and more prominent than it can be in theory which wholly denies the existence of specifically mental entities.'[49]

In 1918, fourteen years after the publication of James' 'Does "Consciousness" Exist?', Russell himself adopted the position of neutral monism. This position and the changes which it entailed in his view of sensation, perception, memory, belief, the claim to immediate knowledge, and the distinction between acquaintance and descriptive knowledge are most clearly seen in *The Analysis of Mind*. He had originally adopted the view of sensation as relational, consisting of subject, act, and object, by an amendment of Meinong, in an effort to oppose idealism with a realistic view of perception. He had become uncomfortable with the concept of the subject, unsure of such an entity occurring in experience, and finally had become convinced by James' argument that there is no such empirical entity.[50] He came to see that it might be possible to give up his former view and adopt neutral monism while avoiding the 'lingering influence of idealism' involved in James' notion of 'pure experience'.[51] He was further attracted to neutral monism because it promised a metaphysical simplification. Formerly it had seemed necessary to assume the existence of two different kinds of entities, material, as are most objects of sensation, and mental, as the subject must be supposed to be; now this dualism could be dispensed with. The sensed particular, taken in one way, was a member of a class of particulars described by the laws of physics, the object; taken in another way, the same particular was a member of a class of particulars which could be described according to the laws of physiology and psychology, the person whose sensation it was.[52] In addition to these persuasions, Russell's reading of psychology, especially behaviouristic psychology, led him to find neutral monism more compatible with its evidence than any other hypothesis.[53]

However, Russell's version of neutral monism was significantly different from that of James, Perry, and Holt. Russell maintained throughout a causal theory of perception, defining perception, and distinguishing sensations from images in terms of their different causal origins.[54] In the case of images he treated these particulars as belonging to a class described by psychological laws, but not physical laws (unlike sensations). He also wished to leave open the possibility of unsensed particulars, filling the gaps in the series of perspectives constructed on the basis of sensed particulars, but not members of the class described by psychological causal laws.[55] In the case of memory, and belief, and truth and falsehood, Russell, in opposition to pragmatism, maintained a realist and relational view in which the referent, the remembered, believed about, and asserted object is outside of the memory, belief, and assertion.[56]

The adoption of neutral monism which marks the single most revolutionary change in Russell's theory of knowledge had far-reaching consequences on the position which he had developed in *The Problems of Philosophy*, *Mysticism and Logic*, and *Our Knowledge of the External World*. Under this influence and the influence of Wittgenstein and the contemporaneous development of logical atomism, almost every aspect of Russell's theory of knowledge underwent change, although it took some time for the full extent of the change to be apparent.

It was immediately apparent that the adoption of neutral monism meant a change in the relation of perception to sensation. Since there is no longer any distinctive sensation-relation as formerly described as immediate and two-term, sensation and perception are not sharply distinguished, and the psychology which had inclined Russell toward his new position emphasized how little of perception could be seen as free from the influence of memory, habit expectation, and so forth.

'Theoretically, though often not practically, we can, in our perception of an object, separate the part which is due to past experience from the part which proceeds without mnemic influences out of the character of the object. We may define as "sensation" that part which proceeds in this way, while the remainder, which is a mnemic phenomenon, will have to be added to the sensation to make up what is called the "perception". According to this definition, the sensation is a theoretical core in the actual experience; the actual experience is the perception.'[57] A further implication of the changed view of sensation is that sensation is no longer considered knowledge. Russell makes the logic of the argument clear when he says that it *seems* that when I see a person I know approaching, the seeing itself is the knowing, but that if this view is taken, it is necessary to distinguish between the seeing and what is seen. If this distinction between the sensation and the sense-datum is made, it requires the admission of the subject which has the sensation. But this 'appears to be a logical fiction', and such a gratuitous assumption must be avoided. Hence, when I see a patch of colour, all that is there *is* the patch of colour, and thus there is no cognition. Russell quotes Dewey to the same effect with approval.[58]

As we shall see in another context,[59] at the same time that the adoption of neutral monism was causing Russell to abandon his claim that sensation yields immediate, direct knowledge by acquaintance, other changes in the development of his logical theory had been gradually lessening what was required in the way of a direct knowledge of universals, relations, and classes. By 1918 or 1919 the influence of Wittgenstein had persuaded him that all logical and mathematical truths are tautologies. Hence the need to assume *a priori* intuitive knowledge of logical truths, as seen in *The Problems of Philosophy*, had evaporated, as had much of the apparatus of universals and logical truths assumed to be known by acquaintance in 'Knowledge by Acquaintance and Knowledge by Description'. It seemed, then, that there could be no claim to direct, immediate knowledge of any kind, or any need to claim it.

The 'impact of Wittgenstein' on Russell's thought is described by Russell as coming in 'two waves';[60] one prior to 1914 was due to conversations and unpublished notes and is expressed in 'The Philosophy of Logical Atomism' lectures delivered in 1918 before communication was renewed following the war; the second followed and was attributable to Wittgenstein's *Tractatus*. This is more evident in the essay 'Logical Atomism'.[61] The major significance of the point of view of logical atomism was the justification and use of a method of analysis to 'logical atoms' by which complex propositions could be reduced by truth-functional analysis to propositions of simple atomic form.[62] Such an atomic proposition was said, if true, to be identical in structure to the fact which it symbolized. As a method of analysis this technique, based on truth-functions and on theory of types, supplemented and complemented the method of construction Russell had been using. There were epistemological aspects of this theory which bore on the problem of perception, however. For, below the level of fact and its representation in a proposition of atomic form are the 'constituents' of the proposition, and these particulars can be named but not asserted, while facts can be asserted but not named.

In the earlier presentation of logical atomism there are elements of an earlier epistemology. Russell requires that for a proposition of atomic form to be verified there must be acquaintance with the particulars which are constituents of the proposition.[63] We also find in the early essay a passage in which Russell expresses indecision regarding the truth of neutral monism. The lectures were given early in 1918 and the adoption of neutral monism is said to be 'in 1918', so presumably both of these statements which are incompatible with the full adoption of the new position were shortly to be modified. In the later essay of 1924, we find no reference to acquaintance with particulars, but in speaking of the distinction of 'simples' and 'complexes', which are respectively named as constituents of facts and referred to in propositions stating facts, Russell says, 'When I speak to "simples" I ought to explain that I am speaking of something not experienced as such, but known only inferentially as the limit of analysis'.[64] There is no reference to any *a priori* knowledge of logical truths, and Russell tells us that Wittgenstein convinced him that all logical and mathematical systems are just different ways of saying the same thing.[65] This omission may mark a further influence of Wittgenstein and a further reduction in what might be said to be known immediately. The other points on which Russell was influenced by Wittgenstein have to do with the philosophy of logic, and little to do with the points in epistemology which have been discussed in this chapter.

In *The Analysis of Matter* the change to neutral monism and the influence of Wittgenstein seem to be absorbed. We find Russell treating mathematics and formal logic as analytic.[66] His view of matter is that of neutral monism, and in analysing the connection between perception and the developed propositions of physics he specifically adopts a causal theory of perception as an alternative to phenomenalism.[67] In treating perception he comments that much of what is ordinarily called perception is due to the influence of memory, habit, and interpretation. He writes, 'the elements of interpretation can only be eliminated by an elaborate theory, so that what remains—the hypothetical bare "sensation"—is hardly to be called a "datum", since it is an inference from what actually occurs'.[68]

This second period culminates in *The Analysis of Matter*, and Russell's work in theory of knowledge is not renewed in any systematic way until the publication of *An Inquiry into Meaning and Truth* in 1940. In the course of this second period in Russell's treatment of experience, 'neutral monism' and 'logical atomism' were set forth, and the changes which they introduced were worked through in Russell's theory of knowledge. The outcome can be seen through a rough sketch of the contrast between the view of experience and how its material yields knowledge in the period of *The Problems of Philosophy* and *Our Knowledge of the External World*, with the very different views of the later period.

The very striking change in the view of sensation and perception resulted in the original claim for sense-data which were given in direct, error-free, and immediate presentation being modified to finding a 'sensory core' as the portion of perceptive experience which would be left if all of the contributions of memory, habit, and inference were analysed out of it.

The study of psychology and physiology provided more empirical material, which, with the careful attention to experience itself, persuaded Russell that there could be no place in his analysis of knowledge for the subject or 'consciousness'. At the same time, these studies suggested means by which the distinctions of sensation, imagination, and memory could be analysed out of ordinary perceptual experience.

The refinement and development of the logical techniques

which had originally been set forth in *Principia Mathematica* yielded the philosophical methods of construction used throughout these two periods. The analysis of levels of meanings became the analysis of levels of propositions in logical atomism. Russell became aware of the metaphysical confusions and the philosophical errors due to the uncritical acceptance of the structure and vocabulary of ordinary speech. Henceforth, care must be taken in using a language in which levels of complexity of form are made to correspond to levels of complexity in the structure of fact.

Hence one might say that the dominant effects of the changes in Russell's thought were: first, in removing the early conviction of the possibility of using sense-data and given logical truths as the building blocks of the method of construction; second, in showing the need for, and the possibility of, new kinds of analysis of meanings and of psychology. As the lack of a secure starting place became more marked, the need for analysis in order to uncover some more or less reliable units for construction became more emphatic. The total effect, then, was to place more stress on analytic techniques, especially those of the levels of language and those of physiological and behavioural psychology. Another effect was to make the claims of Russell's 'scientific method in philosophy' somewhat more modest[69] and to make him more conscious of the gap between the problem, that of making a continuity between experience and the beliefs of common sense and of science, and the only means so far developed for solving the problem, the somewhat tentative constructions and temporarily postulated hypotheses by which he had been trying to bring the two together.

Accordingly, we find that the dominant motifs of the later phase of Russell's treatment of experience emphasize the need for analysis and the attempt to supply both the behaviouristic and the linguistic means of carrying out the analysis to come as close as possible to the reliable experiential, that is, 'sensory core' of perceptual experience as is possible. This is the principal theme of the *Inquiry*. In *Human Knowledge* Russell attempts to formulate in a systematic fashion what principles of inference are required if experience is to yield the beliefs of common sense and of science. These required principles are to be postulated to bridge the gap between the too-meagre products of a restricted, purified empiricism, and the desirable limits of a critically analysed and scientific realism.

The work of the third period can be seen, then, as the culmination of that of the earlier phases. 'But new problems, of which at first I was not fully conscious, arose as a consequence of the abandonment of "sense-data",'[70] Russell tells us, and makes this the transition between *The Analysis of Mind* and *Inquiry*. 'This change [adopting neutral monism] in my opinions greatly increased the difficulty of problems involved in connecting experience with the outer world.'[71] That Russell made no major change in his opinion during this period is testified to by his statement that 'I am conscious of no major change in my opinions since the adoption of neutral monism'.[72] The third phase of Russell's thought on experience and its relation to knowledge is to be regarded, then, as a period of consolidation when the consequences of earlier changes were worked out and this theory of knowledge was developed in detail into what can be considered its mature form.[73]

The third phase of the changes in Russell's analysis of experience extends from 1928 to the present. For almost ten years following *The Analysis of Matter* Russell published nothing on the theory of knowledge. During 1936 and 1937, however, Russell wrote three articles which foreshadow the work which culminated in the two major books of this period. These articles were 'On Order in Time',[74] 'The Limits of Empiricism',[75] and 'On Verification'.[76] The first of these was a technical work of construction, adding to the work he had done earlier on the same topic in *Our Knowledge of the External World;* the second of these posed problems concerning exactly how much or how little knowledge could be properly said to be 'derived from' our experience; the third concerned a similar problem, the relation between a 'basic proposition' and that experience which could

be said to verify it. These suggestive articles were followed in
1940 by *An Inquiry into Meaning and Truth*, in which the connection between experience and those propositions which are
'derived' from it was explored in depth. In 1944 *The Philosophy
of Bertrand Russell*, in the 'Library of Living Philosophers'
series, appeared. It contained Russell's intellectual autobiography,
and the very valuable response to criticisms. In 1945 Russell
published *History of Western Philosophy* which is less relevant
to our present topic, and this was followed in 1948 by *Human
Knowledge: Its Scope and Limits*. This book could be looked
upon as the culmination of Russell's work in theory of knowledge up to that time. It re-stated the basic principles of his
analysis of empirical knowledge and dealt with two new topics,
the nature of inductive inference in general, and specifically,
it formulated what he regarded as those postulates of non-
deductive inference which were required if the materials provided
by experience could become the basis of our scientific and common
sense knowledge. Since 1948 his work on theory of knowledge
has been chiefly polemical, criticisms and replies to criticism
vis-à-vis linguistic analysis and logical empiricism.[77] The other
major contribution is the 1957 publication of *My Philosophical
Development*, an invaluable help in reconstructing the development of Russell's thought.

In 'The Limits of Empiricism' Russell's conclusion indicate
the direction his mind was taking:

'It seems clear, therefore, that we all in fact are unshakeably
convinced that we know things which pure empiricism would
deny that we can know. We must accordingly seek a theory of
knowledge other than pure empiricism.

Collecting the results of our argument up to the present,
we have found reason to believe:

(1) That if any verbal knowledge can be known to be in any
sense derived from sense experience, we must be able, sometimes,
to "see" a relation, analogous to causation, between two parts of
one specious present.

(2) The facts about universals can sometimes be perceived when the universals are exemplified in sensible occurrences; for example, that "preceding" is transitive, and that blue is more like green than like yellow.

(3) That we can understand a form of words, and know that it expresses either a truth or a falsehood, even when we know of no method of deciding the alternative.

(4) That physics requires the possibility of inferring, at least with probability, occurrences which have not been observed, and, more particularly, future occurrences.

Without these principles, what is ordinarily regarded as empirical knowledge becomes impossible.'[78]

The foregoing 'conclusions' are to be interpreted rather as a budget of problems yet to be solved in Russell's empiricism than the avowal of a non-empirical point of view. These problems are pointed out here because they are the very ones which the *Inquiry* and *Human Knowledge* attempt to answer. The first, second, and third of the enumerated points above refer to problems which are central in the *Inquiry*: the difficult question of just what the connection is between a particular experience, and the knowledge which is expressed in a proposition, which it is somehow said to 'justify' or 'cause'. This is the problem which Russell attacks the following year (1937) through a treatment of 'basic propositions'. We see him in the earlier essay stating the problem but not on the track of the solution of it. In the essay, 'On Verification', he makes the connection between the proposition and the subsequent experience which 'verifies' it. In the *Inquiry* the whole topic is explored from the standpoint of the 'perceptive experience', the analysis of its 'sensory core' and accompanying inferences, and from the stand-point of the proposition in terms of its form, the experience which it 'expresses and the fact which it 'indicates'. This argument is the nub of Russell's mature empiricism; there are experiences, 'spontaneously' expressed in a proposition of atomic form which indicates a fact. Such propositions are the basic premisses of empirical knowledge, with the smallest degree of error between the analysed and the perceptive experience, and between the perceptive experience and the basic proposition. An example of such a proposition would be 'hotness-here-now' or 'I am hot'.[79] Some of the difficulties centering around the apparently perceived universals are approached in the *Inquiry* through a different analysis of qualities and relations in which qualities such as 'red' are said to be particulars rather than universals.[80] The fourth point concerning the 'limits' of empiricism enumerated in the early article concerns the necessity for postulating certain principles of inference which go beyond the 'momentary empiricism' which Russell regards as the proper consistent philosophical definition of empiricism. This is the topic discussed in *Human Knowledge*. This book concludes with the statement of certain 'postulates' of non-demonstrative inference; these postulates are assumptions which are required to supplement experience in order that beliefs may be justified which we do, in fact, hold to be highly credible. They concern causal connection, relative permanence of structures, continuity of causal influences, and analogy.

'Each of these postulates asserts that something happens often, but not necessarily always; each therefore justifies, in a particular case, a rational expectation which falls short of certainty. Each has an objective and a subjective aspect: objectively, it asserts that something happens in most cases of a certain sort; subjectively, it asserts that, in certain circumstances, an expectation falling short of certainty in a greater or less degree has rational credibility. The postulates collectively are intended to provide the antecedent probabilities required to justify inductions'.[81]

Accordingly, when Russell concludes his early essay by saying that we must 'seek a theory of knowledge other than pure empiricism', he must be understood as recommending a modified empiricism in which certain added postulates and certain incompletely fulfilled analyses render the empiricism 'impure.'

We have next to consider how Russell's analysis in the *Inquiry* yields the 'basic premisses' of his theory of knowledge. We have indicated that this depends upon two kinds of analysis. First, there is an analysis which attempts to strip off the layers of habit, expectation, and inference from the immediate perceptive experience to arrive (or almost arrive) at the sensory core of the perceptive experience. This may be called behavioural analysis since it is largely concerned with the application of considerations derived from psychology and physiology. Secondly, there is the necessity of analysing the connection between the having of the perceptive experience and the occurrence of propositions which are derived from it. Since this is concerned with the psychological connection between having an experience and using symbols to refer to this experience, it is also a kind of behavioural analysis. In addition, consideration must be given to the nature of symbols, sentences, and propositions and various kinds or levels of meaning involved. This may be termed linguistic analysis.

In calling the kind of analysis used by Russell in uncovering the different aspects of perceptive experience 'behavioural', certain liberties are taken with Russell's own terminology. Russell himself used the term 'behaviourism' to refer to the kind of psychological analysis which he employed in *The Analysis of Mind* and the *Inquiry*. It was derived from his reading of Watson and other psychologists of the same school. Russell said he thought it valuable to see how far this kind of explanation could go in explaining the behaviour of men in perception, in the use of symbols, and in emotive and purposive behaviour, by treating them as the subject of inquiry in the same manner that other animals were studied, that is, externally and in terms of their behaviour. Much could be learned from this kind of scientific study. However, Russell qualified his acceptance of behaviourism by pointing out that the information provided by this kind of study of human behaviour ought to be supplemented by what could be known introspectively by an analysis of our own thought processes and emotions. Behaviourism of the Watsonian kind could not give a complete and adequate account of all aspects of human behaviour, including cognitive behaviour, but such results as it had attained should be used by the philosopher in developing a theory of knowledge.[82] The use of behaviouristic psychology is analogous to Russell's use of physics. The conclusions, tentative as they may be, which physical science has attained are to be taken account of by the philosopher in his working out of a hypothesis of the construction of space and time orders, or causal laws, for instance. Physiology and psychology are on the same basis and have similar usefulness. Therefore, in terming this aspect of Russell's analysis 'behavioural' I am including all the scientific theories which he employed in his analysis of perception: the scientific explanation of the emission and transmission of light rays, for instance, the explanation of the workings of the eye and other sense organs, the explanations of such reflexes as the 'eye blink', the explanations of memory, anticipation, the selectivity and interpretation involved in sensation, habits, language habits, emotional responses, and so forth. Physics as well as physiology and psychology is involved here, and also data derived from the study of non-human animals.

As an example of the use of behavioural analysis, Russell begins his analysis of knowledge by considering cases of knowledge on the non-human level. In some sense animals may be said to 'know' when they respond to some stimulus in a way appropriate to an absent situation with which the stimulus is connected.[83] They evince the formation of habits of expectation, the fulfilment and non-fulfilment of expectations, forethought, indecision. Russell has many whimsical examples from animal behaviour; the dog which shows he interprets his master's getting his coat as a sign of an impending walk by jumping and wagging his tail, the pigeon which mistook another pigeon for his own mate with appropriate advance and retreat, the cat which hesitated between two equidistant kittens.[84]

What might be called the next step in cognitive behaviour is the non-verbal behaviour of man, not primarily the 'eye-blink' kind of reflex, but the learned or habitual response, such as jumping to the kerb at the sound of an approaching car or ducking at the sight of an oncoming missile.

The connection of this kind of pre-verbal knowledge with the problem of perception can be seen in Russell's example of the walker who silently steps around the puddle. His response of avoidance is one he has learned from past experience. It may not be one of which he is conscious but may be the result of habit; yet, if he is challenged as to why he stepped aside, he would reply that he noticed the puddle and wished to avoid getting his feet wet. (If he were silent, we could make this interpretation of his actions.) The 'noticing' is the nub of immediate experience in the whole perceptive experience in which physics may describe the movements of light refracted from the water, physiology may describe the co-ordination of foot and eye and the visual image resulting from the stimulus of the optic nerve, and psychology may describe the way in which previous experience of walking in puddles has left an unpleasant memory and a resultant tendency to avoid repetition of the unpleasantness. When this incident is regarded as a case of knowledge derived from sensation, and the elements of it which can be scientifically explained as due to neural impulses, habit, memory, and so forth, are set aside, what is left is the noticing of the puddle as a patch of colour, the sensory core of that perceptive experience.[85]

The same kind of behavioural analysis can be applied to knowledge at the verbal level. For the use of language can be treated in the same way as any other behaviour; we can observe what sounds people make and what responses are made to the sounds. We can observe that the utterance of certain words, such as 'Fire!' in a crowded theatre, will be followed by the same kind of response as would the fire itself. We can observe the generality of meaning which various sets of sounds and 'heaps of ink' have in terms of common responses. Hence, when a perceptive judgment is made, expressed in words, we can make allowances for the habits of using language which are incorporated in the judgment. In paring that perceptual judgment down to its core of immediate meaning we may re-word it to take account of the habits of association, interpretation, and generalization inherent in our language. For instance, 'I see a dog' might be re-worded, 'I see a canoid patch of colour' in order to take account of the fact that 'dog' means a certain kind of animal with an independent existence and certain observable features such as bark, tail wagging, and so forth and that in the case in question, all that is actually observed is a visual perception of a dog-like patch of colour, the rest being the result of memory associations and interpretations.[86]

By 'whittling away' the elements not due to immediate perceptive experience, partly through a behavioural analysis, theory of knowledge may eventually arrive, or nearly arrive, at a 'pure datum', that part of the experience which is due to present sensation, that which is noticed, selected, become aware of, even though this element is embedded in the associations and interpretations which, together with the sensation, make up the whole perceptive experience. It is this 'sensory core' which gives the judgment based on perception its authority, and that is why it is also necessary to re-word the language in which the perceptual judgment is made so that a minimum amount of inference is involved in the sentence itself. Russell admits that neither in the case of the experience nor in the case of the judgment is the whittling away complete or definitive; in some cases it may reduce the element of interpretation to such a degree that the judgment may be taken as a 'basic proposition' and, eventually, serve as an 'epistemological premiss'.[87] In order that basic propositions may be distinguished from other empirical judgments, however, it is necessary that a further kind of analysis be carried out, one specifically related to the structure of language itself.

The linguistic analysis which is a major theme of the *Inquiry* owes much to the earlier analysis of 'The Philosophy of Logical Atomism'. The same distinction between propositions of atomic form and molecular propositions is made. However, since the distinction between knowledge by acquaintance and knowledge by description has been dropped, a difficulty develops in linguistic analysis in distinguishing between words as names of simples and propositions as referring to facts. For this reason, and because of the addition of more behavioural analysis, a somewhat different analysis of language is given in the later book. Russell begins by distinguishing levels of language in terms of levels of meaning. The 'object-language' is defined as a first level of language in which words refer directly to elements of experience which may be denoted; on this level at least some of the words are, and all of the words could be, learned ostensively. It is also the level on which a word, by itself, could have meaning, or be used as a significant sentence.[88] A second level of language is the level of logical words; here logical connectives such as 'and' and 'or' are introduced, and terms like 'true' and 'false' are appropriate. Such words always function on a level which refers to the primary level of language. A sentence on the primary level is judged from the standpoint of the secondary level to be 'true' or 'false'. The 'or' or the 'and' refer to an alternation or conjunction of meanings given on the primary level; there are no 'ors' in nature, Russell thinks. Similarly, negative facts are now not considered part of nature, but 'not' expresses an attitude of disappointed expectation on the part of the utterer of the sentence in which it occurs. 'Some' and 'all' also belong to this second, logical level of language. There are further levels of language as they are required to make reference to a secondary or a tertiary level already constructed. Hence 'I am hot' would be on the first level of language; the 'it is true that I am hot' would be on the second level of language; 'John believes that the proposition "I am hot" is true' on a third level.[89]

In addition to 'object-words' and 'logical words' there are words which Russell calls 'egocentric particulars'.[90] These are words such as 'I', 'now' and 'this'. These words are very important because they carry the denotative function of pointing to specific aspects of the immediate situation, in distinction from object words which always carry some generality of meaning, although in a given context they may refer to specific referents. Yet, the egocentric particulars refer to different particulars in each sentence. The 'this' referred to in a sentence will change from moment to moment, the 'now' always refers to the time of utterance of the sentence and this changes from sentence to sentence, while the 'I' refers to the utterer of the given sentence, whoever that may be. These words function as names, and that function of being what Russell calls 'a logically proper name' is vitally important to Russell's theory of meaning and theory of knowledge, as it is in this relation of naming that the present perceptive experience is directly referred to. Russell accordingly develops a way of referring to the present experience which will be equivalent in meaning to the use of 'egocentric particulars' but at the same time will be descriptive of the present experience. Taking the given present experience as a 'complex of compresence' he believes it is possible to describe it in terms of sets of co-ordinates in which visual and tactual space orders of up and down, right and left, and temporal orders of succession and simultaneity, for all senses, can order the qualities of sensations. This involves him in a new treatment of sense qualities in which a colour, say red, which occurs in different places and times in the succession of visual fields can be treated as a particular, not as a universal. Such careful and detailed descriptions of the present complex of compresence will give the unique reference required of 'logically proper names'.[91]

In discussing this problem of 'egocentric particulars' we have been led into a discussion which is properly concerned with the meaning of sentences and propositions, rather than of individual words. Although rudimentaty meaning may be carried by a single object-word used alone, as in the cry of 'fire!', in most cases meaning is carried in a sentence not through the office of each separate word but through the unity of the sentence itself.[92] In the sentence 'x precedes y', for instance, the unity of meaning is clear in that the order of the words is part of the meaning itself. While an atomic sentence could be described as one in which there is a single subject and predicate, this description is superficial, and it is not until we discuss the 'proposition of atomic form' that we deal with the basic unit of meaning.[93] The 'proposition of atomic form' is defined by Russell as one composed of a finite number of proper names and another word, usually a relation-word, for instance '*A* gave the book to *B*' or '*x* precedes *y*'. Such propositions will exclude all object-words which are not logically proper names (since these involve generality and hence do not refer directly to a specific portion of space-time) and all logical words (since all conjunctions, negative terms, and words of 'quantity' refer to a second level of meaning and are properly to be expressed in a molecular proposition). Propositions of atomic form, therefore, refer to an analysable complex of the given compresent complex of qualities. It turns out that there is a fact which verifies them and renders them true or false. Russell defines a basic proposition as true by definition when the sentence in which it is symbolized 'spontaneously', that is, immediately and nondeceptively, expresses and indicates the same fact.[94] 'The sentence expresses what it indicates' means that it expresses the utterer's immediate experience and it indicates, that is, refers to the fact which is what the utterer is experiencing, and this is the same experience, or the same fact. There is a direct causal connection between the experience and the uttering of the sentence.

The implications of this linguistic analysis of propositions of atomic form are connected with derivative meanings and truth values, because, as in the earlier logical atomism, molecular propositions are built up out of atomic propositions, or perhaps it would be better to say, molecular propositions are analysable into their component atomic propositions, and it is through such analysis that they are testable. The theory of truth and the metaphysical implications of this theory are to be discussed later, but it should be pointed out here that there are important differences between the linguistic analysis developed in the *Inquiry* and the earlier analysis of 'The Philosophy of Logical Atomism', in spite of the similarity of method and of terminology. First of all, there is no implication that the 'simples' which the constituents of the atomic proposition 'name' are there to be named as ultimate units of experience. The qualities which are named by 'logically proper names' are analysable out of the complex of compresence;

they are not given. This may require considerable effort of attention and of the tracing of distinctions and the inventing of a vocabulary to distinguish differences. Nor is there any assumption that such analysed out components are ultimate in any sense; the analysis is simply carried as far as is required by the particular purpose of the discourse in question.[95] The original programme of logical atomism at least suggested the possibility that all molecular propositions could be reduced to the appropriate atomic propositions and hence verified. Russell no longer believes this to be possible. In the *Inquiry* there is a long argument against the verifiability theory of meaning and the verifiability theory of truth of logical positivism. In this argument Russell maintains that there are meaningful propositions which are not capable of verification, and true propositions which cannot ever be known to be true. Both science and common sense require the acceptance of generalizations which cannot be analysed in the desired empirical method of logical atomism and yet cannot be rejected. In fact, the amount of knowledge which could be completely verified by such methods would be very limited and would not even extend to one's own more remote memory or to the experience of others.[96]

Another distinction between the later use of linguistic analysis in the *Inquiry* and the earlier programme is that the original idea of the isomorphism of proposition and fact is no longer accepted. There will always be at least one more relation in the proposition than in the fact, Russell argues.[97] Even a logically perfect language cannot be expected to mirror perfectly the structure of the complex of compresence, as Russell's attempts to do this demonstrate.[98]

The particular points at issue between the earlier and later versions of logical atomism include the change from the uncomfortable early position, that there were both negative and general propositions of atomic form and hence that they mirrored negative and general facts, to the later position, that negative and general statements are not propositions of atomic form and hence that there are no negative or general facts. Russell's early hesitancy about accepting the treatment of 'non-truth functional propositions' according to the model of '*A* believes *p*' as equivalent to '*p*' hardened. He also became more convinced that it was possible to make statements concerning the correspondence of propositions of atomic form with facts by using a language of a higher level, rather than to accept this as something to be 'shown' and not 'said', as Wittgenstein held. His early openness to Wittgenstein's criticisms of his own treatment of identity was replaced by the assurance that Wittgenstein was wrong. Similarly Russell became more convinced that it is possible to make a statement that the description of the elements of a complex is complete, as against Wittgenstein. The discussion of atomicity and extensionality indicates grave reservations on Russell's part concerning the logical implications of the original assumptions of logical atomism which Wittgenstein's influence had led Russell to accept.[99]

The survival of the original programme of logical atomism with its linguistic analysis can be seen in Russell's later work in the attempt to work out a way of describing a present complex of compresence in such a way that the description would be nondistortive of what is actually perceived, shorn of accompanying inferences and linguistic misinterpretations, and in such a way that a complete analysis of what is so perceived may be given. This would be the primary level of language, the one closest to what is immediately perceived, and the first level to which a second, logical level of language would refer. As this analysis of levels is a survival of 'logical atomism', so the attempt to make this primary language a 'minimum vocabulary' with the smallest number of undefined words is a survival of the method of construction. Both play an important role in Russell's mature empiricism.

The two main themes of the later phase of Russell's work in theory of knowledge involved the treatment of perception and its relation to knowledge. One theme is the connection between the immediate perceptive experience and the judgments, or propositions, which are said to be derived from it. The other theme is the limits of empiricism, the degree of which the directly derived and testable judgments of perception can justify what we regard as reliable knowledge. Since Russell had come to realize that the 'immediate perception' involved many inferential elements which were fused with the directly given sensation, it became a problem to see how the perception could yield any 'knowledge'. And, on the side of language, the various inferential leaps involved in the most modest statement made it difficult to see how such 'knowledge', if it were available, could be put into words without distortion. We have seen that Russell attempted to solve this problem by using two kinds of analysis: a behavioural analysis by which scientific explanations of sensation and of the workings of the nervous system and of habits and associations could guide the philosopher in uncovering the core of 'sensation' in the experience of perception; and secondly, a linguistic analysis by which the reduction of complex to simple language forms and the framing of careful vocabularies could reduce the distortions of language to a minimum. Russell claimed only partial and limited success for these methods of analysis, and, accordingly, the remaining gap between perception and what we want to say we know has to be filled in by the formulation of the 'postulates of non-demonstrative inference'. These postulates permitted the empiricist to add to the limited store of almost completely vindicated judgments of immediate perception certain inferences. Inferences to the existence of the objects causing his perceptions such as physics suggests are permitted by postulates of causality, quasi-permanence, and continuity of structure. Inferences to the existence of minds and bodies similar to our own as causing the words we see and hear and interpret as we would if they came from us are permitted by the additional postulate of analogy. Finally, inferences to the existence of a world in which scientific generalizations have a range far wider than one's own experience or that of others would suggest, to the farthest nebulae, to the future events, and to the distant pre-human past are permitted by all these postulates. Such postulates are said to be not in conflict with any experience or scientific evidence, compatible with what is known, plausible, and true as far as we can decipher, and a demonstrably necessary minimal supplement to the limits of empiricism.[100]

In order to see the way in which Russell's empiricism and his method of analysis were combined to make his distinctive theory of knowledge, we must turn our attention to his treatment of 'data'. No term in Russell's theory of knowledge is so difficult to trace through a multitude of uses and meanings. Yet it is central to the direction and purpose of his theory of knowledge, as the Introduction to the *Inquiry* attests:

'My main problem, throughout, will be the relation of basic propositions to experiences, i.e., of the propositions that come first in the epistemological order to the occurrences which, in *some* sense, are our grounds for accepting these propositions.'[101]

This is the problem of data. One of the sources of confusion in Russell's treatment of data is that he uses the term in two distinct contexts: one is the context of experience, and the other is the context of belief or proposition. In the first context Russell, throughout his early career, used the term 'sense-data'. The sense-datum is an element of immediate experience, either given or analysed out. In the *Inquiry* it is the latter, and the datum is said to be 'the 'sensory core' of the perceptive experience. However, this sense of 'data' is not the same as the sense in which Russell speaks of propositions or beliefs as being 'data'. In this latter meaning, data can sometimes be referred to as 'premisses' of our knowledge. In addition to this confusion of two different contexts of the use of the term, which runs throughout Russell's writings on theory of knowledge, there seem to be four separate meanings of data in the sense in which data are the premisses of knowledge.

We might begin the disentanglement of the four meanings of data by referring to the distinction made by Loewenberg of pre-analytical and post-analytical data.[102] Pre-analytical data are elements of knowledge 'given' prior to any analysis, or to the making of any distinctions. Sometimes in epistemology these are referred as to 'the given'. Post-analytical data, on the other hand, are data which are the product of analysis. Using this distinction we may describe four possible meanings of data, all of which occur in Russell's theory of knowledge. These four meanings are: data as what is given, temporally first in experience, that with which inquiry begins, the pre-analytic; data as what is causally prior in experience, the origin or genesis of later beliefs; data as what is logically prior, the basic logical premisses from which other beliefs may be inferred; and, finally, data as what is epistemologically prior, the product of the analysis which judges certain beliefs to be what ought to be accepted as premisses.

The first meaning of data, as the pre-analytically given, has had a long history in Russell's thought; we have had occasion to refer to it in connection with the method of analysis in which data, in this sense, are the starting point of the analysis, that which we seem to know with certainty but which is vague and confused.[103] It is data in this sense which initiates the inquiry which is epistemology. But in Russell's early work in epistemology there is another context in which he speaks of data as given. In *The Problems of Philosophy*, Russell distinguishes between the immediately given, the intuitively known, and what is known indirectly and derivatively.[104] In a similar sense, knowledge by acquaintance, the direct two-term relation by which the 'particular facts of sense' and the 'particular truths of logic' are presented without the possibility of mediation or error, provides us with data which are pre-analytical.[105] However, there is also a suggestion of post-analytical data when in the early writings it is suggested that it may be necessary to submit our beliefs to analysis in order to determine which are immediately given and which are not.[106] An element of epistemological priority is involved in this case. After the adoption of neutral monism the meaning of data as given immediately with no possibility of error is rejected. Data are defined as the product of analysis rather than as prior to analysis.[107] The only pre-analytical meaning of data which survived neutral monism is that of data as the vague starting point of inquiry. This is a less important meaning of data.

The meaning of data as causally prior refers to the elements of our knowledge which are, in fact, the sources of our beliefs. These include sensations as the common causes of beliefs, and sensations, in turn, refer causally to events inside and outside the nervous system—the light emanating from the star and travelling through space, stimulating the retina, and through the nervous system causing the event called 'seeing the star'. Russell sometimes makes a distinction between the causally prior, which is to some extents accidental, varying from one individual to another, and the epistemologically prior, that which constitutes good grounds for accepting a belief. We may believe that the earth is spherical because we were told it at school, but this is not the grounds for believing it; rather, the observations of horizons, eclipses, and rocket photographs would constitute grounds.[108] (It might happen that the two were identical, as presumably it was with Magellan.) Of the two kinds of priority, that of grounds is more important in epistemology than that of cause. However, the causes of belief are important epistemologically; when one tries to differentiate between reliable and unreliable perceptual beliefs, an investigation of causes of belief is the first method used. On this ground Russell rejects Humes' argument and claims that only if one looks into the operation of the nervous system and into what is happening in the environment can one distinguish between an impression and an idea, a sensation and an image, a dream and a reality.[109] It turns out that finding a given belief to have causes in a normal experience of perception is the best grounds for accepting it as data in a logical or epistemological sense. The treatment of the causally prior data changes according to Russell's analysis of perception. With the adoption of neutral monism Russell emphasized that no subject or act of sensing could be distinguished in experience; hence, he spoke of sensed particulars, and it became necessary to employ a causal analysis in order to distinguish the sensory element in perception from the 'en-crustation' of memory, anticipation, and interpretation. We have seen how behavioural analysis, which is essentially causal analysis, was employed in *The Analysis of Mind* and the *Inquiry* to achieve this. In this latter work stress was placed on the importance of the causally direct link between the sensory impact of the imme-diate perception and the consequent judgment derived from it as being the source of the basic proposition.[110]

The concept of the logically prior appears early in Russell's treatment of data. In *The Problems of Philosophy* there is said to be intuitive knowledge of principles of inference and logical laws; and knowledge by acquaintance included direct awareness of logical truths.[111] These truths, given directly, serve as premisses for both inductive and deductive arguments. The programme of the construction of the external world was intended to show how the beliefs of common sense and of science could be constructed logically from the sense-data of a single person; hence, these data would serve as logical premisses for the logical construc-tion.[112] This programme was never carried out successfully, but the attempt to implement it assumed the concept of the logically prior data.

Russell entered one important qualification of the meaning of logically prior as applied to data. He pointed out in 'The Philosophy of Logical Atomism' that there is a difference between the logical premiss of a developed and completed deductive system such as that of a mathematical or logical system, and the logical premiss of a body of knowledge which is not completed but in process and is empirical rather than formal. In the first case it would be possible, as in the *Principia Mathematica*, to survey the entire system and to select those premisses as logically basic which would best serve that function, the most economical, simple, and elegant. In this sense the basic concepts or axioms of a formal system are chosen as truly 'logically prior'. But in the case of theory of knowledge, one cannot see how the whole inquiry is going to turn out when the premisses are chosen, nor can considerations of logical consistency and elegance be the sole determinants of choice.[113] Therefore, what will serve as logical premisses will be those beliefs which seem to be the best available foundation of further inference, or, as it turns out in *Human Knowledge*, are those required in order that the beliefs which are to be derived from the premisses be given a logical foundation. However modified the claim for the logical premisses may be, Russell continues to maintain that theory of knowledge is interested in the basis of logical inference and that producing this foundation is an important function of data in theory of knowledge.

The fourth meaning of 'data' is that of the epistemologically prior, and this has been described as what ought to be believed rather than what is believed, what ought to serve as the premisses of our knowledge, rather than what is, in fact, its basis.[114] Throughout his work in theory of knowledge Russell stressed this as an important meaning of data. In the early period of *Our Knowledge of the External World*, Russell distinguished between 'hard data' and 'soft data'.[115] There are many beliefs or element of knowledge which seem to be certain and indubitable, but when philosophic doubt is introduced, and the apparent data are subjected to questioning, it is found that some become doubtful, while others continue to resist doubt and to be indubitable in the sense that scrutiny increases rather than decreases one's confidence in the belief. The former are 'soft', and the latter are 'hard' data. The soft data are no longer considered candidates for epistemological premisses, while the data which, as hard, survive the method of doubt become premisses of further knowledge. For instance, it might become impossible to doubt that one sees a red patch, but at the same time, very doubtful that one sees an apple, as further analysis suggests sources of error and deception in the interpretation of the experience. What remain as hard data, the survivors of epistemological doubt, are the 'particular facts of sense' and 'the particular truths of logic'.

If we look back at the early period of Russell's thought, prior to the adoption of neutral monism, we see that his hope for the epistemological method of analysis and synthesis, of scrutinizing doubt, and doubt-resistant data, seemed to depend, at least in part, on merging the four meanings of data. As far as data are the product of direct acquaintance, they are pre-analytic; as far as they are the cause of later inferences, they are casually prior; as far as they can serve as the premisses of further inference, they are logically prior; and as far as they survived the test of doubt, they ought to be believed and are epistemologically prior. It does not seem to be too strong a statement to say that Russell's programme of using the material of perception as the basis for a method of logical construction depended upon the fusing of these four meanings of data. However, there were already difficulties in the carrying out of the programme and in the consistency of his meanings of data. The concept of pre-analytical data could hardly be consistent with the necessity of analysis; or, to put it into other words, directly given data are hardly compatible with the necessity of logical, causal, or epistemological ordering. In addition, as we saw, Russell was puzzled about the question of the given sense-datum, the object of acquaintance, sometimes containing complexities within it that required analysis. He was troubled about whether one ever experienced oneself as the subject of awareness.[116] There was the complication that some of the items mentioned as 'data', particular *facts* of sense and particular *truths* of logic, would have to be in the form of judgments or propositions; yet these, by definition, could not be given in a two-term relation of acquaintance.[117]

In any case, after the adoption of neutral monism, it became impossible to identify the pre-analytical, the directly given, with causal, logical, or epistemological data. The two-term relation of acquaintance had dropped out, and with it the claim that sensation is itself knowledge. Perception is now seen to involve mediation and interpretation, and the sensory element must be analysed out of it before a premiss can result. Further, the 'truths of logic' are now considered to be tautologies, and any principles of inference other than formal or demonstrative ones must be found to be based in experience. Observed particulars are given, but given in interpreted, organically conditioned, psychologically distorted form, requiring analysis before they can be made the basis of further inference. In *The Analysis of Mind* and *The Analysis of Matter* the programme of showing how the causal laws of psychology and the causal laws of physics could be constructed from the perspectives derived from the range of sensed particulars without resorting to metaphysical postulates of matter or mind is the centre of attention. The concept of data is of less importance.

In the later phase, that of the *Inquiry* and of *Human Knowledge*, the concept of data returns to importance. In the Introduction to the *Inquiry*, the ordering of our beliefs according to their degree of credibility is said to be one of the important tasks of epistemology, and epistemologically prior beliefs are distinguished from those which are causally or logically prior.[118] The outcome of the analysis of the *Inquiry* is to establish the importance of what are called basic premisses or perceptual premisses. Here the propositions which most closely express and most directly indicate a fact of perception are given first place as epistemological premisses. But this order is justified on causal and logical grounds. Causal grounds are important in that such propositions are closest to what they are caused by. The 'canoid patch of colour' is more credible than 'the dog', and 'the dog' than the species 'canis', because of the closeness of the first symbol to what is actually seen. In the same way, 'hotness-here-now' is better qualified as an epistemological premiss than 'you are hot' or 'the sun is hot'. This ordering of preference is justified on logical grounds because it is argued that there must be some source for new beliefs, otherwise one belief would be derived from another in a kind of coherent reciprocally derived system. Hence, an epistemological premiss provides logical grounds for believing something that is not believed on other grounds.[119] In *Human Knowledge* a datum is defined as a belief which is believed on its own account independent of any other reasons for believing it. Here again the concept of degress of objective credibility appears as a description of the search for data.[120]

That there are other basic beliefs in addition to those derived as directly as possible from perception is stressed in *Human Knowledge*, and the postulates of non-deductive inference are introduced as postulates which there is reason to accept, but for which there is no conclusive evidence.

It would be a mistake to think that the more recent treatment of data in which epistemological priority is emphasized, and in which this priority is partially determined on the basis of logical and causal priority, has resolved the earlier confusions and conflicts in Russell's concept of data. It is true that the incompatible concept of pre-analytical data has all but disappeared and that one could avoid the confusion of data as elements of perception with data as beliefs, restricting the usage with which we are concerned to the latter. A problem still remains, however, for Russell is in the position of a Descartes who has neither the *cogito* nor self-evident truths. The scrutiny of doubt which is required before any belief can be accepted as a datum is made as objective as possible by making the criteria of objective credibility first, the directness of the causal connection between datum in question and perceptive experience and second, the order of inference from premiss to derived inference. Yet the first criterion involves a somewhat incomplete analysis by which the results of science are applied to pare the perception down to its veridical nub, and, in the case of the important non-deductive inferences, principles of inference which are not capable of complete empirical justification are accepted. This dilemma is apparent when Russell raises the question of the relation between psychological indubitability and objective credibility:

'Scientific method, broadly speaking, consists of technique and rules designed to make degrees of belief coincide as nearly as possible with degrees of credibility. We cannot, however, begin to seek such a harmony unless we can start from propositions which are both epistemologically credible and subjectively nearly certain. This suggests a Cartesian scrutiny, but one which, if it is to be fruitful, must have some non-skeptical guiding principle. If there were no relation at all between credibility and subjective certainty, there could be no such thing as knowledge. We assume in practice that class of beliefs may be regarded as true if (*a*) they are firmly believed by all who have carefully considered them, (*b*) there is no positive argument against them, (*c*) there is no known reason for supposing that mankind would believe them if they were untrue. On this basis, it is generally held that judgments of perception on the one hand, and logic and mathematics on the other, contain what is most certain in our knowledge.'[121]

All that empirical epistemology can do, in being guided by this non-sceptical principle, is to order its beliefs according to their degree of credibility, putting first in logical and epistemological order those that seem least doubtful, and putting last in logical and epistemological order those which seem most doubtful, but for which there is no reason for rejection. Such an epistemological search for data will have the effect of purging from knowledge its inconsistent, erroneous, or highly dubious elements and of bringing forth for closer examination those premisses which have been accepted without careful scrutiny. If the essence of rationality is, as Russell says it is, to put the degree of confidence in a belief which the evidence in favour of it justifies, then this procedure will render the structure of human knowledge more rational, if it cannot render it completely empirical.

NOTES TO CHAPTER IV

1. Russell, *The Problems of Philosophy*, p. 116.
2. Russell, *My Philosophical Development*, p. 132.
3. Russell, *Inquiry*, p. 329. 'It is customary now-a-days to dismiss contemptuously the atomic view of sensation as it appears in Hume and his followers. We are told that the sensible world is a continuous flux, in which divisions are unreal, the work of the mind, purely conceptual, and so on. This is said as something obvious, for which only a stupid

man would demand evidence. Now the word "sensation" or "sensible", as is often pointed out, stands for something hypothetical—broadly speaking, for what *could* be noticed without change in the environment or the sense-organs. What is not hypothetical is what *is* noticed, not what *could* be noticed; and what *is* noticed has, I maintain, just that atomicity and discreteness which the critics of Hume reject. They do not, as empiricists should, start from data, but from a world that they have inferred from data but use to discredit the kind of thing that can be a datum. In theory of knowledge, what is fundamental is noticing, not sensation.'

4. *Ibid.*, pp. 328–9.
5. *Ibid.*, p. 56.
6. *Ibid.*, pp. 56–7.
7. *Ibid.*, p. 338.
8. *Ibid.*, p. 55.
9. *Ibid.*, pp. 57–8.
10. Russell, *Our Knowledge of the External World*, pp. 121–2.
11. *Ibid.*, p. 122.
12. Bertrand Russell, 'On the Nature of Acquaintance', *The Monist*, Vol. XXIV, Nos. 1, 2, 3, 1914; republished in *Logic and Knowledge*, pp. 127–74. For the restrictions placed upon present experience, see pp. 133 *f.*
13. Bertrand Russell, 'On the Experience of Time', *The Monist*, Vol. XXV, No. 2, 1915. The 'specious present' is defined in the following passage: 'a momentary total experience is the period of time within which an object must lie in order to be a sense-datum' (218). The definition of 'succession' is 'a relation which may hold between two parts of one sensation, for instance between parts of a swift movement which is the object of one sensation; it may then, and perhaps also when one or both objects are objects of immediate memory, be immediately experienced, and extended by inference to cases where one or both of the terms of the relation are not present' (213). In both cases, a foundation is laid for an experienced basis of temporal order in the given experience.

    For the history of the term 'specious present', see William James, *Principles of Psychology*, Henry Holt, New York, 1890, Volume I, Chapter XV, 'The Perception of Time'. For a recent discussion of certain difficulties with the concept, see J. D. Mabbott, 'Our Direct Experience of Time', *Mind*, LX, No. 238, April 1915, pp. 153–80.
14. *Ibid.*, 227–33.
15. Russell, *Inquiry*, pp. 336–7. 'The argument demands that the total of our experience at any one time should always be such a whole, and

so must certain complex parts of this total. The parts of such a total are bound together by the relation of compresence.' In another work Russell says: 'There are complexes composed by compresent qualities. I give the name of a "complete complex of compresence" to a complex whose members are all compresent with each other, but not all compresent with anything outside the complex.' *My Philosophical Development*, p. 171.

16. Russell, *The Analysis of Mind*, pp. 151 *ff.*

17. Russell, *Human Knowledge*, pp. 188–9.

18. Russell, 'Knowledge by Acquaintance and Knowledge by Description', *Mysticism and Logic*, pp. 211–12.

19. Russell, *Inquiry*, pp. 49–51.

20. Russell, *The Problems of Philosophy*, p. 171. 'Our immediate knowledge of things, which we called *acquaintance,* consists of two sorts, according as the things known are particulars or universals. Among particulars, we have acquaintance with sense-data and (probably) with ourselves. Among universals, there seems to be no principles by which we can decide which can be known by acquaintance, but it is clear that among those that can be so known are sensible qualities, relations of space and time, similarity, and certain abstract logical universals. . . . Our immediate knowledge of truths may be called *intuitive* knowledge, and the truths so known may be called *self-evident* truths.' See also *Mysticism and Logic*, pp. 213–14.

21. Bertrand Russell, 'The Philosophical Importance of Mathematical Logic', *The Monist*, Vol. XXIII, No. 4, October 1913, pp. 481–93. The quotation is from page 492.

22. Bertrand Russell, 'The Limits of Empiricism', *Proceedings of the Aristotelian Society*. Vol. 36, 1936, pp. 131–50. Russell says: 'Collecting the results of our argument up to the present, we have found reason to believe:

(1) That if any verbal knowledge can be known to be in any sense derived from sense experience, we must be able, sometimes, to "see" a relation, analogous to causation, between two parts of one specious present.

(2) That facts about universals can sometimes be perceived when the universals are exemplified in sensible occurrences; for example, that "preceding" is transitive, and that blue is more like green than yellow,' p. 148. It should be noted that this position was considerably modified in Russell's next book, *An Inquiry into Meaning and Truth*, as will be shown later.

23. In spite of the first point of the quotation in the preceding foot-note; this position is expressed in no other of Russell's writings.

24. 'There is a great tendency among a very large school to suppose that when you are trying to philosophize about what you know, you ought to carry back your premisses further and further into the region of the inexact and vague, beyond the point where you yourself are, right back to the child or the monkey, and that anything whatsoever that *you* seem to know—but that the psychologist recognizes as being the product of previous thought and analysis and reflection on your part—cannot really be taken as a premiss in your own knowledge. That, I say, is a theory which is very widely held and which is used against that kind of analytic outlook which I wish to urge.' Russell, 'The Philosophy of Logical Atomism', *Logic and Knowledge*, pp. 180–81. See also Bertrand Russell, 'Professor Dewey's "Essays in Experimental Logic",' *The Journal of Philosophy, Psychology, and Scientific Methods*, Vol. XVI, No. 1, January 2, 1919, pp. 5–26.
25. Russell, *My Philosophical Development*, pp. 134–7.
26. Russell, *The Problems of Philosophy*, p. 17.
27. Russell, *The Problems of Philosophy*, pp. 73–5; Russell, 'Knowledge by Acquaintance and Knowledge by Description', in *Mysticism and Logic*, pp. 209–14.
28. Russell, *The Problems of Philosophy*, pp. 82 *ff*; Russell, 'Knowledge by Acquaintance and Knowledge by Description', in *Mysticism and Logic*, pp. 214–21.
29. Russell, *Our Knowledge of the External World*, p. 75.
30. *Ibid.*, p. 76.
31. *Ibid.*, p. 76.
32. *Ibid.*, pp. 76–80.
33. *Ibid.*, pp. 88–9.
34. Russell, *The Problems of Philosophy*, p. 236.
35. Russell, *Our Knowledge of the External World*, pp. 77–9.
36. *Ibid.*, pp. 94 *ff*.
37. Russell, 'Knowledge by Acquaintance and Knowledge by Description' in *Mysticism and Logic*, pp. 211–12, for a tentative conclusion that it is possible to be acquainted with the self. See Russell, *Our Knowledge of the External World*, for a tentative statement that it is not possible to be acquainted with the self. 'The bare subject, if it exists at all, is an inference, and is not part of the data; therefore, this meaning of Self may be ignored in our present inquiry.' p. 81.
38. Russell, 'Knowledge by Acquaintance and Knowledge by Description', in *Mysticism and Logic*, p. 211.
39. Russell, 'The Relation of Sense-Data to Physics', in *Mysticism and Logic*, p. 147.
40. See below, pp. 115 *ff*.

41. Russell, *Our Knowledge of the External World*, Preface, pp. 7–8.
42. *Ibid.*, pp. 88–9.
43. *Ibid.*, pp. 103–4.
44. Russell, 'The Relation of Sense-Data to Physics', in *Mysticism and Logic*, p. 157.
45. *Ibid.*, p. 157.
46. *Ibid.*, pp. 148 *ff.*
47. Russell, *Our Knowledge of the External World*, pp. 116–17.
48. Russell, 'On the Nature of Acquaintance', in *Logic and Knowledge*, pp. 139–59.
49. *Ibid.*, p. 159.
50. Russell, *The Analysis of Mind*, p. 25.
51. *Ibid.*, p. 24.
52. *Ibid.*, pp. 25–6.
53. *Ibid.*, pp. 9–10.
54. *Ibid.*, pp. 145–56. *The Analysis of Mind* has frequently been said to belong to a phenomenalist point of view, and, in this interpretation, the causal explanations of perception and imagination given in this book are to be viewed as constructions, as were the common sense objects and the matter constructed in *Our Knowledge of the External World*. While this theory has some plausibility, it conflicts with the evidence that Russell, in this book, took as part of his data the results of physics, physiology, and psychology, and the causal explanations which they offered. In the absence of these scientific explanations the distinction between sensations and images would fail, as his criticism of Hume indicates. In addition to evidence internal to *The Analysis of Mind*, there is additional evidence in that Russell explicitly states as an assumption in *The Analysis of Matter* the causal theory of perception. This caused Stace to attribute phenomenalism to the earlier but not to the later book, but Russell in his reply to Stace's article said there was no difference between the two books. See W. T. Stace, 'Russell's Neutral Monism', *The Philosophy of Bertrand Russell*, ed. Paul Arthur Schilpp, Northwestern University Press, Evanston and Chicago, 1944, p. 355
55. *The Analysis of Mind*, p. 25.
56. *Ibid.*, Chapters IX to XIII inclusive.
57. *Ibid.*, pp. 131–2.
58. *Ibid.*, pp. 141–3.
59. See below, pp. 175–6.
60. *My Philosophical Development*, p. 112.
61. Russell, 'The Philosophy of Logical Atomism', in *Logic and Know-*

ledge (first published, 1918); Russell, 'Logical Atomism', in *Logic and Knowledge* (first published, 1924).

62. Russell, 'The Philosophy of Logical Atomism', in *Logic and Knowledge*, pp. 178–9.

63. *Ibid.*, p. 194. "All analysis is only possible in regard to what is complex, and it always depends, in the last analysis, upon direct acquaintance with the objects which are the meanings of certain simple symbols.'

64. Russell, *Logic and Knowledge*, p. 337.

65. Russell, *My Philosophical Development*, p. 119.

66. Russell, *The Analysis of Matter*, p. 171.

67. *Ibid.*, pp. 209–17.

68 *Ibid.*, p. 189.

69. In commenting on the change in his own views, Russell quotes from the 1914 essay, 'The Relation of Sense-Data to Physics', in which he stated his aim as the giving of equations of physical objects in terms of sense-data. Russell writes, 'I soon, however, became persuaded that this is an impossible programme and that physical objects cannot be interpreted as structures composed of elements actually experienced'. He had hoped eventually to dispense with the hypotheses of 'sensibilia' and of other minds, but 'gave up the attempt to construct "matter" out of experienced data alone, and contented myself with a picture of the world which fitted physics and perception harmoniously into a single whole'. *My Philosophical Development*, p. 105.

70. Russell, *My Philosophical Development*, p. 136.

71. *Ibid.*, p. 13.

72. Conversation with B.R., June 1964.

73. The picture we have been drawing of a consistent direction and method to Russell's work in theory of knowledge has, as a consequence, that the books published from 1940 on can be seen as the more fully developed outcome of this work.

74. Bertrand Russell, 'On Order in Time', first read to the Cambridge Philosophical Society, March, 1936, published in their *Proceedings*. Published in *Logic and Knowledge*, pp. 345–63.

75. Bertrand Russell, 'The Limits of Empiricism', *Proceedings of the Aristotelian Society*, Vol. 36, 1936, pp. 131–50.

76. Bertrand Russell, 'On Verification', *Proceedings of the Aristotelian Society*, Vol. 38, 1938, pp. 1–20.

77. Bertrand Russell, 'Logical Positivism', originally in *Revue Internationale de Philosophie*, 4, 11, Janvier, 1950, pp. 3–19, in *Logic and Knowledge*, pp.366–82; Bertrand Russell, 'Logic and Ontology', *Journal of Philosophy*, Vol. 54, April 25, 1956; reprinted in *My Philosophical Development*, pp. 231–8. This is a comment on Warnock. Bertrand Russell, 'Philosophical

Analysis', *Hibbert Journal*, Vol. 54, July, 1956, pp. 319–29; reprinted in *My Philosophical Development*, pp. 215–30. This is a response to Urmson. Bertrand Russell, 'What is Mind?' *The Journal of Philosophy*, Vol. 55, Jan. 2, 1958; reprinted in *My Philosophical Development*, pp. 245–54. This is a review of Ryle's *Concept of Mind*. Bertrand Russell, 'Mr. Strawson on Referring', in *My Philosophical Development*, pp. 238–45. This is a response to Strawson's criticism of his theory of descriptions in 'On Referring'.

78. Russell, 'The Limits of Empiricism', p. 148.
79. Russell, *Inquiry*, p. 139.
80. *Ibid.*, pp. 103 *ff.*
81. Russell, *Human Knowledge*, p. 487.
82. Russell, *My Philosophical Development*, pp. 128–30.
83. Russell, *Human Knowledge*, p. 433.
84. *Ibid.*, p. 428, *Inquiry*, p. 84.
85. Russell, *Inquiry*, pp. 49 *f.*
86. *Ibid.*, p. 151.
87. *Ibid.*, Chapter IX.
88. *Ibid.*, Chapter IV.
89. *Ibid.*, pp. 62–3.
90. *Ibid.*, Chapter VII.
91. *Ibid.*, pp. 127 *f.*, 337 *f.*
92. *Ibid.*, p. 36.
93. *Ibid.*, p. 45.
94. *Ibid.*, p. 215.
95. Russell, *My Philosophical Development*, pp. 221–3.
96. Russell, *Inquiry*, Chapters XXI, XXII.
97. Russell, *My Philosophical Development*, pp. 113–14.
98. Russell, *Inquiry*, Chapter XXIV.
99. Russell, *My Philosophical Development*, pp. 114–27.
100. Russell, *Human Knowledge*, Chapter IX, Part 6.
101. Russell, *Inquiry*, p. 18.
102. J. Loewenberg, 'Pre-Analytical and Post-Analytical Data', *The Journal of Philosophy*, Vol. XXIV, Jan. 6, 1927, pp. 5–14.
103. Russell, 'The Philosophy of Logical Atomism', in *Logic and Knowledge*, pp. 179–80.
104. Russell, *The Problems of Philosophy*, Chapter XI.
105. Russell, 'Knowledge by Acquaintance and Knowledge by Description', in *Mysticism and Logic*, pp. 209–14.
106. Russell, *The Problems of Philosophy*, pp. 210 *f.*
107. Russell, *The Analysis of Matter*, pp. 187–9.
108. Russell, *Inquiry*, pp. 16–17.

109. Russell, *The Analysis of Mind*, pp. 145–50.
110. Russell, *Inquiry*, p. 135. 'Speaking psychologically, a "perceptive premiss" may be defined as a belief caused as immediately as possible by a percept.'
111. Russell, *The Problems of Philosophy*, pp. 176–7.
112. Russell, 'The Relation of Sense-Data to Physics', in *Mysticism and Logic*, p. 157.
113. Russell, 'The Philosophy of Logical Atomism', in *Logic and Knowledge*, p. 180.
114. *Ibid.*, p. 181. Also Russell, *Inquiry*, pp. 16–17.
115. Russell, *Our Knowledge of the External World*, pp. 77 f.
116. Russell, 'Knowledge by Acquaintance and Knowledge by Description', in *Mysticism and Logic*, pp. 211–13.
117. Difficulties in the pre-analytical meaning of data were evident prior to Russell's complete adoption of neutral monism in his response to John Dewey's criticism of Russell's concept of data. Russell argues that Dewey had misunderstood the meaning of data for him. He does not mean the historically primitive. 'When I speak of "data", more particularly of "hard data", I am not thinking of those objects which constitute data to children or monkeys: I am thinking of the objects which seem data to a trained scientific observer. . . . The state of mind that I am imagining in investigating the problem of the physical world is not a naïve state of mind, but one of Cartesian doubt.' Bertrand Russell, 'Professor Dewey's "Essays in Experimental Logic",' *The Journal of Philosophy, Psychology, and Scientific Methods*, Vol. XVI, No. 1, January 2, 1919, p. 7.
118. Russell, *Inquiry*, pp. 15–18.
119. *Ibid.*, pp. 122–5.
120. Russell, *Human Knowledge*, pp. 380–4.
121. *Ibid.*, p. 397.

CHAPTER V

REALISM

The term 'realism', unlike 'empiricism' or 'analysis', requires special clarification. For, not only is 'realism' itself a term which is used in philosophy with a variety of meanings, but also its application to Russell's philosophy might be questioned.[1] The topic discussed here can be described as the question of how Russell's philosophy stands on the problems of 'what there is'.[2] This question should be interpreted as widely as possible as including several distinct philosophical problems. What assumptions or conclusions are made (if any) about the nature of the world which surrounds us? The possible answers to this question would be kinds of metaphysical theories such as idealism, materialism, and so forth. 'What there is' would include the question of what is said to be the status and nature of the referent of our knowledge. When we know something, what is it that we know? The possible answers to this query would include phenomenalism, naïve or representative realism, and idealism. 'What there is' would include, as well, the question of the status of the referents of such symbols as class names, quality terms, relation terms, numbers, logical or mathematical terms, that is, the so-called problem of universals. The possible answers to this question would include nominalism, conceptualism, Platonic realism, Scotistic realism.

The problem with which this chapter is concerned is the extent to which Russell's theory of knowledge answer these questions. The discussion will follow the order of the preceding list of questions. The question of what metaphysical *assumptions* Russell makes about the nature of the world can be dealt with by way of introduction. The question of the nature and status of the referent of knowledge is more lengthy and difficult. It will be discussed under the concepts of 'belief', 'truth', 'knowledge', and 'probability'. The problem of the status of universals, classes, relations, logical or mathematical entities will be dealt with in a historical manner, since on this topic Russell's position shifted considerably. The final portion of the chapter will draw these threads together in a discussion of Russell's imaginative construction of a metaphysical hypothesis, a description of 'what may be'.

It is clear that, for Russell, philosophy is not chiefly concerned with speculative metaphysics. Yet, as an item of intellectual autobiography, he has confessed on more than one occasion that he approaches the world with a bias towards the vast non-human sweep of space and time. His picture of the world is the one which science gives us, a world of history and extent, stretching for millions of light-years, which reduces human existence and human concerns to triviality.[3] This imaginative framework produces two kinds of emotional response: awe and admiration of the grandeur of the universe, and revulsion towards the stuffiness of a humanistic bias which looks at the world only through the desires and the knowledge of man. Yet, there is an element of conflict in Russell's feelings, since he believes it is inappropriate to value or revere anything non-human or impersonal.[4] Perhaps for this reason he terms his own perspective on 'what there is' a 'prejudice';[5] it might better be termed a pre-disposition toward scientific realism. He does not attempt to build any metaphysical structure on this 'prejudice', but it is reflected in his resolve to accept as largely true what science and common sense tell us of the nature of the world.[6] This assumption that the world has the characteristics described by science is compatible with the hypothesis which he constructs as a possible picture of the nature of the world.

The question of realism concerning the status of the object of knowledge is related in an important way to the discussion of Chapter IV. For the analysis of perceptual knowledge is, on the one hand, directed toward a faithfulness to experience and on the other hand, to the problem of finding in it the source of what we think we know, that is, the beliefs of common sense and of science. The epistemological scrutiny of beliefs, their arrangement in an order of credibility, is designed to sift the true from the false, the more reliably known from the less reliably known. In this sense, a description of belief, truth, and knowledge is the outcome of an empiricist analysis of experience, an outcome in the light of which the adequacy of the analysis of experience itself is to be judged. In addition, the topics of belief, knowledge, and truth are those on which Russell differentiates his own position from other contemporary and historical points of view. It is on these issues that the combination of an analytic method and an empiricist description of experience require the addition of a new set of postulates to extend the limits of empiricism. This will bring us to the topic of probability.

Two words of caution are required before we follow Russell's treatment of the key concepts of belief, truth, and knowledge. The first warning is to the effect that these terms are defined in terms of one another; that is, truth is defined in terms of a belief and what the belief refers to, knowledge is defined as a sub-class of true beliefs, and belief itself is discussed in several different contexts. The second warning concerns the shifting terminology used by Russell in these contexts. Sometimes he refers to beliefs or judgments as true or false, sometimes he refers to sentences as true or false, and sometimes it is a proposition of which it is said that it is true or false. Similarly, knowledge is sometimes put in the context of behaviour, sometimes in the context of discourse, and sometimes in the context of 'fact'. These shifting terms usually do not indicate a difference between an earlier and a later position, but a difference in the context of the discussion, whether it is a psychological, a linguistic, or a logical analysis which is in question.

Since both knowledge and truth are defined in terms of belief, analysis may well begin with 'belief'. It is necessary to discover what Russell meant by 'belief' and how beliefs are related to judgments, propositions, and sentences.

In the first place, the terms 'belief' and judgment' belong to the psychological aspect of knowledge and truth. A belief or a judgment is something that belongs to a thinking organism; it is psychological and physiological. Although the treatment of belief changed somewhat throughout Russell's work, it ended by being defined as an 'organic state'.[7] As a belief, the organic state itself is either true or false. However, in order for the belief to have any public existence, it must be expressed in some way. It may be expressed in the actions of the holder of the belief, or in his words. For instance, an organic state of fear may be expressed by running away, or by words stating that the person is afraid. Or, a belief may include not only the organic state itself, but the objective referent of that state; one may put up an umbrella, or one may say, 'it is raining'. Both the action and the words may be said to be true or false in so far as they express a true or false belief concerning the weather. Hence, one who raises an umbrella when no rain is falling may be said to be mistaken, and the belief which his action expresses may be said to be false in the same way that the sentence, 'it is raining', is false, because the fact what both action and words purport to indicate is not as stated. Russell adds that the terms 'true' and 'false' may be applied 'derivatively' to sentences. That is, the terms 'true' and 'false' apply to beliefs, but since beliefs are expressed in sentences, those sentences themselves may be said to be 'true' or 'false'.[8]

What is meant by a sentence? A sentence is a group of words which has significance by virtue of its conforming to certain grammatical rules, and by virtue of its relation to the beliefs of the user and the hearer of the sentence. There are several points to be noticed here. First, Russell distinguishes between the sentence and the sentential utterance; both, as he points out, involve a certain generality. Any symbol has a kind of generality. The word 'book', for instance, is really a group of visible squiggles and audible squawks, which, for convenience, are grouped together and referred to as one word. There is no uniformity or unity in the sounds and the squiggles which justifies the denomination of one 'word'; there is only a 'family resemblance'

unified by the fact that, when the language is commonly understood by utterer and hearer, or writer and reader, a communication occurs concerning whatever the referent of the symbol
may be.[9] The same is true for sentences as it is for individual
symbols; a sentence is a larger and more complex group of
squiggles or squawks, uttered or written by different persons
on different occasions. For convenience, however, we may call
the group of squiggles or squawks with similar significance
and a certain degree of similarity of structure one sentence. Of
course, the precise significance will be different depending on
the unique use and the context of that unique use: a sentential
utterance is the unique occasion on which a specific sentence
is uttered by a specific speaker in a specific tone of voice.[10]

It is also important to note the qualifications for the application
of the terms 'true' and 'false' to sentences and sentential utterance.
In the first place, there are many sentences which have no or
minimal relevance to the property of 'true' or 'false'; they ask
questions, give directions, but neither express an organic state
nor indicate a fact. Furthermore, there may be sentences which
meet the grammatical requirements of good form, but not the
requirements of significance. Russell's example of this latter
group is 'quadruplicity drinks procrastination'. This has a subject
and a predicate, hence it conforms to grammatical sentence
form; but we cannot even imagine what it might mean to assert
this sentence. There must be a psychological criterion of significance as well as a syntactical one.[11]

The context in which sentences and sentential utterances
are discussed is linguistic. That is, a sentence is always in English
or French or some language; it has six or seven or some number
of words; it is punctuated in a certain way; it is spoken or
written. Although it is possible to say that 'Christopher Columbus
discovered America' is the same sentence when lisped by a
schoolboy, written on a blackboard in script, printed in a text,
or carved on a stone monument, this is not the most important
kind of unifying principle to look for among sentences. The
important unity is that of meaning; this is what we recognize

when we read a number of sentences in different languages and in different words and recognize that they have one meaning. This meaning is a proposition; for instance, 'it is raining', '*il pleut*', and 'the rain is falling' are all different sentences but they are one proposition.[12] The proposition, like the belief, has a psychological and physiological status, but the usual context in which propositions are discussed is in terms of their status as 'true' or 'false', and in terms of their logical function.

We have three kinds of items to which the terms 'true' and 'false' may be applied; the psychological terms, belief and judgment; the linguistic terms, sentence and sentential utterance; and the logical term, proposition. A proposition is the meaning common to a number of sentences which are all true together and false together; it is the meaning of the sentence in a logical sense. Basically, there is 'belief' which refers to an organic state; this belief may be expressed in linguistic form, a sentence, and the sentence may be said to 'mean' the proposition. Although it is appropriate on some occasions to refer to a given sentence as 'true' or 'false', it would make for too much multiplicity to call each sentential utterance, or even each sentence, individually, 'true' or 'false'. A kind of useful economy results from saying that the proposition which is the meaning of the sentence 'Christopher Columbus discovered America' is true. Accordingly, one simply says that the proposition 'Christopher Columbus discovered America' is true.

When either a belief or a proposition is interpreted, there are two aspects to the meaning of it; one is what is expresses, and the other is what it indicates. Although in one sense the sentence or proposition may be said to be the expression of the belief, in another sense the sentence or propositions may be said to 'express' an organic state.[13] For instance, if one says 'I am hot', the meaning of this sentence or proposition, assuming that one is telling the truth, is a certain organic state of feeling hot, which the sentence expresses. Whatever a belief or proposition or sentence is about, one aspect of its meaning is the expression of the organic state which is the underlying pre-verbal belief.

The other aspect of the meaning of belief or sentence or proposition is what it indicates; for instance, the statement about Christopher Columbus expresses a 'yes-feeling' concerning the assertion of a certain sentence; it also refers to a person and an event which happened in the fifteenth century. The facts to which this historical proposition refers are what it indicates.[14] In the interesting case of 'I am hot', Russell says that what is expressed and what is referred to are the same. Hence this proposition cannot be false.[15] As we shall see, it is because in most propositions there is a gap between the organic state of belief which the proposition expresses and the fact which it indicates that the possibility of its being true or false arises. If one is speaking sincerely, the statement about Christopher Columbus cannot but be an adequate expression of one's own organic state; but whatever may be one's organic state, the historical event referred to is what it is, and it may be not what it is believed to be. It is here that falsity may occur.[16]

It is noteworthy that the qualification that the belief be sincerely expressed must be accepted for the co-ordination of psychological, linguistic, and logical contexts to be successful. Russell refers to a 'spontaneous sentence', one in which neither intentional nor unintentional deception is employed.[17] There is a direct causal connection between the occasion, the feeling hot, and the sentence which expresses it. This limitation to 'spontaneous sentences' is similat to the restriction to indicative sentences. Other uses of language are not relevant to the discussion of truth and belief. Russell's theory of knowledge requires a rigour concerning the relation of belief, symbol, and fact which is possible only if one limits one's consideration to the kind of language and language use which is truly indicative.

In discussing the relation of belief, proposition, and sentence, we have relied on the most recent statements on this topic in the *Inquiry* and in *Human Knowledge*, but it is important to follow the development of Russell's thought concerning the description of belief, since this is a central theme in his epistemology. In *The Problems of Philosophy* Russell does not make a psychological analysis of belief, nor does he give any specific description of belief, but he treats believing as a relation holding *from* the subject *to* the terms of the complex of what is believed. This relation is said to have a certain sense or direction.[18] Beliefs, he says, depend on minds for their existence but do not depend on minds for their truth. In 'The Philosophy of Logical Atomism' even this limited mention of belief drops out. There the emphasis is on the correspondence of fact and proposition; the proposition is analysed into its terms rather than into its psychological antecedents.[19] This shift of emphasis has two explanations; one is that Russell was feeling doubts about the empirical existence of the entity 'subject' or 'consciousness'; the other is that his primary concern was with logical analysis in this context.

In *The Analysis of Mind* Russell is interested primarily in psychological analysis, and he drops the reference to the knowing mind or subject as part of that analysis, having adopted the position of neutral monism. He recognizes the importance of the analysis of belief, and we find here a more careful treatment of what can be called belief, which he calls 'the central problem in the analysis of mind'.[20] A belief is analysed into three elements, the believing, the content of the belief, and the reference of the belief. The believing is the individual's possession of the conviction of a certain meaning, either in words or in images; the content of the belief is the meaning, for example, *that* Caesar conquered Gaul; the reference of the belief is the event or fact to which the belief, if it is true, refers, the historical event of the conquering of Gaul. This last, the 'objective reference' of the belief, may be derived from the meaning of the individual words, if one is trying to understand a given proposition. But, at the same time, there may be a considerable gap between the belief and the content, which is remote in space and time, and which may not itself be the cause of the occurrence of the belief. For instance, if I say 'it is raining', the objective reference of my belief is the water now streaming down my face from the clouds, and my belief is caused by the same fact which is the objective referent of the belief. However, this is not the case with respect to 'Caesar conquered Gaul'. In this case, the causal connection between the event referred to and my belief is remote and indirect.

Another point of importance in the description of belief in *The Analysis of Mind* is that what is included under the heading of belief is wider in extent than the description in previous discussion. Although the behaviourist analysis of belief, that a belief is equivalent to the actions which would ordinarily be said to follow from it, is rejected, at the same time, the propositional form of belief, which had been emphasized in earlier statements, is extended to take in beliefs had in the form of images, and, more significantly, beliefs which are had only as expectations without being consciously entertained.[21]

In *Human Knowledge*, Russell has a statement of what he means by belief, a statement which summarizes the description of belief given in the *Inquiry* as well as that of the later book. There are several points on which Russell had modified his description of belief. This description is still predominantly a psychological analysis, but one which incorporates a good deal of behaviouristic psychology. The actions of the body may not *be* the belief, but they, as well as words, may express it. He says that he treats belief as something that can be pre-intellectual, as displayed in the behaviour of animals; a purely bodily state may be called a belief; it is a state of the organism.[22] He defines belief as a state of the organism in which 'the presence of *A* causes behaviour appropriate to *B*.[23] He differentiates between active and static beliefs, the latter consisting of an idea or image combined with a 'yes-feeling'.[24] But he also retains the connection of beliefs with external referents. His final definition of belief is 'a collection of states of an organism bound together by all having in whole or part the same external reference'.[25]

Whether the increasingly behaviourist analysis of belief is consistent with the emphasis on the external referent as the basis for the evaluation of the truth or falsity of the belief is a question to be discussed later. In any case, an organic state and an external reference remain important throughout the analysis of belief.

Throughout his career Russell gives two characteristic descriptions of truth: truth is a property of a belief which depends upon something outside of the belief, and truth is the correspondence of a belief with a fact.[26] These definitions stress the essential features of his view of truth. His is a correspondence theory of truth in that what is believed must correspond with, that is, be closely similar to, the fact to which it refers. Russell's theory of truth is realist, that is, the correspondence is between something psychological, or internal to the believer, and something real, existent, and external to the believer, something which is unchanged by the belief itself.

As we noted in the discussion of belief, truth may be said to be a property of a belief, a judgment, a proposition, or a sentence. The sentence is the verbal expression of the belief, so its truth is 'derivative'; the proposition is the logical form of the belief, but is also thought of as something psychological and physiological.[27] One particular problem concerning the definition of truth arises because of the variations in usage in Russell's application of the terms 'true' and 'false' to beliefs, propositions, and sentences. Since basically truth is a property of propositions and beliefs, and only derivatively of sentences, how can Russell say that any sentence may be true or false, whether there is any evidence for its truth or falsity or not? It would seem that if there were evenly balanced evidence, or a sheer lack of evidence, no belief or conviction could be sincerely held. If no belief is held, then it would seem that it would be impossible to use the terms 'true' and 'false'. Yet Russell says, 'On what may be called the realistic view of truth, there are 'facts', and there are sentences related to these facts in ways which make the sentences true or false, quite independently of any way of deciding the alternative'.[28] As appears in his defence of the 'logical' version of the correspondence theory of truth, one motive for accepting the position that a sentence or proposition must be true or false in the absence of either evidence or conviction as to which it is, is that the truth of each atomic proposition is independent of that of every other, and it is desirable to hold that if a given atomic proposition, say one whose truth is directly given in experience, 'I am hot' has one of its terms replaced, 'Tom is hot', the resultant proposition is true or false, although one may have no evidence as to what Tom's organic state is. Accordingly, Russell extends the definition of truth to call a proposition or a sentence true or false, even though no one believes it, if it would be true or false, if some one *did* believe it.[29] The logical requirements of the theory of truth cannot be permitted to be restricted by accidental psychological limitations.

As far as the history of the concept of truth is concerned, although there is consistency in the correspondence and the realism of the theory of truth, there are interesting changes in the description of what is meant by the terms 'true' and 'false'. In *The Problems of Philosophy* truth is defined as the correspondence of belief and fact, and some of the problems which arise with the definition are discussed. Truth and falsehood are properties of beliefs and statements, but they depend upon something which lies outside the belief itself, that is, the fact. It is in the precise definition of fact, and of the correspondence with fact, that Russell's views change. The initial definition of the correspondence between belief and fact is developed in *The Problems of Philosophy* as a mode of relation in which the 'subject' is in a relation of believing to a complex 'object'. Othello believes that Desdemona loves Cassio. Then the belief may be held to be true when there is another relation existing which corresponds to, or is the same as, the relation between the 'object terms' of the belief, that is, when there is a fact of Desdemona, of Cassio, and of the relation of love between them. If there is no such identical complex fact, the belief is false.[30]

In 'The Philosophy of Logical Atomism' a similar definition of truth is given. It is said to be a property of beliefs, and a property which depends upon a relation external to the belief, a relation to fact. The correspondence is somewhat differently stated, however, than in the earlier work. The emphasis upon the believing subject is dropped, and the correspondence becomes that of identity of structure of proposition and fact. The propo-

sition is analysed into its elements, and this results in the distinction between atomic and molecular propositions, the latter
reducible by truth-functional analysis to the former. The relation
of correspondence is said to hold if the atomic proposition points
to its objective and if the proposition and the fact are closely
similar in structure. In the case of the atomic propositions this
can be determined by correlation of the terms of the proposition
with the components of the fact. If there is a one to one correlation, then the proposition is true (the proposition pictures the
fact). If there is no close correlation, then the proposition points
away from the fact and is false. In changing the definition of
correspondence, Russell's motive appears to be the elimination
of the believing 'subject' as an integral part of the complex in
the interests of an economy of metaphysical assumptions. There
is also more of a logical and less of an epistemological bias in
this analysis, since the concept of the atomic proposition and the
method of truth-functional analysis is dominant. The truth of
molecular propositions may be inferred from the truth of their
atomic components according to this truth-functional method.[31]

In *The Analysis of Mind* one reservation with regard to the
theory of truth of his earlier work is indicated. Russell says that
the earlier treatment had failed to show reasons for preferring
true to false beliefs and that an adequate theory of truth would
show how true beliefs lead to more appropriate responses, and
thus help us fulfil our purposes more satisfactorily.[32] This remark
is prophetic of Russell's later concern with what may be called
the psychological, organic, and pragmatic aspects of the theory
of truth. This emphasis fits somewhat oddly with the formal
aspects of Russell's definition of truth and might be thought to
be a modification of the correspondence theory. It leads to a
further consideration of the relation of truth to verification and
a consideration of the contemporary theories of truth which
make verification the basis of the definition of truth.

In similar terms, in the *Inquiry* truth is defined as a property
of belief and as dependent on a reference external to the belief
itself. The treatment of fact and the relation of fact to belief

give evidence of some modification of Russell's position. In the *Inquiry* Russell considers the simplest kind of belief which has the most direct relation to fact as a prototype of a true proposition. A belief which expresses and indicates the same thing, such as is expressed in the sentence 'I am hot', would be an example of fact and belief being identical, and hence of there being no possibility of error. This spontaneous utterance of 'I am hot' in which there is no attempt to deceive is a case of the smallest gap between expression and indication.[33] In this sentence we have the expression of a present situation and the indication of a future sensation. In this case, we can say that 'an expectation as to an experience of my own is *true* when it leads to confirmation, *false* when it leads to surprise'.[34] This seems close to a verifiability theory of truth, but it is meant to apply only to cases where the fact indicated is a future experience of my own, whereas most of the beliefs in the truth of which we are interested make statements going far beyond these limits. This leads Russell to the concept of the 'verifier' of a belief. When a belief is relatively simple, there will be one or more possible causal relations which it will have to certain other occurrences. The other occurrences are called 'verifiers' of the belief; if the occurrence of the 'verifier' makes the belief true, the non-occurrence makes it false.[35] In *Human Knowledge* the verifier of a belief is said to be analogous to the husband of a given lady—the description of a person who would be the lady's husband if she had one, applies to a given man, if she has a husband, to no one, if she is unmarried.[36]

This concept of the relation between belief and fact makes judgments of perception the preferred kind of judgment, since in this case it is possible for a verifier to be specified and for confirmation to occur. This fits in with the importance of perceptual knowledge in Russell's theory of knowledge in general. There is a direct causal link between the perceived fact and the proposition in the case of 'I am hot', an indirect causal link between the perceived fact and the judgment in the case of 'you are hot'. In the case of the indirect causal link, more analysis is required to uncover the perceptual datum in the derived complex perceptive experience and its expression.

A similar treatment of factual propositions in *Human Knowledge* supports the contention that the concept of the verifier, as it is used to relate beliefs to the facts to which they must correspond if they are to be true, has the effect of using perception as the link between what is believed on the basis of experience and what is, by virtue of external fact, true.

In *Human Knowledge* Russell gives a definition of truth in which this perceptual causal link is apparent. 'A sentence of the form "This is *A*" is called "true" when it is caused by what "*A*" means.' When this definition is extended to refer to past and future referents, Russell concludes that the definition covers all sentences asserting facts of perception and animal inferences from a percept, and, thus, the definition 'covers all the factual premisses of empirical knowledge'.[37] Two implications of the treatment of truth in the two later books should be noted. One is that the relation of fact to percept is not a 'given' but a causal one, which must be uncovered prior to the acceptance of the perceptual judgment. Secondly, the definition of the verifier allows us to infer that there may be propositions for which the verifier is completely inaccessible; yet the proposition would remain significant, and it would be true or false, even though there might not be a shred of evidence.

Russell offers his theory of truth as an alternative which satisfies the requirements of a theory of truth better than any historical or contemporary theory. There are, accordingly, two parts to the justification of his theory, the requirements which any theory of truth should meet and the weaknesses of alternative theories.

According to the account given in *The Problems of Philosophy*, the requirements of a theory of truth are that it must take account of error, that it must apply to beliefs, and that it must refer outside itself.[38] Similar requirements seem to be implied in later discussions of the same topic. In the *Inquiry* he mentions that a theory of truth must show that truth is wider than knowledge in two respects, first, that there are true sentences as to which we have no opinion, and that there are true sentences which we believe and yet do not know, because we arrived at them by faulty reasoning.[39] It seems to be assumed throughout that a common-sense meaning of what it is for a statement to be true or false is to be incorporated into the theory.

What are the alternative views to which Russell considers his own to be preferable? In *The Problems of Philosophy* the only alternative considered is the coherence theory of truth, and this is rejected on the grounds of the possibility of more than one logically consistent system of thought and on the grounds that the notion of coherence itself must be true in some other sense than that of coherence.[40] In later discussion Russell defends his correspondence theory against some of the criticisms which have been made of it. In *The Analysis of Mind* he defends his own views against definitions of knowledge in terms of response to the environment, and truth in terms of appropriate response. He claims that, contrary to behaviourist psychology, there are some aspects of our knowledge which can be known through introspection.[41] In this book he gives attention, also, to the concept of verifiability, but it is more relevant to the degree of certainty different kinds of confirmation may give than to a theory of truth.[42]

In the recent discussion of theory of truth in the *Inquiry*, it is evident that Russell is conscious of the need to defend his view of truth as a relation dependent on the existence of fact external to knowledge. The defence is called forth by the widespread objection to using the description 'true' of a belief where there is no possibility of knowing that it is true. In this book Russell distinguishes four theories of truth: Dewey's theory of warranted assertibility, Reichenbach's theory which substitutes probability for truth, the coherence theory (as advocated by the Hegelians and by some logical positivists), and the correspondence theory. The correspondence theory is defined as that 'according to which the truth of basic propositions depends upon their relation to some occurrence, and the truth of other propositions depends upon their syntactical relation to basic propositions'.[43] There are two forms of the correspondence theory; in one version the basic propositions must be related to experience, and if they are not so related, then the propositions are neither true nor false; in the other version the basic propositions must be related to 'facts', not necessarily to experience, although if they are not related to experience, they cannot be known.[44]

Of the five possibilities outlined—the coherence theory, warranted assertibility, probability, the 'experience' version of the correspondence theory, and the 'fact' version of the correspondence theory—Russell affirms his choice of the last. He gives his reasons for this choice in terms of criticisms of the other points of view. His criticisms of the Hegelian coherence theory have not changed. The logical positivists' version of the coherence theory is criticized on the grounds that it results in the development of an encyclopædia of interrelated meanings with no reference to experience, since it stops with protocol statements but refuses to discuss what these statements refer to. Russell's arguments against the other theories of truth turn on three points: first, he insists on the importance of basic perceptual propositions and finds that neither Reichenbach nor Dewey pay sufficient attention to these; second, he believes that truth is wider than knowledge and defends the law of excluded middle; and third, he finds that the definition of truth must be such as to provide a satisfactory goal of knowledge.

Russell's criticisms of Dewey's concept of truth centre around the interpretation of truth as the satisfaction of the requirements of the situation of perplexity and doubt which initiates inquiry. Russell first interprets this as a subjective definition of truth, truth as anything which is personally satisfying in quieting doubt. But if Dewey's meaning is wider, truth is anything that is socially or biologically satisfying in a situation of doubt. When Dewey rejects this interpretation and insists that the doubt and the perplexity are objective and not subjective and that the satisfaction of the doubt must meet the objective requirements of the situation,

Russell then says that this is just the old-fashioned correspondence theory of truth in different language.[45]

Another criticism of Dewey and of other contemporaries made by Russell is that, by limiting truth to the outcome of inquiry or to what is within the range of possible knowledge, they have removed the concept of truth as the goal beyond inquiry toward which the search for truth is directed. This criticism is related to another point of attack against both Dewey and Reichenbach and some logical empiricists, that is, that no distinction is made between the verifying of the proposition and the fact that makes it true or false. The proposition 'Caesar conquered Gaul' may be verified by books and documents now existing, but what makes it true or false is an event which occurred in the past. 'It snowed on Manhattan Island in the year 1 A.D.' may be a proposition for which no evidence can be obtained, but there is a fact by virtue of which it is true or false. Even a proposition concerning a world which is said to be forever inaccessible to observation from this world has a truth status, although by definition it can never be known. Russell concludes that a distinction must be made between the verification of a proposition and the truth of a proposition. There may be propositions which are true but are not known to be true. Truth is a wider concept than knowledge. This conclusion fits in with the distinction which common sense makes between the truth of a statement and the verification of a statement; it fits in with the common-sense belief that it makes sense to talk of things of which we can have no direct perceptual experience. In addition, Russell's own analysis of empirical knowledge has shown that the limits of what can be known by experience are so narrow that we are forced to go beyond them. It also has shown the importance of the new data derived from perceptual knowledge. In addition to these reasons, the restriction of truth to the verifiable would require a large part of mathematics, logic, and scientific and common-sense knowledge to be placed beyond the scope of the law of excluded middle.

The concept of 'knowledge' can be seen in its outlines as a

consequence of the treatment of 'belief' and 'truth', and the details of this concept and that of 'probability' complete the answer to the second question of what there is, that of the status of the object of knowledge.

In *The Problems of Philosophy* Russell's preliminary definition of knowledge is that knowledge is true belief, which is believed for good reasons.[46] This definition remains the fundamental description of knowledge for Russell. But important changes occur in the specification of what are 'good reasons' for believing any proposition. In *The Problems of Philosophy* Russell's specification of good reasons brought him to the distinction between derived and intuitive knowledge.[47] The latter is direct and indubitable, and known by acquaintance. The former is validated by being deduced more or less directly from intuitive knowledge. The evaluation of beliefs as knowledge depends on this distinction. However, when our beliefs are scanned, it appears that there are very few of them which are certain, as is intuitive knowledge. Russell says that, although self-evidence is an absolute guarantee of truth, the difficulty is in knowing, in the case of any given judgment, whether it is absolutely self-evident. For we pass from the self-evidence of the fact of sun's shining to the analysis of this complex and the statement of it in a judgment, and the analysis and the judgment lack the infallibility of the fact.[48] Also, although perceptions are the prototype of self-evidence, there are some faint or very complex perceptions of which it is difficult to be certain what they are. The other model of self-evidence is inferences of logic, that from certain premisses, a certain conclusion must follow. Although such inferences may be self-evident for simple arguments, complex arguments are not self-evidently valid or invalid. Much of what we think we know turns out to be in the class of probable opinion rather than of knowledge.[49]

The problem of knowledge is the problem of estimating whether a given belief has intrinsic self-evidence, or whether it has a clear title through logical implication from a self-evident belief, or whether other considerations such as those of logical coherence tend to support or reduce its degree of probability. It is noteworthy that the criteria of knowledge, as described in *The Problems of Philosophy*, are based primarily on psychological certainty, for the most part derived from perception with some support from logical objectivity.

In *The Analysis of Mind*, the distinction between intuitive and derived knowledge has been dropped, and with it the claim for any certainty of self-evidence. Here the evaluation of belief as knowledge is based upon relative criteria such as coherence and the verification of expectations. While the truth of a belief is dependent on its reference to fact, its credibility is dependent upon the feelings of assent which occur when a given belief fits in with other beliefs, or when it meets confirmation in the form of subsequent experience, or when it possesses a high degree of subjective certainty. Although the method of confirmation is not infallible, it is the way by which a belief is rendered more probably true. The method of confirmation as used in science shows how it serves to increase our knowledge.[50]

In the *Inquiry* the problem of the definition of knowledge is important in the plan of the book, the problem described as 'the relation of basic propositions to experiences, i.e., of the propositions that come first in the epistemological order to the occurrences which, in *some* sense, are our grounds for accepting these propositions'.[51] The emphasis is on perceptual beliefs and the way in which they may form the foundations of our know-ledge. In the order of credibility, the most credible are those in which indication and expression are one, such as 'I am hot'. The next most credible are those which express a fulfilled expectation; then come those based on recent and vivid memory. Later in the order of credibility are those propositions which go beyond the immediate and direct perception to judgments concerning events remote in space and time, and which involve more interpretation and generalization. In order to include as knowledge the beliefs of common sense and of science which we think we know, we must go far beyond the limits of immediate experience.[52]

There are many sources of possible error in this putative

knowledge. Even a simple and immediate judgment of perception is sometimes unreliable and must be submitted to a critical analysis to make sure, by means of an investigation of the cause of the perceptive experience, that it points to the interpretation which has been given.[53]

In addition there is the difficulty that the percept and the derived perceptual proposition refer to an event in the biography of the observer. How can a proposition of perception be valid beyond the experience of the one having the perceptual experience? The assumption of the existence of other minds, and of the existence of the external world, can be justified only on a pragmatic basis. On the level of both common sense and scientific knowledge it seems that we continually go beyond our experience, and even beyond all possible experience, even in our simplest judgments. Russell concludes that we must accept the existence of fact which can never be experienced and the consequent limitations on the possibility of our having any experiential validation for our beliefs.[54] Much of what we are accustomed to call knowledge has little claim in the order of credibility.

A simliar conclusion seems to follow from the argument of *Human Knowledge*. Knowledge is there defined as 'a sub-class of true beliefs'.[55] The differentia narrow the class to those beliefs which, as well as being true (and we have no way of telling from the nature of the belief whether it is true or not), are believed on the basis of sound evidence. Sound evidence is taken to mean, in the common-sense interpretation, what we believe on the basis of matters of fact, known in perception and memory, and on the basis of principles of inference, both inductive and deductive. The same difficulties remain in relating our beliefs to these sources, and finding either the sources as simple and reliable as they are at first taken to be or most of our beliefs derived from them, except by devious means not recognized by the canons of inference.[56] It seems that if we try to define 'knowledge' in such a way as to fit our common use of the term, the sense in which we say we 'know that the sun is shining' and 'the square on the hypotenuse of a right-angle triangle is equivalent to the sum of the squares on the other two sides', we find that defining it as true belief, believed for sound reasons, leads to a critical evaluation of the 'sound reasons'. This evaluation reveals the weaknesses of what are usually taken to be reasons, and causes us to scale down our claims for knowledge. Russell concludes that knowledge is a vague term requiring us to specify degrees of knowledge, in analogy to the term 'baldness'.[57] If knowledge is defined as true belief, then this makes knowledge an ideal far above the achievement of any specific beliefs which we are accustomed to call knowledge. On the other hand, if knowledge is defined so that it applies to the beliefs which we usually think we know, then we are forced to accept criteria of knowledge which lack the cogency of either perceptual foundation or logical validity. This dilemma is revealed in the attempt to distinguish between subjective certainty and objective credibility.

Russell defines subjective certainty as a state of belief in which no further evidence could render belief more certain. The degree of subjective certainty must be psychologically estimated, since this is a subjective concept. The degree of objective credibility of a belief is a measure of its objective standing against certain accepted standards of belief: closeness to perception, logical consistency, and connection with other accepted beliefs. If knowledge is to be possible, these two concepts must be linked. To forge a link between certainty and credibility Russell begins with propositions which are both epistemologically credible and subjectively nearly certain.[58] In order to find these propositions Russell undertakes a 'Cartesian scrutiny' guided by a non-sceptical guiding principle, that is, the principle of confidence that there is some connection between subjective near-certainty and objective high-credibility. This scrutiny results in the conclusion that in practice a class of beliefs may be regarded as true 'if (*a*) they are firmly believed by all who have carefully considered them, (*b*) there is no positive argument against them, (*c*) there is no known reason for supposing that mankind would believe them if they were untrue'. This leads to the acceptance of judgments of perception and of logic and mathematics as containing the highest degree of certainty and of credibility.[59]

Russell's conclusion with respect to the concept of knowledge is expressed in the following passage:

'I think that, if we are to be allowed to know any empirical generalizations except those derived from a census, the word "know" will have to be used rather more liberally than hitherto. We could be said to "know" a proposition if it is in fact true and we believe it on the best available evidence. But if this evidence is not conclusive, we shall never know whether we know it. It is hoped that inductive evidence may make an empirical generalization probable. This takes us, however, into a region that lies outside the scope of the present work. . . .'[60]

A complete statement of Russell's concepts of belief, truth, and knowledge requires a consideration of the solution which Russell offers of the problem of 'induction'. Russell's title for this topic is the problem of 'non-demonstrative inference', a title chosen in preference to the term 'induction' to indicate that the problem is wider than that of the traditionally formulated problem of induction. For Russell, there are three main components of knowledge: sensory experience or perception, deductive inference as discussed in *Principia Mathematica*, and other forms of inference needed to bridge the gap between bare perceptual experience and the judgments, inferences, interpretations, and generalizations based upon it. One among these forms of inference would be the kind which passes from a limited number of perceptive experiences to a generalization concerning a class of similar cases. This topic of non-demonstrative inference was discussed in full in *Human Knowledge*, but Russell had been aware of the problem since the beginning of his career and had referred to it throughout his writing. Gradually he came to see the scope of the problem and the way it was linked with other topics in his thought.

The first occasion on which Russell discussed the philosophical 'problem of induction' was in *The Problems of Philosophy*, and, on this occasion, he formulated it as the problem of generalizing from a limited number of instances.[61] Granted that we are accustomed to generalizing from limited experience, why do we do so, and on what grounds? Russell uses the example of to-morrow's sunrise. We have all observed a number of sunrises, and we imagine that there will be one every twenty-four hours; and, even if we do not think about it, we expect a sunrise to-morrow. This is accepted by everyone. But what are the grounds of this expectation? Are they empirical? No, not in the sense of observational evidence, for there can be no observational evidence of tomorrow's sunrise. Are they deductive? No, for the expectation of tomorrow's sunrise is not a conclusion of any recognized form of deductive argument, of which we possess the premises. If we try to deduce the belief in the sunrise from an astronomical theory about the relation and movement of the sun and the earth, we will find, first, that the theory itself is a set of generalizations of the kind that we are questioning and, second, that even if the theory is accepted, there is no logical reason to believe the relations will continue in the future, for the generalizations, at best, are descriptive of the past.

Russell points out that the problem is an important one, for all the knowledge of common sense and of science rests on the expectation that the future will be like the past, on the relative reliability of inductions, yet we can find no basis for induction in the recognized sources of knowledge. Why we have these expectations, and why they are fulfilled, on the whole, and why we find it reasonable to be guided by them in some cases and not in others—all these questions are left unanswered in *The Problems of Philosophy*.

In an essay entitled 'On the Notion of Cause',[62] Russell linked the problems of induction with the problem of causal laws. He defends the modern and scientific view of cause as the observed uniformity of sequence of events, ideally expressed in the differential equations of physics, in opposition to the traditional metaphysical concept of cause as something operative, in analogy to voluntary action. But if cause is to be identified with the causal laws of physics, inferences to the future are involved, since such laws are predictive as well as descriptive. Russell again finds that some principle, such as the uniformity of nature, is required in order to justify inferences to the future. But what justification could be offered of a principle of induction such as that of the uniformity of nature? If one offers the justification of the past success which has attended the acceptance of the inductive principles, then the argument is circular, since you are assuming that past succcess is relevant to future success. The only other alternative seems to be that the principle of induction is an *a priori* logical law; but if it is, it is a strange one. It does not appear to be self-evident, since one could easily imagine it not to hold; it does not seem to be known directly; and its formulation is full of difficulties. Again Russell leaves the problems of induction unsolved.

At the time Russell wrote this essay, he was at the peak of his confidence in the logico-analytic method, the method of construction. He hoped to construct the whole of common sense and scientific knowledge from the sense-data of a single person.[63] Hence, the problem of generalizing from a limited number of observed instances was a vital one for his theory of knowledge. Perhaps he hoped to find some inductive logical law, as he found deductive logical laws, among the 'hard data' from which the structure of knowledge could be built. However, the changing status of logical laws, as syntactical rather than *a priori*, which followed the influence of Wittgenstein on Russell, made this unlikely. Nor could an inductive principle, dealing with generalizing from experience, be treated as linguistic. At the same time, the limitations on the immediacy and cognitive status of perception involved in the adoption of neutral monism made the problem more difficult.

In addition to the general problem of how one is to infer a generalization from a restricted number of instances, there is a technical aspect to the problem of particular interest to the logician. Russell's early work had keen concerned with bringing into adequate and consistent formulation the principles of inference and argument forms of mathematics and logic. But he deplored the fact that logicians had made so little progress with the formulation of non-deductive argument forms. It is evident in the analysis of scientific inquiry that deductive arguments, although important, are not the sole kinds of inference employed, yet little had been done to submit inductive inference to the precise formulation of deductive inference. This was an uncompleted part of logical analysis.[64]

While there had been little progress with respect to the generalized formulation of the principles of inductive argument, there had been a good deal of progress and agreement in the mathematical study of probability. Part of Russell's purpose in *Human Knowledge* was to state the agreed upon principles of mathematical probability and to survey the proposed postulates which would permit its application to empirical inquiries. The problem is this: logicians and mathematicians agree on the mathematical procedures for dealing with finite collections of items of determinate kinds, the white and black balls drawn out of the bag, the perfect dice, or die, or evenly balanced pennies; but the difficulty is to use these techniques in the study of nature where the collections are neither finite nor determinate, nor the kinds and extent even known to be finite or infinite. To some extent successful application of the methods of mathematical probability has been achieved in limited areas where the items studied are finite and where each item can be treated as a uniform unit. For instance, population statistics are complete enough to enable statisticians to compute within a limited range of accuracy the number of deaths among certain age groups in the population. In other words, by making certain assumptions concerning the uniformity of all cases of a given kind and by making assumptions concerning the irrelevance of some factors of the investigation, statisticians have been able to employ the concepts of mathematical probability beyond the limits of the artificial cases used in developing the theory. Logicians have tried to formulate these assumptions in a way which would make them applicable, within the restrictions of their formulation, to all empirical studies.

Three of these philosophical interpretations of probability theory are singled out for critical analysis by Russell; these are the Mises-Reichenbach theory, the Keynes theory, and the finite-frequency theory. He re-states the agreed on mathematical formulae and compares analytically the different assumptions which each requires. It is here that his attention is centred, since his concern is to formulate assumptions of his own which will be adequate to the needs of the application of probability theory to scientific inquiry.

Russell mentions as one possibility a blanket postulate that the future will be like the past; this might be a satisfactory way of dealing with one part of the problem, that of prediction as opposed to description, but it is only one aspect of the problem. This assumption does not solve the problem of the presently existent unobserved entities to which the generalization refers, for it is not only in time, but in range of observations that the problem exists.[65] Another blanket-type assumption which is sometimes recommended is that of the uniformity of nature. It is assumed that nature does exhibit regularities and that, all else being equal, what has been found to be a regularity in an area which has been investigated will also be a regularity in another area which has not been investigated. The trouble with this assumption is that it is very wide and indiscriminate; it proves no way of predicting which cases will turn out to be uniform and which will not. For instance, on the basis of a large number of cases of swans observed to be white, and assuming the uniformity of nature, a generalization would be justified to the effect that 'all swans are white'. Yet, as the subsequent appearance of black swans in Australia showed, this inductive generalization was not a reliable one. Of course, one might say that colour in animals is not a good basis for generalizing about species, that is, compared with means of reproduction or skeletal structure. Yet, it seems that whatever postulate or postulates are used, it ought to be possible for the postulate to help one to discriminate occasions when it is and occasions when it is not likely that uniformity will be found.[66]

Keynes' inductive postulate of 'limited variety' seems to be more discriminating than that of uniformity. This principle postulates that in nature there is not an infinite number of kinds of things, but that things fall into a finite number of kinds or classes, and the latter have some common characteristics. In biology, for instance, although it may be that there is an infinite number of individual organisms, there is a finite number of species and genera with common characteristics into which these individuals may be categorized. In the same way there may be an infinite number of cells, or stars, or pieces of matter, but we are justified in expecting a finite number of *kinds* of cells, stars, and pieces of matter. Russell finds this postulate unsatisfactory because it is based on a kind of generalization characteristic of biology. He believes that the generalizations of physics are of a more highly developed kind and represent a further refinement towards which biology may be moving. When this happens, references to 'kinds' will drop out. Thus, Keynes' assumption is based on a potentially outdated aspect of scientific inquiry.[67]

Although Russell accepts as valid much of the logic of probability developed by Keynes and others, he concludes that what is needed is not one but several postulates which will be more specific, but more comprehensive than any so far put forth.

The problems which the postulates of non-demonstrative inference are intended to solve include the tradional problem of induction, but include as well the problems which Russell's analysis of empiricism had shown to be involved when one tried to find in experience the justification for common sense and scientific knowledge. These problems could be described as those of perception, of language, of psychological analysis, of the limitations of empiricism, and of the statement of empiricism.

We have seen how problems connected with perception increased during the development of Russell's thought. The early problems centred round the necessity of adding to the sense-data; the data themselves were thought of as immediate, direct, and yielding truth. But with the adoption of neutral monism, the given was found not to have the simplicity, clarity, and freedom from error required of the building blocks of knowledge. Perception involves habits of inference, organic tendencies, expectations based on past experience. Analysis is required to uncover and discount the interpretative factors. All that can be hoped from perception is an approach to the sensory core of perceptive experience.

Russell's analysis uncovered problems when the perceptual experience is converted into a perceptual judgment. This step involves the use of language, and language is by no means a transparent medium. Even when linguistic analysis uncovers levels of language, the primary level itself is not directly representative of the components of experience. Even with care in using an artificial language to minimize the metaphysical implications of class and substance which are built into the ordinary object language, the linguistic analysis of a presented complex is a difficult task. There is a kind of dubious generality involved in the use of the 'same' symbol on different occasions. Even more difficulties develop on the second level of language with the use of terms such as 'or', 'some', 'all', 'true' and 'false'.

The use of psychological and physiological analysis in addition to linguistic analysis did not resolve all the difficulties in passing from the given perceptive experience to the sophisticated and guarded perceptual judgment. As we have seen, the complexities of the development of habits, attitudes, and emotional accompaniments to judgment require extensive analysis of their own. As Russell developed his theory of knowledge, the problems of this kind of analysis increased as he became more aware of the involvements. His reservations about behaviourist psychology did not prevent him pushing the analysis as far as it would go, while holding that it must be supplemented by introspective analysis.

Another set of difficulties concerns the assumptions which were found to be necessary and for which Russell admitted he could provide no ultimately satisfactory empirical justification.

Some of these centre round perception and some concern the realistic theory of truth. One of these is the causal theory of perception. As we have seen, Russell never held any view of perception other than that the perceptive experience is the causal product of a series of events which begins with the physical object and continues through the reflection of light, light waves, the stimulation of the retina, and subsequent events in the nervous system, and ends with the visual sensation of a seen colour and shape. But, in trying to construct the world of common sense and of science from the given elements of perception, it is necessary to start with the end of the process and infer backwards to the cause. This is a 'shaky inference'. Causal inferences are shown to depend on the correlation of observed sequences of events, but in this case the physical object, the light waves, the stimulation of the retina, in fact, all events prior to the seen visual shape, are unobserved. Russell saw this difficulty[68] and admitted it was necessary to postulate the causal theory of perception. Although he earlier had hoped to replace the postulation with justified inferences, this never became possible. The postulation of the causal theory of perception remains a limitation of empiricism.

Another assumption which remains an unsupported postulate is that of the existence of other minds. As we saw, Russell had hoped that he would at some time be able to construct the world of common sense and of science from the sense-data of a single person. But, until he was able to do this, he was forced to postulate the existence of other minds. This means that what one observes of the behaviour of other persons, including their speech, allows one to infer that this behaviour means that the cause of the behaviour is a person, like oneself, and that what that person says, as a report of his experience, means for him what it would mean as a report of one's own experience. This is an assumption which common sense does not hesitate to make, yet it lacks the justification of direct experience since we cannot experience the experience of others, nor can it be logically inferred from our own experience. The method of constructing and correlating perspectives described in *The Analysis of Mind* and

The Analysis of Matter depends on accepting testimony based on the assumption of the existence of other minds. The further analysis of perception made the hope of replacing the postulate with a construction more remote. Hence the existence of other minds remains a postulate which must be accepted unless one were able to accept Berkeley's God or solipsism.[69]

Another assumption of a similar kind, required by Russell's theory of knowledge, but not justifiable within it, is the existence of the external world as the cause and the referent of our judgment of perception. As with the existence of other minds, it must be assumed, if solipsism is to be avoided. It is necessary for the realism with respect to perception, and the realistic correspondence theory of truth, both of which were persistent positions in Russell's theory of knowledge. But, as is the case with the causal theory of perception, no inference to the existence of the external world is possible without circularity.[70]

With respect to all of these assumptions, then, it had been found to be necessary to postulate these three beliefs if an empiricist and realist epistemology were to provide support for the beliefs of common sense and of science. These assumptions are justified only to the extent that there is no evidence against them, that they are consistent with our experience, and that they are necessary in order for us to know what we believe we know. Making assumptions concerning the causes of our perceptions, the external world, and other minds is the alternative to accepting an empiricism which would be a 'solipsism of the moment'. The position of solipsism is 'logically impeccable', but impossible to accept with sincerity; hence the making of assumptions going beyond experience is preferable.[71]

Another limitation of empiricism is mentioned in both the *Inquiry* and *Human Knowledge*; that is, that the statement of the position of empiricism cannot be proven by experience. By this Russell means that the basic assumption of empiricism is that there is no basis for our knowledge other than experience and the inferences derived from experience. But this proposition itself cannot be known to be true, for it is a universal claim going beyond all evidence. It is at least conceivable that some new development in evolution or some new invention could provide man with direct insight into the structure of his world. However, the limitations of empiricism have been found by an empirical method, and this method is less inadequate than that of any other theory of knowledge.

In *Human Knowledge* Russell tries to bring together the problem of induction and the other problems of the limitations of empiricism which his analysis has uncovered, and then to ask: By what set of minimal assumptions can all these limitations of empiricism be overcome and the possibility of common sense and scientific knowledge established? His method might be compared to that of an impoverished but prudent businessman who found that he could not keep his potentially profitable business in operation until it could become self-sustaining without some extra funds. It would be possible for him to negotiate a loan for each need as it arose; several thousand for needed tools several thousands more for wages, and more for raw materials. This policy would exhaust his credit, and yet leave him insecure. A better alternative would be to estimate with care all the financial needs he is likely to meet until profits can be expected to overtake expenses and to negotiate a single loan for the total sum, a sum adequate for his needs but not more extended than necessary. In a similar manner Russell estimates just what extra-empirical assumptions are required if an empiricist theory of knowledge is to fulfil its function. He then formulates the necessary minimum of such assumptions. This is the basis for his choice of five postulates of non-deductive inference as they are formulated in *Human Knowledge*.

The postulates which Russell chooses are intended to perform these important tasks for empiricism: make generalizations and the application of mathematical probability logically justifiable; close the gaps between the 'pure datum' and the perception, and between both and the validated perceptual judgment; make reasonable a structure of more indirect beliefs which are derived from perceptual judgments. These postulates are stated under the following five headings: the postulate of quasi-permanence, the postulate of separable causal lines, the postulate of spatio-temporal continuity in causal lines, the postulate of a common causal origin of similar structures ranged about a centre (or the structural postulate), and the postulate of analogy.[73]

Each of these postulates has its role to play in the structure of empirical knowledge, and this is sketched out by Russell in the last few chapters of *Human Knowledge*. One might conveniently think of these as modern substitutes for the older concepts of cause, substance, and an absolute order of space and time. In two early essays, Russell demonstrated that the metaphysical concept of cause as active, operative, and as a nexus between events must be abandoned in the light of Humean criticism and of modern physics. He had replaced it with the view of cause as the observed uniform sequence of events. But later analysis showed that the uniform sequence view of cause would not serve to give empirical grounding for the causal theory of perception, or for the imputation of causal sequence by which we interpret the 'behaviour' of objects, and the interaction of processes. This was admitted by Russell in *Human Knowledge* when he said that 'invariable sequence would not do' and when he formulated causal postulates involving more than uniform sequence.[74]

As far as 'substance' is concerned, this concept has all but disappeared from philosophy, as well as from science. Russell had early sought to show how the idea of persistent 'objects' of science or of common sense could be replaced by the construction of objects from sense-data and 'sensibilia'. Although in some senses the construction of such objects was successful as far as the analysis of empirical knowledge was concerned, yet it did involve the uncomfortable postulation of sensibilia. And beyond that, the assumption that objects or events of the world of fact, external to our knowledge, were the causal agents in the order of existence, seemed to involve the assumption of the persistence of whatever did exist in the world of fact.

Russell had shown that the space-time order of physics could be constructed from the space-time orders of each experiencer once some publicly accessible co-ordinates could be established. But in order for empirical knowledge to be possible, this construction of perspectives must be brought into relation to the persistence of 'causal lines', that is, the continuity of a process with limited change through a time sequence, with relative independence of occurrences outside that process. This involved reliance on the postulates of persistence, continuity, and separability of causal lines where causal lines were defined as 'a temporal series of events so related that, given some of them, something can be inferred about the others whatever may be happening elsewhere. . . . Throughout a given causal line, there may be constancy of quality, constancy of structure, or gradual change in either, but not sudden change of any considerable magnitude'.[75]

In addition to the postulates providing the persistence, separability, and continuity of causal lines, some assumption was required by which connections could be made cross-sectionally between one causal line and another, as the light emission and reflection process interacts with the light-eye response process in vision. And a cross-sectional assumption is required when a number of co-existing and similar events are permitted to be grouped together, and a common 'causal ancestor' is inferred. Russell calls this a 'structural postulate', and it would be necessary, among other things, for the imputation of common cause for the experiences of different observers.

The assumption of the existence of other minds similar to our own which is necessary to the acceptance of the testimony of other observers requires another postulate, that of analogy. The statement of this postulate clearly connects it with the postulates of cause. '*If, whenever we can observe whether A and B are present or absent, we find that every case of B has an A as a causal antecedent, then it is probable that most B's have A's as causal antecedents, even in cases where observation does not enable us to know whether A is present or not.*'[76]

As far as the needs of induction and the calculus of probabilities are concerned, all five of the postulates together will serve to give a probabilistic basis for scientific or common-sense generalizations. That is, if we are permitted to have assumptions about the persistence and continuity and interaction and relative independence of causal lines, and about the common causes of similar sets of events, we have all that is required to make generalizations based on perceptions, as long as it is understood that these generalizations have the status of a certain degree of probability. With the help of the postulates, of the evidence derived with care and stated with care from perception, and of the rules of deductive logic, the programme of empiricism can be carried out.

As far as the ultimate justification of the postulates is concerned and as far as an answer to the charge that empiricism is self-refuting can be given, all that can be said is that the postulates themselves are not anywhere in conflict with experience; they are self-confirmatory; and they allow us to believe what in fact we do believe and what it is necessary that we believe if any empirical knowledge is to be possible.[77]

The second class of questions concerning 'what there is' has to do with the status of the referents, if any, of numbers, quality words, relation words, class words, and mathematical and logical terms, such as logical constants. A related question has to do with the epistemological and metaphysical status of 'logical truths' or 'principles of deductive inference', such as the law of non-contradiction, or the implicative principle. An additional kind of principle might or might not be considered to be logical and caused Russell some difficulty. This kind of statement might be thought to be synthetic *a priori*, for example, 'if *A* precedes *B*, and *B* precedes *C*, then *A* precedes *C*'. These questions were particularly vital to Russell because of his interest in the philosophy of mathematics. Russell's first philosophical works were attempts to construct a philosophy of mathematics on an idealist basis, to correct the deficiencies of the over-subjectivist treatment of space by Kant and the dialectical logic of Hegel.[78] His failure to create an adequate philosophy of mathematics was one reason for his abandonment of idealism. From that time on Russell was pulled in two different ways: as a mathematician and a logician he could accept no theory of meaning or of knowledge as adequate unless it gave grounds for the development of mathematical and logical systems; as an empiricist he wished to introduce no non-empirical entities into his theory of knowledge, as Occam's razor dictated, to seek a minimum of inferred or postulated entities. It was not open to Russell to regard the matter of whether one admitted certain kinds of universal concepts into one's logical or epistemological language as a choice of linguistic convenience. Throughout the development of his thought Russell saw these questions as a problem of 'what there is', and believed that something could be learned about the structure of nature from the symbols and structures of language.[79]

In spite of Russell's constant preoccupation with the problem of universals and of principles of inference, and in spite of his repeated conviction that something could be learned from the nature of the symbolism that it is necessary to use, his opinions on the matter changed more radically and more frequently than on any other topic. Nor are his final conclusions easy to understand.[80] However, if we consider the shifts in his treatment of these topics in the light of what we have already learned about the development of Russell's thought, it may be possible to see the logic of the development of his ideas.

At the beginning of this century, Russell and G. E. Moore led a movement of rejection of idealism and affirmation of realism. As far as Russell was concerned, there were four main elements in the rejection of idealism: dissatisfaction with the idealist treatment of mathematics, the conclusion, which followed his work on Leibniz, that the doctrine of internal relations must be rejected, the rejection of monistic metaphysics and theory of truth, and the affirmation of the independence of the object of knowledge.[81] Russell records that in the enthusiasm of 'escaping from a hot-house', the rebels hastened to accept as real everything that idealism had held to be unreal. For Russell this produced an exuberant version of realism in which objects, subjects, material particles, tables, men's minds, concepts, classes, number, universals, even referents for all symbols were thought to be real, including chimeras and the Golden Mountain.[82] This was the high water mark of realism for Russell, and from then on his version of reality became more 'clean-shaven' as new developments in his thought caused him to reinterpret the significance of many of these concepts.

The first phase of Russell's realism with respect to universals could be appropriately called a Platonic realism. The logical phase of this realism can best be seen in *The Principles of Mathematics*, in which Russell regards classes, numbers, and logical constants as reals. In a passage which Russell himself quoted later in order to correct, he writes:

'Whatever may be an object of thought, or may occur in any true or false proposition, or can be counted as *one*, I call a *term*. . . . A man, a moment, a number, a class, a relation, a chimaera, or anything else that can be mentioned, is sure to be a term; and to deny that such and such a thing is a term must always be false.'[83]

In this same book, however, Russell had already followed Peano in developing a logic of relations and a definition of number in terms of classes. Russell says that Peano taught him two things, the distinction between a proposition and a propositional function, and the distinction between a class of one member and that member. Although these ideas were on their way to their full development in *Principia Mathematica* in which they would allow Russell to dispense with numbers and classes as entities, at this time only propositional functions were regarded as expressions, while numbers and classes were still regarded as real.

Russell comments that this extreme Platonism, while it was agreeable to him emotionally, arose from a mistaken interpretation of language in which it was assumed that if a sentence is meaningful, this meaning must be derived from the meaning of the individual symbols which compose the sentence. Hence, he assumed that each symbol *in isolation* has meaning. He followed

Meinong in assuming a nebulous realm inhabited by non-existent existences, the referents of symbols which seem to be names but for which no corresponding reality exists. It seemed that if the proposition 'the present king of England is bald' has meaning, and is true or false, by virtue of its referent, the man who is the king of England, then the proposition 'the present king of France is bald' should have meaning, and be true or false, by virtue of its referent. Russell felt that this position offended against logical common sense, however, and in 1905 developed the theory of descriptions to solve the problem which these seeming name symbols created. In the essay 'On Denoting', he proposed a way of treating propositions of this kind. 'The present king of France' or 'golden mountain' are not names, as they appear to be, but denoting phrases or incomplete symbols. This means that they cannot function significantly as symbols by themselves as names can but must be interpreted in the context of the propositions in which they occur. As we have seen,[84] this theory makes it unnecessary to assume the existence of referents for propositions 'referring' to non-existent entities. In *Principia Mathematica* this was given a full and symbolic treatment. The theory of types also persuaded Russell that one word could not be substituted for another without taking account of the context since, if there were a difference of the level of language, the substitution of one symbol for another would produce nonsense. Hence both of the new techniques in logic invented by Russell had the effect of drawing him away from his early realism in regard to the referents of individual symbols.

Further applications of the theory of description embodied in *Principia Mathematica* interpreted classes, and numbers as classes of classes, in terms of propositional functions, and hence it was no longer necessary to interpret classes and numbers as reals. Whitehead went further and suggested that the same technique could be used to construct points, instants, and particles as sets of events. We have seen how Russell continued this programme in the construction of the external world.

In spite of the new definitions of number and class and the

new techniques which allowed Russell to dispense with the metaphysical assumptions of real 'golden mountains', real numbers, real classes, real points, real instants, real 'things' and real scientific 'objects', Russell's position in 1911 was one of a dualism of universals and particulars. This is shown in the essay, 'On the Relations of Universals and Particulars'.[85] In this essay he considers arguments which would establish that only particulars exist (Hume and Berkeley) and that only universals exist; he finds reason to reject both kinds of arguments and concludes with the statement of a dualism of universals and particulars. The argument turns on the criticism of a view which Russell finally came to accept. He considered whether it would be possible to eliminate particulars as subjects in which qualities inhere, replacing them with bundles of qualities. Russell's reasons for rejecting this hypothesis were based on his concept of spatial and temporal order; he thought it would be necessary for unique positions in space and time to be assigned to such bundles in order that one be diverse from another. Since he did not see how this could be done on his interpretation of spatial and temporal order and since he thought the diversity of two identically similar minds or objects must be due to some ultimate diversity of 'substance', he rejected the argument and held to the duality of particulars and universals.

In *The Problems of Philosophy* the same duality is given a less subtle treatment. In this book there are particulars which are known directly in acquaintance, by way of sensation; and there are universals which are known *a priori*; both are important elements of intuitive knowledge.[86] In addition, in this book, Russell argues that logical truths, principles of deductive inference, and such propositions as 'if *A* precedes *B*, and if *B* precedes *C*, then *A* must precede *C*' are known *a priori*.

One further important change occurred prior to 1920 which altered Russell's treatment of logical 'truths' and *a priori* concepts. This change was due to Wittgenstein and consisted in his persuading Russell that the truths of logic and mathematics are tautologies. It was no longer necessary to postulate some logical intuitions since their supposed content is merely linguistic, different ways of saying the same thing. This was not a welcome conclusion, but Russell incorporated it into his philosophy. It is clearly evident in the treatment of analytic truth in *The Analysis of Matter*. This change, however, did not lead Russell, as it did Carnap, to regard the syntactical structure of language as having no extra-linguistic implications. The ways in which it is necessary for us to symbolize our experience and to structure our language may tell us much about the nature of the world in which we live.

Another theme of the logical atomism period was the search for propositions of atomic form, the components of which were thought to have some status as ultimate simples. The atomic proposition was to contain a relation term and what Russell called non-relation terms, that is, terms for particulars or for predicates or for qualities, those items which were the terms of the relation. The question was whether any of the non-relation terms, or all of them, could be regarded as logically proper names. A logically proper name would be the name for a component of the proposition with which the asserter of the proposition was directly acquainted. Syntactically it is described as a word not denoting a predicate or a relation which can occur in a proposition containing no variable. But it proved difficult to resolve all or any of the non-relation terms into logically proper names to meet both the syntactical and the epistemological requirements of such proper names. The use of an artificial language might resolve some of the difficulties by reformulation, but it seemed difficult to carry out the programme completely.

In addition to the problem of the treatment of 'particulars' treated in 'The Relations of Universals to Particulars', and the problem of logically proper names which appears in 'The Philosophy of Logical Atomism', there are still unresolved problems with the formulation of predicates, such as 'colour', which seem irreducible; with the formulation of 'synthetic *a priori* propositions such as the one 'if A precedes B, and B precedes C, then A precedes C'; and with the irreducibility of such relations as 'similarity'. It seemed that the dualism of particulars and universals remained; if the new logic had removed the necessity of realism with respect to mathematics, to logical truths, to classes, and to fictitious entities, it had left the status of qualities, relations, and predicates, and proper names unresolved.

The latest development in this aspect of Russell's philosophy can be seen in the *Inquiry, Human Knowledge*, and *My Philosophical Development*. The greatest change occurs in the treatment of qualities. In the 1911 essay we found him arguing that one could not replace 'particulars', as subjects having qualities, with bundles of qualities. He now argues that this can be done; he has become persuaded that the subjective spatio-temporal order is objective in the sense required by this new theory, so that it is possible to name the 'centrality of purple', for instance. He also argues that the diversity of any two complete complexes of compresence are sufficiently accounted for empirically by our experience being so varied as to have no completely identical recurrences of such a complex. Accordingly, in the *Inquiry* colour quality is accounted for by saying that the 'white' of the paper, the book, the cloud, is simply the same white in different places and times, but this does not make the quality a universal 'whiteness' but a particular quality which happens to occur in scattered positions and times.[87]

It now appears that the given complexes of compresence can be analysed and stated in propositions of atomic form in which the logically proper names are quality words referring directly to sense qualities and in which the relation words refer directly to given spatial and temporal relations as occurring in the presented complex. Would such a vocabulary be sufficient to describe our experience? If so, would any duality of universal and particular be required?

In *My Philosophical Development*, Russell summarizes his conclusions on the subject of universals. He reviews the chief candidates for the status of universals.[88] He finds that qualities no longer require to be treated as universal. His new theory has the 'complete complex of compresence' take the place of particulars, and qualities such as 'white' are identified as components of a given complex. With respect to predicates such as 'colour', he has found no way of reformulating or dissolving the terminology of predicates. It is obvious, he says, that all colours have something in common, since they shade into one another, and that they are generically different from sounds. Hence predicates cannot all be dispensed with, and to this extent retain their status as universals. With respect to relations, Russell finds it impossible to do without relational propositions; no language could describe the world without being relational. Relations such as 'before' seem irreducible; even were we to find ways of reformulating most relations, they would still need to be cast in terms of *some* relation, perhaps that of similarity. It could seem, perhaps, that Russell might make a distinction between relations as given in experience, which could be treated, perhaps, as qualities are treated, and relations which are not spatio-temporal, and hence not given but constructed. But he argues that since *some* relation is required, we might as well admit relations as universals which cannot be eliminated. The other qualification which Russell makes concerning universals is that words themselves must be regarded as universals. A word is a class of more or less similar noises or marks, but it is treated as one, of which each of the noises or marks is an instance. In these respects, extreme nominalism is ruled out.

When Russell asks, What is the metaphysical status of universals?, he replies only that it seems clear that there are relational facts and that it would be impossible to have a language describing the world without relation words. Quoting his own words in the *Inquiry*, he says that 'complete metaphysical agnosticism is not compatible with the maintenance of linguistic propositions. . . . For my part, I believe that, partly by means of the study of syntax, we can arrive at considerable knowledge concerning the structure of the world'.[89] The difficulty is to interpret what this 'considerable knowledge' is, beyond the fact that there are relational facts.

A clue to the possible answer to this last question may be

found in Russell's treatment of 'logically proper names' and 'minimum vocabularies'. We have seen that, from its early period, Russell's epistemology has required some elements of knowledge which are the premises rather than the inferred, the directly known rather than the derived. The search for data was a consequence of this concept, and the 'sense-data' were early candidates for this position; these were said to be directly apprehended in the relation of acquaintance. This epistemological principle was linked with a principle of the interpretation of propositions, that any proposition which we can understand must be made up of components with which we are acquainted. In the basic proposition, called by logical atomism 'the proposition of atomic form', there must be some direct denotative reference of its meaning to a fact, if no longer a word by word correlation, at least a structural correlation. This assumed some more or less ultimate 'simple' as a constituent of the complex fact. In addition, later linguistic and psychological analysis suggested that there must be words which are learned ostensively rather than verbally, and data which are directly causes of, and directly referred to, in the simplest kinds of perceptual judgments. In all these roles some elements of 'fact' were required which were not further analysed (at least in the given context) which were date-able, locate-able, and name-able, within the experience of the person in question. The closest approach to this kind of reference in ordinary language would be what Russell called the egocentric particulars—'this', 'I', 'now', and 'here'. But such terms are too unstable in meaning to serve the purpose of philosophical analysis. Proper names, as unique in reference, seem appropriate; but we find that often we use a proper name when there is no acquaintance with its referent, and, in fact, the proper name may be a disguised description. Also, we often make a proper name from a common noun by adding 'this' to it, as we say 'this book' to indicate the presented individual object in question. It is necessary, then, to create our own language in order to illuminate the function of what Russell calls 'logically proper names'.

'Logically proper names' have two characteristics: syntactically they are those words in a proposition without variables (i.e. propositions of atomic form) which are not relation words, and epistemologically those components of the proposition with which the asserter of the proposition is acquainted. The 'complete complex of compresence' within which certain qualities occur allows us to indicate this particular quality 'hot' as part of the given complex of compresence which is attributed to an individual's experience at a certain time and is given some kind of space-time co-ordinates within it. The immediacy of the perceptual judgment 'I am hot' or 'hotness-here-now' can then be more fully, accurately, and objectively described by means of this language. Empirical analysis should seek to reduce all complex propositions to their basic propositions of atomic form, and formulate them in terms of the language which allows us to notice and analyse out the 'logically proper names'.[90]

When this kind of empirical analysis, that is, the reduction to the basic component 'logically proper names', is applied to a developed body of knowledge, say a science, we may speak of 'minimum vocabularies'. It is Russell's contention that any empirical science must have some points at which it touches experience; for instance, astronomy may be largely concerned with geometric patterns and mathematical formulae and abstract theories, but if it is to be the astronomy of our universe, and not just mathematics, there must be some point at which some of its symbols are defined ostensively, or are denoted, or are related to objects of acquaintance, that is, are logically proper names. It may be a matter of skill to reduce the number of reference points, rendering the theory as formal and deductive as possible; it may be a matter of choice whether Sirius, or the earth, or the sun is the reference point. But the desire for an economy of assumptions and a desire for logical completeness cannot dictate an absence of empirical reference. The search for minimum vocabularies is a development of Russell's early method of construction, and the role of the logically proper name is akin to the role once played by the sense-data and sensibilia. In this search we see the leading direction of Russell's thought: to construct a theory connecting science and experience such that the empirical elements be named, and denoted, and validated (as far as possible) and that the structure of the theory connecting these elements with the conclusions (the beliefs of science which are to be supported) be as logically tight, consistent, and complete as possible. The application of Occam's razor and the commitment to empiricism are the two themes involved, but both are followed out in the context of what may be called 'scientific realism'. That is, it is not questioned that the conclusions to be reached and justified are those beliefs of science which, on the whole, are sure to be more true than any other.

The description of the world that is there or, perhaps, may be there is given by Russell in two contexts, neither of which is the epistemological context with which we have become familiar. The first context is what might be called a philosophically non-technical context; of this context the chapter in *My Philosophical Development* entitled 'My Present View of the World' is representative. The second context is more technical both philosophically and scientifically and is best represented by the analysis given in Parts I and IV of *Human Knowledge*. Since we are concerned with theory of knowledge, a brief description of the less technical aspect of Russell's realism will suffice.

Russell begins his survey of 'what there is' by reviewing and interpreting the results of science; physics for him is the primary description of the world, and whatever the world is, it must be something which permits and requires what our physical science tells us. Russell imagines the universe to be made up of overlapping series of events; the series of events have continuities which may be called (roughly) causal; overlapping clusters of events have a certain kind of persistence or stability which may be called (roughly) substantial. Space and time orders of these overlapping series of events can be thought of by way of the Leibnizian perspectives. Russell uses the analogy of a theatre in which all the seats are filled with cine-cameras, each recording what is going on on the stage and in the theatre, but each with its own perspective slightly different from that of its neighbours.[91] But from a study of the film shot by all the cameras, it would be possible to construct a space-time order for the theatre and its contents. This is itself an analogue of the space-time order of the universe. The calculation of the means of constructing points and instants and continua leads into more technical discussions. In this view of the universe, matter has no existence in the older 'solid' sense; clusters and continuities of events which can be described by scientific 'causal' laws replace matter. That small part of the physical world which is living has been studied by biology; but this science is in a rudimentary stage of development, and we may hope that its generalizations will eventually be included within the scope of physics. That much smaller and, indeed, infinitesimal part of the universe which is man requires, at the present stage, the study of psychology. This study, supplemented by the evidence derived from our own experience, tells us a good deal about the way in which we come to know the rest of the world and about our interactions with the physical world. In the light of our limited knowledge, all that can be hypothesized about the overall nature of reality is a guess, and all that a philosopher can say is that it may be so.

When this view of the world, as an hypothesis based on science, is combined with the tentative conclusions of epistemological analysis, it seems that some overlapping series of events enter our experience as perceptive experiences (with all that this implies about light waves, the nervous system, habit and memory). Within this perceptive experience it is possible for us to denote qualities as part of a complex of compresence (itself the endproduct of the light-eye-brain causal series) and to find these qualities related to one another in various ways, notably visually and tactually in spatial and temporal relations. This is the psychological aspect of the space-time order, and the complex of compresence is itself in the middle of several complicated causal continuities.

The picture of the world and of our place in it which science provides is the end, the conclusion to be justified. The analysis of theory of knowledge which we have been considering works its way back from the beliefs of science to their ultimate justification in the fully analysed perceptual 'data' and the required postulates and inferences. When this epistemological analysis has been completed, a metaphysical hypothesis concerning the nature of the world, its causes, substance, and space-time structure can be formulated to be compatible both with our scientific and common-sense knowledge and with the empirical theory of knowledge which has been constructed. This 'bridge' or 'tunnel' may be useful as a speculative hypothesis which someday may serve science as the origin of scientific hypotheses.

In this chapter we have seen how much realism is a part of this analysis, a realism concerning the object of knowledge, the status of truth, a modified realism concerning universals, and scientific realism which sets the problem for theory of knowledge and for metaphysics. In subsequent discussion we will ask how successfully this analysis of theory of knowledge has been carried out and how compatibly the themes of analytic method, empiricism, and realism have been fused.

NOTES TO CHAPTER V

1. See above, pp. 26–7.
2. The phrase 'what there is' was used by Russell in the sense intended here as part of the title of one of the lectures which comprise 'The Philosophy of Logical Atomism'. 'Excursus into Metaphysics: What There Is' is the title of Lecture VIII of that series. See Russell, *Logic and Knowledge*, p. 269. The phrase has been put into current use in the work of W. V. Quine on the problem of the ontological implications of logic. See Quine's essay entitled 'On What There Is' which appeared in *The Review of Metaphysics* in 1948, and 'lent its title to a symposium of the joint session of the Aristotelian Society and the Mind Association at Edinburgh, July 1951, and was reprinted . . . in the Aristotelian Society's supplementary volume *Freedom, Language, and Reality*, Harrison, London, 1951'. This reference is quoted from W. V. Quine,

From a Logical Point of View, Harvard University Press, Cambridge, Mass., 1953. A second revised edition was published by the same press in 1961 and reprinted in paperback for Harper Torchbook edition in 1963. The current reference is to the paperback edition, p. 169.

3. Russell, *My Philosophical Development*, pp. 130–1.
4. Russell, 'My Mental Development', *The Philosophy of Bertrand Russell*, pp. 19–20.
5. Russell, *My Philosophical Development*, p. 128.
6. *Ibid.*, p. 205.
7. Russell, *Human Knowledge*, pp. 144–6.
8. *Ibid.*, pp. 116 *ff.*
9. Russell, *Inquiry*, p. 25.
10. *Ibid.*, p. 36.
11. *Ibid.*, p. 170.
12. *Inquiry*, pp. 166–7.
13. *Ibid.*, pp. 205 *f.*
14. *Ibid.*, pp. 214 *f.*
15. *Ibid.*, p. 215.
16. *Ibid.*, p. 227.
17. *Ibid.*, p. 204.
18. Russell, *The Problems of Philosophy*, pp. 198 *f.*
19. Russell, 'The Philosophy of Logical Atomism', in *Logic and Knowledge*, pp. 187 *f.* The dropping of the subject term of the analysis of belief is coincident with the dropping of the subject term of sensation in neutral monism.
20. Russell, *The Analysis of Mind*, p. 231.
21. *Ibid.*, pp. 238 *f.*
22. Russell, *Human Knowledge*, pp. 144–5.
23. *Ibid.*, p. 145.
24. *Ibid.*, p. 148.
25. *Ibid.*, p. 145.
26. *Ibid.*, p. 148.
27. Russell, *Inquiry*, pp. 249–51.
28. *Ibid.*, p. 245.
29. Russell, *Human Knowledge*, p. 148.
30. Russell, *The Problems of Philosophy*, pp. 186–203.
31. Russell, 'The Philosophy of Logical Atomism', *Logic and Knowledge*, pp. 187, 196, 208 *f.*
32. Russell, *The Analysis of Mind*, p. 278.
33. Russell, *Inquiry*, p. 206.
34. *Ibid.*, p. 271.
35. *Ibid.*, p. 223.

36. Russell, *Human Knowledge*, p. 149.
37. *Ibid.*, p. 118.
38. Russell, *The Problems of Philosophy*, pp. 188–9.
39. Russell, *Inquiry*, pp. 226–7.
40. Russell, *The Problems of Philosophy*, pp. 190–3.
41. Russell, *The Analysis of Mind*, pp. 257 f.
42. *Ibid.*, pp. 270 f.
43. Russell, *Inquiry*, p. 289.
44. *Ibid.*, p. 289.
45. *Ibid.*, pp. 289–326. For John Dewey and Bertrand Russell's exchanges on the subject of Dewey's theory of truth, see *The Philosophy of John Dewey*, 'The Library of Living Philosophers', edited by Paul Schilpp, Northwestern University Press, Evanston and Chicago, 1939. Bertrand Russell, 'Dewey's New Logic', and John Dewey, 'Experience, Knowledge, and Value: A Rejoinder'.
46. Russell, *The Problems of Philosophy*, pp. 205 f.
47. *Ibid.*, pp. 174 f.
48. *Ibid.*, pp. 214 f.
49. *Ibid.*, p. 217.
50. Russell, *The Analysis of Mind*, p. 271.
51. Russell, *Inquiry*, p. 18.
52. *Ibid.*, p. 234.
53. *Ibid.*, p. 151.
54. *Ibid.*, p. 245.
55. Russell, *Human Knowledge*, p. 154.
56. *Ibid.*, pp. 154–6.
57. *Ibid.*, p. 158.
58. *Ibid.*, p. 397.
59. *Ibid.*, p. 397.
60. Russell, *Inquiry*, p. 323.
61. Russell, 'On Induction', in *The Problems of Philosophy*, Chapter VI.
62. Bertrand Russell, 'On the Notion of Cause', first published in the *Proceedings of the Aristotelian Society*, 1912–13; reprinted in *Mysticism and Logic*.
63. Russell, 'The Relation of Sense-Data to Physics', in *Mysticism and Logic*, p. 157.
64. Russell, *My Philosophical Development*, pp. 190–1.
65. Russell, *Human Knowledge*, p. 317.
66. *Ibid.*, p. 317.
67. *Ibid.*, p. 318.
68. Russell, 'The Ultimate Constituents of Matter', first published in *The*

Monist, July, 1915; reprinted in *Mysticism and Logic*, pp. 134–5. See also Russell, *My Philosophical Development*, pp. 103–4.

69. Russell, *Human Knowledge*, p. 181.

70. Russell, *My Philosophical Development*, p. 105.

71. Russell, *Human Knowledge*, pp. 175–81.

72. *Ibid.*, p. 506.

73. *Ibid.*, pp. 487 f.

74. *Ibid.*, pp. 455 f.

75. *Ibid.*, p. 459.

76. *Ibid.*, p. 486.

77. *Ibid.*, p. 496.

78. Russell, *My Philosophical Development;* see Chapter IV, 'Excursion into Idealism'; see also Russell, 'My Mental Development', in *The Philosophy of Bertrand Russell*, pp. 10–12.

79. Russell, 'Logical Atomism', in *Logic and Knowledge*, p. 338. Russell writes, 'The purpose of the foregoing discussion of an ideal logical language (which would of course be wholly useless for daily life) is two-fold: first, to prevent inferences from the nature of language to the nature of the world, which are fallacious because they depend upon the logical defects of language; secondly, to suggest, by inquiring what logic requires of a language which is to avoid contradiction, what sort of structure we may reasonably suppose the world to have'. See also *My Philosophical Development*, p. 157, where Russell quotes his own former writing: 'The sole point of this parable is that the question of "universals" is not merely one of words but one which arises through the attempt to state facts.'

80. Russell, *My Philosophical Development*, p. 173. Here Russell says, 'This does not answer the metaphysical question, but it comes as near to giving an answer as I know how to come'. In the *Inquiry*, p. 347, Russell says, 'The result I have in mind is this: that complete metaphysical agnosticism is not compatible with the maintenance of linguistic propositions . . . I believe that, partly by means of the study of syntax, we can arrive at considerable knowledge concerning the structure of the world'. But see also in 'Reply to Criticisms', in *The Philosophy of Bertrand Russell*, p. 688, where he writes, 'If it is true, as it seems to be, that the world cannot be described without the use of the word "similar" or some equivalent, that seems to imply something about the world, though I do not exactly know what. This is the sense in which I still believe in universals'.

81. Russell, *My Philosophical Development*, Chapter V, 'Revolt into Pluralism', pp. 54–64.

82. *Ibid.*, p. 62. See also, 'My Mental Development', *The Philosophy of Bertrand Russell*, p. 12.
83. Bertrand Russell, *The Principles of Mathematics*. George Allen and Unwin, London; first published 1903; second edition, 1937. The quotation is cited from Chapter IV, p. 43, of the second edition; this passage is quoted by Russell in rejection in the new preface to the second edition of *The Principles of Mathematics*, p. x. See also the reference and quotation in *My Philosophical Development*, pp. 159–60, where he again rejects the view of 1903.
84. See above, pp. 72 *f.*
85. Bertrand Russell, 'On the Relations of Universals and Particulars', *The Proceedings of the Aristotelian Society*, 1911–12; reprinted in *Logic and Knowledge*, pp. 103–24.
86. Russell, *The Problems of Philosophy*, Chapters IX and X.
87. Russell, *Inquiry*, pp. 97 *f*, 230 *f*, and 337 *f.*
88. Russell, *My Philosophical Development*, pp. 171 *f.*
89. Russell, *Inquiry*, p. 347.
90. *Ibid.*, Chapter XXIV.
91. Russell, *Human Knowledge*, p. 462. See also, Russell, *My Philosophical Development*, pp. 18–24.

CHAPTER VI

CONCLUSION

The appraisal of Russell's theory of knowledge involves several factors. In the first place, it was noted earlier that there has been widespread misinterpretation of Russell's epistemology. These misconceptions, as well as criticisms of Russell's thought, can now be evaluated in the context of the development of his complete theory of knowledge. Secondly, each of the main topics, the method of analysis, empiricism, and realism, has revealed points of ambiguity or difficulty which need to be restated and evaluated. Thirdly, we are now in a position to draw all the separate threads together and to ask: What is the outcome of Russell's theory of knowledge? Did he succeed in what he was trying to do? What prospects for further fruitful development can be seen in his mature theory of knowledge?

The charge that Russell's philosophy changes, contradicts itself, and emerges in constantly different versions is so common an opinion that it is repeated long and often without the critic feeling the need for justifying the charge. Russell has pointed out that his philosophy does not aim at consistency, which he regards as a goal appropriate for a dogmatic theology but not for a philosophy modelled on science.[1] Russell's thought has developed in close connection with changes in scientific theory; Götlind, for instance, documents the care with which he modified his treatment of causal laws in response to new scientific theories. But this criticism of Russell shows not only that the critics may be assuming a standard of philosophizing which is inappropriate, but also that they have missed the progressive nature of Russell's thought, the sense in which one 'phase' or 'period' of his thought is an hypothesis worked through, rejected or amended for good reasons. For this reason the present interpretation of the development of Russell's theory of knowledge puts us in a position to answer the charge of inconsistency in a way which illuminates the progressive nature of his thought. This answer will take the form of showing the unifying principles present in his philosophy by interpreting the changes in his thought in the context of the proposal of hypotheses, the working out of their consequences, the testing, and the subsequent rejection or amendment or search for new hypotheses in the light of his analysis.

The unifying principles which have remained constant in Russell's thought from the time of his abandonment of idealism to the present are: analytic method, empiricism, and realism. The first term, analytic method, refers to Russell's 'logico-analytic method'. From the first adoption of this method applied to the technical problems of *The Principles of Mathematics* to the method employed in *Human Knowledge*, he has used, consistently, a method of analysis in which the techniques of logic are employed to formulate and attempt to solve the traditional problems of philosophy. Two able commentators on Russell's philosophy have chosen the method of analysis as a central theme in his thought. Morris Weitz stresses the method of analysis as a form of real or contextual definition; Charles A. Fritz emphasizes the use of the method of construction. In contrast to the analysis of Weitz and of Fritz, the present analysis concludes that this method is to be described appropriately as a multi-level or complex method. The logical techniques which are adapted in its philosophical application include the use of an artificial language, the concept of levels of language, the truth-functional reduction of molecular to atomic propositions, and the method of construction. These techniques are used to analyse experience itself into sense-data or complex compresences; to analyse the operation of the organism in the process of perception with the help of physiology and psychology; to analyse the space-time complex of the physical world with the help of physics; to analyse the use of language in formulating propositions with the help of both psychology and logic; to analyse the body of common-sense and scientific knowledge in the search for premises; and to order our beliefs according to their degree of credibility. Sometimes the analysis is employed to answer a descriptive question, such as, What can we discover to be the causes of our beliefs? Sometimes the question asked is a logical one, such as, What must be assumed as a premiss if a given conclusion is to follow from it? Sometimes the question for which analysis is to provide the answer is an epistemological one, such as, If our premisses are of this kind, what assumptions must be added to them in order to justify the acceptance of common sense and scientific beliefs? But whatever the specific use which is made of the analytic method and whatever particular subjects are being analysed, this way of 'doing philosophy' seems to be what is most characteristic of Russell.

The second point of unity in Russell's philosophy is his empiricist starting point. From the time he first turned his logico-analytic method to the task of formulating and solving philosophical problems, he has accepted the position that no knowledge comes to us other than by experience. In that sense he was and is an empiricist. He has remained in the tradition of British empiricism, that of Francis Bacon, Hobbes, Locke, Berkeley, Hume, and J. S. Mill. In his *History of Western Philosophy* he comments on the movement of British empiricism by saying that he believes that the empiricists were right in rejecting *a priori* knowledge and in insisting that it is in experience that we should look for the source of knowledge. But he criticizes British empiricism as so concerned with faithfulness to the facts of experience that it neglected the importance of logical order.[2] In this respect Russell might be regarded as one who is correcting the anti-logical bias of British empiricism by his method of analysis.

Russell is also consistent in the description he gives of experience as providing the raw materials of knowledge. He says repeatedly that his view of experience is similar to that of Hume. Experience, for him, is analysable, if not given, in terms of discrete units of sensation, colour, shape, texture, tone, fragrance or taste. Specifically he argues against those who take a different view of experience, holding that it is run together with strands of meaning and does not present any units of sensation except as the interests of a specific philosophy produce them as a product of epistemological analysis. He rejects the view that experience can be given a broad comprehensive meaning, and he insists that, as empiricists, part of our job is to give a very careful and definitive description of just exactly what we do mean by 'experience'. Otherwise, much confusion occurs, and the delineation of empiricism suffers. Experience must always be that of a specific person at a specific time. We can speak of 'my experience' and 'now'. If we speak of past experience, we mean what we now remember, and refer to, some time in the past, a time which was then a present experience.

Another way in which Russell has been an empiricist throughout his career is in refusing to deny that we believe what we do believe, or act as we do act, or infer what we do infer. It is for this reason that he rejects complete scepticism as a possible philosophical conclusion. Russell finds solipsism to be a 'logically impeccable' but unsatisfactory conclusion. For a similar reason, his 'logical common sense' caused him to reject Meinong's solution of the problem of the referent of fictitious names, and a 'robust sense of reality' caused him to accept realism as a release from the unreality of idealism. A similar empiricist conviction lies behind his insistence throughout his career that whatever errors we may find or suspect in scientific and common-sense 'knowledge' and whatever philosophical reasons might motivate us to a suspense of judgment, we must accept the beliefs of common sense and of science as 'on the whole' reliable and formulate our philosophical problems in those terms.

The third respect in which Russell's philosophy is marked by unity from the time of his rejection of idealism to the present is his holding a position of philosophical realism with respect to the object of knowledge. This means that he has always believed that the world consists of a number of particulars which are known, at least partially, by science, and in another way, by common sense. This world, the world of physics and the world in which we live, exists and has specific characteristics regardless of our knowledge of it or our existence in it. Russell's world dwarfs the puny concerns and efforts of man in space, in time, and in force, although man may also act in the world and have effects, including that of blowing part of it up. As far as theory of knowledge is concerned, this means that all our knowledge has a referent outside knowledge, in external, objective fact. When what is said, or believed, conforms to this external reality, we say we have truth; when it does not conform, we have falsity. Neither meaning, truth, nor knowledge is defined by the limits of our experience, but by the characteristics of what is there, whether it is known or not. Furthermore, the relation between our knowledge and its object, or the belief and the fact, is not one of correspondence alone, but it is also causal; that is, the fact, the particulars, the reals, act upon our organisms in perception, and the end of that causal chain is our knowledge of those facts. This explains why, in spite of what appears to be a phenomenalist method of constructing the objects of science and of common sense from sensed particulars, the causal theory of perception is brought in as a required assumption. Here the difference between the order of existence and the order of knowledge is the crucial factor in interpreting Russell as a realist. Occam's razor directs him to minimize all inferences which go beyond the directly observable; but the realist framework of his philosophy still requires that what is there, what exists, has its own determinate characteristics, whether it be 'constructed', 'inferred', or 'assumed'.

It is clear from what has been said in previous chapters that to say that there is consistency to Russell's thought is not to say that his philosophy has been unchanging. He has changed his mind on a number of important issues. It is argued here that not only do these changes not affect the unity of analytic method, empiricism, and realism, but also that the changes themselves fall into a pattern of the development of Russell's thought from his early programme to his later acceptance of modifications to that programme. This is evident if we review some of the important changes in his thought.

There are six chief topics on which this theory of knowledge underwent important changes: the status of universals, logical truths and how they are known, immediate knowledge, perception, the limits of empiricism, and the concept of knowledge. As far as the status of universals is concerned, there may still be some room for a divergence of interpretations. It seems, however, that after the revolt from idealism he began with a Platonic realism concerning the status of numbers, classes, predicates, qualities, and relations. Since then this Platonic realism has been steadily reduced in response to changes in mathematical logic and in obedience to Occam's maxim of reducing the number of inferred entities. However, neither source of change nor the continued attempt to give a new analysis to qualities, relations, and predicates has gone as far as nominalism. First, the independent reality of numbers and classes was given up, following the development of the technique of the resolution of incomplete symbols. This method enabled Russell to dispense with the undesirable pseudo-entities of the referents of fictitious terms; it also enabled numbers to be defined as classes of classes to be understood as logical functions. Consequently, from about 1914 on there was a dualism in which numbers and classes were not thought of as 'reals', but qualities, relations, and predicates were thought of as necessary 'universals'. In the *Inquiry* Russell put forth a new way of treating qualities in which 'red', for instance, was thought of as a particular, a component of a complex of compresence, which was the same particular although occurring at different places and different times. This enabled Russell to get along without qualities as universals. However, he found that although one relation could be re-stated in other terms, eventually the re-statement would come down to some other relational term, such as similarity. Nor could he see how predicate terms such as 'colour' could be dispensed with. Hence the irreducible universals which must be supposed to have some real status are relations and predicates. What looks like a nominalist argument to the effect that a word is a 'set of more or less similar sounds' is used by Russell to conclude that the word is itself a universal. The argument concludes with the inference that there is some connection between language and what language refers to, and hence that the world is such that families of quality words and relation words somehow work in the description of the world and are in some sense irreducible. A modified realism concerning universals has developed from the original extreme Platonic realism.[3]

A parallel movement away from logical realism seems to have taken place with respect to the status and interpretation of 'logical truths'. As we have seen, 'logical truths' were first regarded as intuitively known and among the 'hard data'. Later, however, in *The Analysis of Matter* we are told that the truths of logic and of mathematics are analytic and represent syntactical rules. The change in opinion is credited by Russell to the influence of Wittgenstein in making him see that what had appeared to be an edifice of impersonal and secure truth was and is merely different ways of saying the same thing. In any case the modification of opinion here is similar to that concerning the status of universals, away from full Platonic realism.[4]

A third important change which took place in Russell's thought concerns the possibility of immediate knowledge; he gave up the claim that in sensation there is a two term relation of presentation in which the subject and the sense-datum are directly linked without mediating judgment or the possibility of error. The claims for intuitive knowledge of *The Problem of Philosophy* and the claim for 'knowledge by acquaintance' represented the high-tide of Russell's belief in immediate knowledge. This claim was modified first, by the recognition of the necessity of analysis to separate the 'hard' from the 'soft' data and later, in more revolutionary fashion, by the adoption of neutral monism. This change meant giving up the relational view of sensation with its subject and sensed object, and meant that no sharp distinction could be made between sensation and perception. Experience is immediate, but the perceptive experience is not itself knowledge. It is only by analysis that the 'sensory core' of perception can be distinguished. All knowledge must

CONCLUSION

come back to the present experience as a 'touchstone', but it is only when it is analysed, formulated, and scrutinized that present experience has cognitive status.[5]

These changes from the acceptance to the rejection of immediate knowledge were seen to be involved with an increasing caution in the analysis of perception. Having failed to find either the act or the subject in the analysis of sensation as a relation, and seeking simplicity of metaphysical assumptions, Russell adopted neutral monism and replaced the dualism of body and mind with neutral particulars taken in one way as physical and in another way as psychological. At the same time, his study of psychology made him increasingly aware of the amount of memory, habit, and organic response built-in to the perceptive experience. Perception could no longer provide the incorrigible and doubt-free units from which entities could be constructed; rather, the perceptual experience itself was the starting point of an anlysis designed to uncover the various steps of inference and association between the sensory impact and the experienced perception, and between the perception and the formulation of a perceptual judgment. The result of this is shown in an increasing modesty concerning the claims of perception and an increasing stress on the analysis required to make perception serve as the source of epistemological premisses. For this reason, Russell looked back on his own earlier 'shaky inferences' and warned empiricists that they had failed to realize the limitations of empiricism.[6]

The theme of the limits of empiricism which figures largely in the writings of the last three of his books is a culmination of these changes in Russell's philosophy. When he first formulated his logico-analytic method as the 'scientific method in philosophy', he thought that it would be possible eventually to show the world of common sense and the body of scientific knowledge as constructed from the sense-data of a single observer. This would have been the triumph of his analytic empiricism, to be able by logically controlled inferences and using only the units of direct, given knowledge to show how all our knowledge could be logically inferred from these materials. We have traced the ways

195

in which this hope was disappointed. The original limitations which he had hoped to overcome were those of finding it necessary to postulate the experience of other observers, the external world as the cause and referent of our perceptual knowledge, unperceived particulars, and some principles of inductive inference. These limitations became even more restrictive with the changes which occurred in the giving up of the claim to immediate knowledge and the changing analysis of perception. An increased awareness of linguistic distortions and of psychological influences on immediate perception increased the problem. The gap between what knowledge we wish to be able to establish and what knowledge we can establish became so great as to seem unbridgeable. For this reason, the final portion of *Human Knowledge* suggested the postulates which could enable the gap to be bridged; the cost was the acceptance of the postulates themselves, carefully formulated and empirically supported but not justified. In this respect Russell described the development of his philosophy as 'The Retreat from Pythagoras', and it might also be termed the coming to terms with the limits of his own method and his own empiricism. This Russell called 'the limits of empiricism'; some might call it 'the failure of empiricism'. Instead of considering the changes in Russell's empiricism as a 'failure', it would be preferable to see them as the progressive amendment of the hypothesis of the construction of our knowledge of common sense and of science from the materials of immediate knowledge. In the course of this amendment the claims made for Russell's method become more modest, and the kinds and complexity of the analysis required increase. If *Human Knowledge* is taken as the latest version of Russell's empiricist hypothesis, we can look further to see if new problems and difficulties arise in this hypothesis which remain unsolved or incomplete. But with respect to the consistency and the development of his thought, a steady and logical progression can be seen.[7]

Although it is apparent that Russell was and remained a 'realist', in the meaning that we have given to this term, from the abandonment of idealism to the present, there have been some changes in the conception of the relation of the knower to the known and of the relation of the object of knowledge to the evidence involved in the acceptance of a given belief as knowledge. These developments have paralleled those in empiricism.

In the period prior to logical atomism and neutral monism, Russell accepted an explicit dualism of subject and object. The believing subject was related to what was believed, and both of these terms were psychological; the belief was related to the putative referent of the belief, and the latter was (usually) physical. Hence, both a metaphysical and epistemological dualism were involved in Russell's early 'realism'. With the acceptance of logical atomism, the psychological aspect was minimized, and the relation of belief to referent was thought of as the correspondence of proposition to fact. With the acceptance of neutral monism, the relational nature of sensation, the empirical existence of a 'subject', and the dualism of mind and matter were questioned. The relational natures of belief and knowledge and truth were retained only by accepting the causal theory of perception and the duality of subject and object on the level of belief, knowledge, and truth. This retention required the more complex behaviourist and linguistic analyses of *The Analysis of Mind* and the *Inquiry*. Under the stimulus of the analytic empiricism of logical empiricism and pragmatism, the later development of Russell's treatment of belief, knowledge, and truth set his concepts in opposition to the verifiability theory of meaning and of truth of these other empiricisms. He stressed the distinction of the empirical evidence leading one to accept or reject a belief as knowledge from the actual truth status of a belief. Russell's realization of the importance of the gap between knowledge and truth was one of the reasons for the importance of the degrees of credibility, the analysis of behaviourism and of levels of language, and the postulates as an answer to the problem of non-demonstrative inference.[8]

Commentators on Russell's philosophy have pointed out the extraordinary degree to which his work reflects the influence of other contemporary philosophers. It is consistent with his modelling philosphic inquiry on the cooperative work of science that he should look to the work of others for new hypotheses and learn from them the possible difficulties of his own. Much of his writing has had the work of contemporaries in mind, from the references to idealism in his early work to his polemical answers to the criticisms of Oxford analysis of recent years. In addition, a history of the philosophy of this century could be written around the importance of the influence of Russell on his contemporaries, an influence both leading them toward an analytic empiricism and stimulating in them a reaction in other directions. But the theme of Russell and his contemporaries is the subject of another study; presently we are concerned principally with the interpretation of the development of his own thought. However, the challenges of his critics have had an important part to play in his own development and are relevant to our evaluation of the outcome of Russell's philosophy. We will consider, therefore, the chief contemporary challenges to the central themes of Russell's philosophy and the degree to which these challenges indicate critical weaknesses in his theory of knowledge.

One aspect of Russell's philosophy which has put it in sharp opposition to other segments of the philosophical world has been his analytic method. This method was first formulated in the teeth of a dominant anti-analytic mood in British philosophy. When Russell with G. E. Moore first opposed idealism, their methods as well as their realist position were revolutionary. In the writings of the first two decades of the century it is clear that Russell had his idealistic and his Bergsonian colleagues in mind. In retrospect he tells us that there were four chief points on which he came to reject idealism. The most important issue between him and the idealists concerned the doctrine of internal relations; his study of Leibniz had shown that this leads to the position that all predicates are contained in the subject, and hence that every substance in the universe contains within itself all its present and future predicates. Russell believed that this implied a position in which Bradley is committed to finding all judgments either analytic or contradictory, an unacceptable position to Russell. This kind of propositional analysis cannot deal adequately with relational propositions. Russell thus affirmed the doctrine of external relations in opposition to the idealist doctrine of internal relations.

The second point on which Russell opposed idealism was related to this theory of relations, the view of nature and man as belonging to one reality and one category, that of mind. This metaphysical monism was too confining and offended his 'stubborn sense of reality'. If internal relations lead one to think of the universe as a single web of meaning, the doctrine of external relations leads one to think of a world in which some things are connected with other things, while some entities have no connection whatever with one another. Relations are to be postulated only where they are found to exist, and kinds of reality are to be as diverse as experience shows them to be.

A third point on which idealism was attacked by Russell was on its theory of truth. The doctrines of internal relations and metaphysical monism were connected with a monistic theory of truth. For, if everything in the world is connected with everything else, it is never possible to make a limited statement about a single entity and claim that it has a definitive truth value. Any judgment will necessarily involve all the predicates contained in the given subject. For Russell the model of scientific inquiry suggests that it is precisely by making inquiries of limited scope that the scientist has succeeded where the speculative philosopher has failed. The proper method for philosophy, too, is piecemeal and tentative, and this means an analytic method. In defending his own analytic method Russell makes this reference explicit by pointing out that it is only by analysis that any scientific progress has been made, so that an enemy of analysis is an enemy of inquiry.[9]

The fourth point on which Russell rejected idealism was the unsatisfactory nature of the idealist philosophy of mathematics. For Russell a philosophy must fit in with some way of dealing with problems in the foundation of mathematics. It was for this reason that the logico-analytic method was developed in philosophy as an outgrowth of Russell's and Whitehead's work in *Principia Mathematica*.[10]

Not only did Russell's philosophy develop in specific opposition to an anti-analytic bent in contemporary thought, but he has continued to defend his analytic method against anti-analytic attacks. Two of these are familiar criticisms of analysis: that analysis destroys what it analyses and that when an analysis is complete, something still remains unexpressed. Russell answers that to analyse is to take apart *intellectually*, and it leaves the reality of what is analysed untouched. To analyse water as H_2O is not to render it undrinkable; the analysis does not affect the qualities of water as they exist, but it gives us a set of categories by which the water can be understood. Russell points out that there may be other ways of understanding the reality of nature as intuitionists claim, and he would leave them free to pursue their own methods. But for him, the only available method of understanding is that of patient and painstaking analysis.

With regard to the criticism that when an analysis has been completed something still remains unexpressed, Russell challenges this statement and asks if one compares a statement concerning wholes with its analysis, formulated in a series of propositions concerning units of those wholes, what is left out? He takes the example that Urmson had cited against him, 'England declared war on Germany'. If this were analysed in terms of observable features of what particular English people and particular German people were doing on a certain date, what the headline in the paper said, what the Prime Minister said, and so forth, what would be left out? Is there some ineffable meaning beyond these details, some entity 'England' which cannot be further analysed? Russell thinks not, and can see no basis for the claim that something is lost in analysis.[11]

A point made by Fritz might be said to be similar to Urmson's; after a careful description of the method of construction as used by Russell, he makes the point that Russell never clearly delineated the scope and limits of the method of construction and that he ought to have done this.[12] Perhaps this is like saying that analysis is acceptable in its own place but ought not to be applied to all subject-matters and to all inquiries. But Russell would seem to be on good grounds here if he would answer, I have a right to try out my analytic method on all inquiries and an obligation only to describe its limitations when I find those limitations. In fact, this is what he has done, for the development of his thought has been the unfolding of what the limits of his particular kind of analytic empiricism are.

Another common response to an analytic method on the part of the opponent of analysis is to accuse the analyst of making substantial metaphysical assumptions himself in adopting his analytic method in the way which he does. This criticism is made of Russell by Urmson when he says that Russell assumed the existence in fact, as in discourse, of ultimate simples, the end-point of analysis.[13] If Russell had not made this assumption, he would not have been able to justify the analytic programme of logical atomism. Russell replies, that, even in the days of logical atomism, he qualified the ultimacy of simples and that he would now reject the necessity of any assumption of the existence of ultimate units of analysis of any kind, physical, logical, linguistic, or sensory. All that is assumed is that analysis is permitted by the nature of what is being analysed; otherwise, analysis could not be carried on. But the point at which a given analysis stops is determined by the needs of the inquiry, and that inquiry does not presuppose that no other analysis can go further. For instance, a physiologist might carry his analysis of the human body to the cell and stop, but this does not mean that the cell is an ultimate simple; some other biological inquiry might analyse the cell into its components. Russell points out that a 'logical atom' is not a physical atom, but only a unit of analysis chosen to fit the ends of a logical analysis of knowledge. These disclaimers do not mean that Russell is unwilling to draw any metaphysical inferences from his analytic method. He argues that the successful carrying out of an analysis indicates that some differentiations existed which permitted analysis. In the case of language our analysis may allow us to infer something not only about the structure of language but also about the structure of what language refers to.[14]

The foregoing criticisms of Russell's analytic method might be thought of as put forth against analysis *per se*, rather than against specific points in Russell's kind of analysis. But another kind of criticism is made by those who are themselves committed to an analytic method, but to one of a different kind from Russell's. This is the case with the writings of several contemporary British philosophers who have made extended criticisms of Russell's analytic method. They have criticized the way in which his analytic method is directed to certain goals which they consider illegitimate concerns of philosophy; they have criticized the metaphysical assumptions involved in this method; they have criticized the logical aspects of the method itself; and they have criticized the treatment of language and theory of meaning involved in his analytic method. On each of these points contemporary British analytic philosophy sets itself in opposition to Russell, as he set himself in opposition to the idealists.

In *English Philosophy Since 1900*, G. J. Warnock outlines the main features of the change in philosophy in Great Britain which has occurred during this century. He begins his survey by stressing the importance of G. E. Moore's and Bertrand Russell's revolt against the speculative idealism of the nineteenth century. However, Warnock concludes that both Moore and Russell belong on the earlier side of the 'revolution' in philosophy by virtue of the traditional conception which they share of the nature and task of philosophy. The questions, 'How is knowledge possible?' and 'What is the nature of the world?', although they were judged to have been approached in a loose and fruitless manner by previous philosophers, were accepted by Moore and Russell as legitimate philosophical questions. Contemporary philosophers generally regard such questions as illegitimate.[15] Russell himself notes this difference between his own view and that of contemporary British philosophy and says that 'in common with all philosophers before W II [Wittgenstein in the post-

Tractatus period], my fundamental aim has been to understand the world as well as may be, and to separate what may count as knowledge from what must be rejected as unfounded opinion'.[16] He opposes his traditional view to that of merely analysing the different ways 'in which silly people can say silly things'.[17] Of the concerns with the justification of scientific and common-sense knowledge, with the source of reliable knowledge, with the analysis of language and behaviour, Russell's critics either do not regard these as properly philosophical questions or conceive the problems in very different terms. Philosophy of mathematics and the technical aspects of mathematical logic are seen as non-philosophical inquiries and as having a distorting effect on philosophical logic.[18] The interest in problems of science is outside the range of philosophy.[19] Problems of language and of meaning are philosophical, but were wrongly conceived by Russell.

As we have seen, in *Our Knowledge of the External World*, Russell claimed to have inaugurated a new Copernican revolution in philosophy which would render philosophy scientific by using the method of logical analysis, by attacking philosophical problems in piecemeal and tentative fashion with logical tools yielding precise results.[20] But the irony is that the very problem which Russell proposed as an exemplification of this method is one that current philosophers would regard as beyond the scope of philosophy, that is, the knowledge of the external world. Just as Russell strove to leave behind him the barren controversies of past speculative metaphysics in developing a new revolutionary method, so contemporary critics regard his own work as over-speculative, ambitious beyond the proper scope of philosophy, and insufficiently piecemeal and tentative.[21]

The idea of the task of philosophy which the younger contemporaries of Russell have adopted stems from the work of the later Wittgenstein. One version of this new idea of philosophy has been called 'therapeutic' and could be expressed appropriately in Wittgenstein's phrase, 'For the clarity that we are aiming at is indeed *complete* clarity. But this simply means that the philo-

sophical problems should *completely* disappear'.[22] Other versions
of this basic idea of the task of philosophy would regard the
clearing of linguistically derived confusions as only part of the
task of philosophy, which may use the resources of language to
construct a logic of language having an explanatory value of its
own.[23] In any case, these views of philosophy eschew all claim
to conclusions which will tell us something about the nature of the
world or the nature of our own experience. No claims for a
scientific status for philosophy are justified. Russell's attempt
to understand the world and our experience in relation to it and
his claim that philosophy can be scientific, at least in some sense,
are over-ambitious and speculative on this view.

With regard to Russell's analytic method, while there is
respect for his pioneering work and agreement on the importance
of analysis, there is also major disagreement. As we noted,
Urmson regards Russell's analytic method as an example of the
errors of 'logical atomism'. The analysis is said to be metaphysically oriented since the atomism, the belief in 'irreducible
facts' at which analysis ends, is the real motive and foundation
for the method of analysis.[24] The reductive analysis of logical
atomism errs in assuming some ultimates at which the logical
truth-functional analysis and the empiricist analysis of 'facts'
must end.[25] This is directed by an ulterior motive of the quest
for certainty, the desire to 'justify' the knowledge of science,[26]
and it involves Russell in problems of solipsism, in locating
elusive basic propositions and their referents, and in a reductive
analysis which necessarily fails.[27] In addition, Urmson cites
certain specific problems in logical atomism, problems which
Russell had already pointed out.

In the opinion of these critics, the errors of the metaphysical
motives and the metaphysical assumptions which misdirect
Russell's method of analysis during the period of logical atomism
are compounded by the 'logico-analytic' method itself. This
method is influenced by his interest in mathematics and mathematical logic, an interest which perverts and distorts meanings
as they occur in the native and natural context of ordinary

language. The use of an artificial language, the concept of an 'ideal language' or a 'logically perfect language', is the central and common target of many contemporary critics of Russell. This concept of an 'ideal language' assumes that common language is in some way inferior and that it ought to be reformed and corrected according to the standards of regularity, of precision, of a logically elegant order, and of explicitness of mathematical logic. But ordinary or natural language is itself the standard by which philosophical discourse is to be judged and by which philosophical conclusions are to be tested. Language is perfectly 'in order at it is',[28] and its complexity, subtlety of distinctions, richness, and variety of shades of meaning make it the proper source as well as the vehicle of philosophical meanings.[29] The imposition of the model of the perfect language distorts, over-simplifies, and misinterprets the proper meanings and the proper logic of ordinary discourse. Its use as a primary method of analysis as in logical atomism, leads to many grievous metaphysical errors. The model of the artificial language led Russell to suppose there were such things as 'logically proper names', and it leads W. V. Quine to develop an ontology modelled on the logical notion of quantification.[30]

In addition to the general criticisms of the influence of the model of the artificial language and of the metaphysical assumptions involved in logical analysis, there have been several specific and detailed criticisms of the logic of truth-functional analysis which is generally regarded as Russell's permanent contribution to philosophy. According to P. F. Strawson, the logical forms used by mathematical logic are necessarily standardized and necessarily impose a standard which cannot take account of the 'logical ambiguities' which are part of ordinary speech.[31] In stressing 'entailment rules' in logical analysis, mathematical logicians disregard other rules which are an important part of the meanings of sentences. These other rules Strawson calls 'referring rules', and he maintains that these rules connecting the specific uses of sentences in specific contexts are, or ought to be, of central importance to logic.[32] The 'ideal sentence' confuses sentences with statements and thus by-passes the problems of specific references of sentences. This is the basis of Strawson's noted attack on Russell's theory of descriptions.[33] Giving a standard meaning to a statement of a given form overlooks the fact that only a sentence, uttered at a specific time, by a specific speaker, on a specific occasion, for a specific audience, is properly to be judged true or false. Russell has confused the standard meaning of a statement with the reference meaning of a sentence. A similar error is committed by the logical reduction of different statements in subject-predicate form to affirmatively or negatively existential forms. The interest in mathematics and in elegance of form has misled modern logicians into oversimplifications of form which obscure the many different and important ways in which sentences may be meaningful. This has occurred with the use of existential quantifiers and with the applications of the true-false dichotomy in cases where, in given circumstances, the sentence is meaningless.[34] Like Urmson, Strawson lays a good deal of the blame for the distortions of modern logic on the influence of the model of the perfect language.

Errors similar to those of his analytic method occur in Russell's theory of meaning and analysis of language, according to these critics. The programme of logical atomism was designed to find the constituents of the 'fact' to which the proposition referred, and this was a basic error. For the truth is that propositions do not mean by atoms or by constituents, but more indirectly by their *uses* in *contexts*. The context of Russell's analysis of meaning is too narrow, too restricted to standard situations of making cognitive statements, and too atomistic in assuming that a given proposition refers isomorphically to a given fact. The same criticisms of logical atomism are made by Wittgenstein and by Urmson.[35] The 'picture theory of meaning' has been extensively attacked for the oversimple and metaphysically moulded description of the relation of proposition to fact.[36] It seems fair to say that there are no contemporary defenders of the original programme of the logical atomist theory of meaning, and this includes Russell himself.[37] The errors found in his treatment of meaning and of language are similar to those found in his entire logico-analytic method; he tries to impose a perfection of form and a simplicity of analysis on language and its reference that is false to the way language actually is used and has meanings.

These specific criticisms of his method, its logic, its application to the analysis of meanings and of language, have not gone unanswered by Russell. Although he is willing to concede that the early form of logical atomism is indefensible, he is unrepentant in other respects. He gives a lively argument in defence of the existential quantifier, for instance, turning the argument back on the critics and holding that if it is true that there are multiple and conflicting meanings for the translations of the logical symbol into ordinary English, this demonstrates the ambiguities of ordinary speech which require some correction in order for consistent meanings and patterns of argument to be used.[38] In defending his theory of descriptions against Strawson, Russell argues that in attacking the example, 'the present king of France is wise', and showing that it would be true on some occasions of utterance, false on others, and meaningless on others, Strawson has hit on the word 'present', a symbol with a special problem connected with it. This problem is that of 'egocentric particulars', and Russell has taken great pains to analyse this kind of symbol. But that problem has nothing to do with the theory of descriptions; for that analysis it would have been better to choose 'the king of France in 1920 is wise'.[39]

In a book-length study of Russell's thought, *Bertrand Russell and the British Tradition in Philosophy*, D. F. Pears attempts to analyse Russell's thought in relation to the empiricist tradition.[40] Although the book is aimed primarily at elucidation rather than criticism, it reflects many of the criticisms of contemporary British analysts. The restrictions of the author's consideration to the period 1905–1919, to the topic of meaning and truth, and to the influences chiefly of Hume and Wittgenstein limit the significance of the work and result in serious misinterpretations of Russell's thought. Preoccupation with logical atomism leads the author to overlook important concepts of the period he is considering, such as the discussion of the immediacy of know-ledge. The same perspective results in the failure to deal with topics which arose prior to the time period under discussion, such as the status of universals. The choice of 1919 as the terminal period leaves unsettled the issue of the relevance of neutral monism to the topics discussed. The deliberate omission of any discussion of logical topics leads to difficulties in understanding such topics as the method of construction. But of particular interest to the present discussion of Russell and his critics is the most striking weakness of this book, that is, the way in which taking a perspective limited to logical atomism of the period to 1920 prevents the author from understanding the place of the topics discussed in the progressive development of Russell's exploration of hypotheses in theory of knowledge.

Whatever the outcome of particular points argued between Russell and his linguistic analyst critics, it seems clear that the fundamental points at issue in this opposition cannot be resolved by detailed discussions. Russell has difficulty in grasping the radical departure that these philosophers have made from his kind of analysis; to him they are wilfully turning their backs on the tradition of philosophy, on science, and on the gains made by logic. But to them, Russell is looked upon as a stage they have gone through and overcome, just as Wittgenstein himself lived through and then rejected his own early philosophy to become the source of new ideas to British thinkers. Their criticism of Russell is a delineation of what they have overcome to be them-selves. The two slogans of contemporary analysis in Britain—'don't ask for the meaning ask for the use' and 'every statement has its own logic'—are to be interpreted in this light. The negative reaction to logical atomism is part of their meaning; one is being advised not to expect or to search for a single, standard, formalizable meaning for any statement but for varieties of shades of meaning in different contexts of use, varieties of situations in which such a sentence could be *uttered* with different purposes and different responses. One is being told that formal logic is to be replaced by the logic of the multifarious concrete uses of everyday words. Hence, the method is to invent possible new and unusual contexts in which such-and-such could be said and inquire what different meanings it could have in these different situations. Where Russell used analysis to clarify, simplify, and reduce the possibility of error through the use of Occam's razor, the linguistic analysts use their method of analysis to expand, diversify, enrich the possibilities of meaning in order to avoid simplification in the interests of doing justice to the complex logic of the living language. This opposition in the direction of philosophical analysis cannot be resolved or reconciled; all that can be done is to wait and see what new developments in contemporary philosophy may find methods and concepts of value in the philosophy of Russell or of his critics.

Among the proponents of a method of analysis are those whose debt to Russell is gladly acknowledged, the logical empiricists. Yet, even here there is a foreshortened perspective on the significance of Russell's work. In acknowledging the important influence of Russell, logical empiricists tend to select for emphasis three aspects of Russell's work: the contribution to mathematical logic, the method of construction of *Our Knowledge of the External World*, and the classic Wittgenstein-Russell contribution of 'logical atomism'. Carnap, in the *The Philosophy of Rudolf Carnap*, acknowledges Russell's model for *Der Logische Aufbau der Welt*;[41] Ayer takes the theory of descriptions as the paradigm of philosophical analysis;[42] Quine praises the contribution of mathematical logic and accepts the historical importance of the constructionist method.[43] Yet, along with the acknowledgment goes deprecation; the method of construction is said to have reached a dead end and to be incapable of realization; the limitations of logical atomism are taken to be final.[44] These judgments can be explained in that Russell's philosophical heirs in logical empiricism have accepted the early Russell as having put forth and practised methods of analysis from which their view is derived, but have judged these views to be limited and outgrown. They do not see Russell's philosophy as undergoing a process of growth in which these early methods are themselves surpassed and transformed into new versions of analytic method.

When one attempts to evaluate the different criticisms which have been made of Russell's method of analysis, it seems fair to say that this method has been challenged from the outside by those who espouse different philosophical methods. No conclusion is to be expected from such confrontation. Where the criticisms of his method of analysis have been put forth in terms of the details of the method itself, as by his current British critics, it seems fair to say that weaknesses in logical atomism have been pointed out, but that there has been no criticism offered of his mature practice of the method of analysis. If this method is to be judged internally, that is, in terms of the way he himself worked it out, it will have to be after we have considered its outcome in empiricism and realism.

There are two ways in which criticisms of Russell's empiricism arise. One question concerns the description which he gives of experience and asks, Is this the way experience is? Another question concerns the way in which this concept of experience works in Russell's theory of knowledge, the use that is made of it, and the outcome of the empiricist analysis. The two questions are not to be kept entirely separate since what experience is determines, to a large extent, what philosophical use can be made of it. But from the standpoint of criticism, the questions require separate answers.

Many different arguments have been given which challenge aspects of Russell's description of experience. Examples are: whether sense-data are located in the experiencer, whether the sensory-datum has an aspect of spatial and temporal order in itself or by construction, and so forth.[45] But it seems that the most meaningful opposition is from those critics, such as the pragmatists, who have a very different description of experience. John Dewey took issue with Russell's description of experience, and Russell himself opposed his own view to that of Dewey and James.[46] What is the issue here? The pragmatists see experience as a fused whole, permeated with meaning, while for Russell experience is of discrete units; it is atomistic. Pragmatists use the term 'experience' in an inclusive sense to encompass, among other things, 'death, war, and taxes'; for Russell this breadth deprives the term of all meaning; it ought to be used in a narrow and more precise way to denote the very units of experience which I have before me or have had before me. For pragmatists, experience is a public rather than a private term, as one might speak of 'human experience'. Experience must always, for Russell, be the experience of a specific experiencer, and private to him. In a similar way, experience for the pragmatist extends not only to include all human experience now, but also the experiencings of the past and what may be anticipated for the future; it has no specific or narrow locus in time. For Russell it is always the experience of a specific and limited time period; not of a moment, if by that is meant a split second, but of a specious present, the time of a given person's attention span. It is necessary to distinguish these when one is speaking of a present experience, the content of which is a memory image, and of an experience of the past which was a present at a certain time for a certain observer. But perhaps the most vital difference between the pragmatic concept of experience and that of Russell concerns the kinds of relations which are thought of as given in experience. William James' radical empiricism includes within experience all kinds of actions, relations, structures, feelings, events; all are 'there' in experience. But for Russell, in spite of some interest in a given causal relation involved in perception, his final description of experience has only spatio-temporal relations and order as given within it.

One consequence of this contrast between the view of experience of pragmatism and that of Russell is that, in adopting neutral monism, Russell made a reservation concerning the giving up of the dualism of subject and object, idea and referent. For James neutral monism meant that it was no longer necessary to think of the subject and the idea as within experience, the object and the referent outside of it. While Russell was willing to give up the 'subject' as not to be found in experience, he was not willing to give up the relational view of knowledge in which the idea or belief was in experience, the referent of the idea or belief outside experience in a realm of fact. For this reason, he retained the causal theory of perception through neutral monism with the cause of the perception as outside of the perceptive experience itself.[47]

For pragmatists, Russell's description of experience as composed of discrete units of sensation was a falsification; he had mistaken the results of an analysis of experience for the actual given features of experience itself. But for Russell, the black dog on the field of white snow is representative of the atomistic character of experience.[48]

The criticism of Russell's view of experience, to the effect that it did not describe experience correctly, was connected with another kind of criticism, that of the role which experience plays in his empiricism. Dewey claimed that in portraying experience as given in discrete, directly known, and indubitable units of sense-data, Russell was actually taking the results of an analysis of experience to be descriptive of experience as given. The reason for this transfer of the post-analytic data to the role of pre-analytic data was that Russell desired to find in sense-data the incorrigible, directly-given touchstones of perceptual knowledge. It was the claim for the immediacy of the data of perception which motivated the distortions of Russell's description of experience.

Urmson also criticizes logical atomism on a similar basis, finding in its analysis of experience the search for the incorrigible data on which to build a structure of reliable truth, and this he regarded as an ulterior motive in the description of experience. Not only does assigning this role to sense-data distort the description of experience, but it builds into the view of experience a dualism in which the sense-data are given as inside the perceiver, thus generating the problem of the existence of the external world. The dualism of the relation of sensing subject to the cause and referent of the sense-data imports an unneeded dualism into the very description of experience itself, according to the pragmatists.

Dewey finds that one of the unfortunate implications of Russell's treatment of experience is that, in requiring that the atomistic sense-data provide the basis for a structure of empirical truth, he necessitates importing some *a priori* logical principles in order that these discrete units be able to be put together into some synthetic pattern.[49] In other words, by describing experience as he has, Russell ensures the defeat of his own empiricism because such data cannot support the structure of scientific and common-sense beliefs.

Russell, in facing these various criticisms of his empiricism, refuses to yield on the point that experience does have the characteristics he attributes to it. However, he says that the 'data' with which he is concerned in his method of construction are not to be thought of as primitive but as sophisticated, the product of a mature mind searching for some basis relatively free of doubt on which he might build a theory of knowledge. As his thought developed, he stressed increasingly the necessity of analysis before any perceptual material could be accepted as data, as we have seen. He also gave up the claim for immediate knowledge and the direct two-term relation of sensation. Russell did not abandon the relational view of perception and of know-ledge, however, although he would claim that this is justified by common sense itself and is on stronger empirical grounds than the view of the monist. Russell pointed out that Dewey is primarily interested in tracing the consequences of a given perceptual experience in the ongoing of experience, while he is more con-cerned with tracing the causes of the perceptual experience.[50] Russell has recently remarked that the differences between philo-sophers and schools of philosophy are frequently exaggerated,[51] and it seems that this may well be the case with Russell and Dewey. For, as Russell's theory of knowledge developed, more stress was laid on the post-analytical rather than the pre-analytical aspect of data; more attention was given to the behaviouristic aspects of the analysis of experience and of knowledge, and less was claimed for the results of his empiricist analysis. This brought Russell closer to Dewey.[52] At the same time, if one contrasts

Russell and Dewey with other contemporary schools of philosophy, in terms of what they conceive the task of philosophy to be, and in terms of their attitude to science and to the uses of language, this perspective shows the old antagonists to be on the same side in relation to emerging philosophical issues. Even the beguiling comment that Russell is interested in causes and Dewey in consequences seems to indicate less of a contrast when it is realized that both philosophers recognize the exploration of causes to be relevant to experiences of which the status and meaning are disputed, while both also recommend a method of verification as a test of belief, that is, an interest in consequences.

In most of the criticism of Russell's concept of experience there is merely a confrontation of two different descriptions of experience, or of two different ways of using experience in epistemology. Much of it is rendered outdated by Russell's own development. But one of Dewey's criticisms raises a problem internal to Russell's thought; that is, that by describing experience in atomistic terms, Russell sets up the necessity of importing non-empirical logical principles in order to justify any knowledge derived from experience. It might be thought that there is some truth in this criticism, for we have seen that when Russell has finished analysing the perceptual experience, all he has are complexes of compresence which are ordered temporally and spatially, and this proves to be an insufficient basis for the knowledge which he wishes to show is empirically derived. We saw that this was the reason for the necessity of the postulates of non-demonstrative inference with which *Human Knowledge* concludes and for the lameness of the equation of psychological certainty with 'objective credibility'. This might seem to be a confirmation of Dewey's critical insight.

The problems involved in working out Russell's concept of experience with his overall epistemological purposes of sifting the reliable from the unreliable and from these constructing inferences sufficient to base the knowledge of common sense and science can be seen in his treatment of data. We might rephrase the difficulties with the concept of data this way: How can Descartes and Hume be compatible? For Russell's intention in the search for data is closely akin to that of Descartes; he wished to find somewhere some beliefs which could not be doubted and from these reconstruct the whole of our reliable knowledge by means of logically controlled inference. This was the original meaning of the search for data. But as a Humean, Russell was committed to denying the possibility of *a priori* truths and was opposed to Descartes' depreciation of knowledge of the sense. In his search for the indubitable, Russell sought to find it in directly given knowledge, especially in the sensory elements of direct knowledge. At first it seemed that this combination of empiricism and rationalism could be successful: the sense-data, directly intuited, were what they were and were not subject to doubt; thus, they would provide the premises, and the method of construction would provide the controlled inference from which all knowledge could be reconstructed. But difficulties arose. Some sense-data are not clear and distinct but hazy and complex; direct knowledge can only be error free as long as it is not formulated. Next, it appeared that it was necessary to scan all knowledge, including that of perception, to find its credentials in sense-data that resist doubt. Subsequently, perception was recognized as involving inferences, and the sense-data were found to be not given, but analysed out. It turned out, then, that not indubitables, but relatively more credible data are to be found only at the end of a long linguistic, physiological, psychological analysis. The more-or-less pure datum is the residue of this analysis. We have noted the change in the concept of data and the continued confusion of the different meanings of data which resulted from these developments in Russell's thought. Sometimes he held beliefs to be data, sometime propositions, and sometimes the sensory core of the perceptive experience. There was an additional difficulty in that Russell came to stress the fact that deductive inferences alone are not sufficient to build up our knowledge, but that kinds of inductive inference are required if any body of belief is to be erected on the epistemological premises in question. Not only is there a need for inductive inferences, but the postulates on which inductive inference depend have their own difficulties. Now we may ask, What is left of the hoped for combination of Descartes and Hume when all the changes and confusion have been taken account of?

With all the necessary qualifications on the status and nature of the 'undeniable data', is there any point in retaining the method of analysis of data, the Cartesian scrutiny, when all possibility of finding a secure starting point for inference is gone? Russell seems to answer in the affirmative and to find that it is a limitation, but not a fatal one, on the analysis of data, that the data are difficult to analyse out, lack certainty when arrived at, and require the dubious supplementation of the postulates of non-demonstrative inference. Russell accepts the limitations rather than give up the attempt to evaluate the degrees of credibility of propositions from which inferences follow.

But, even if one agrees that it is better not to give up such an epistemological scrutiny, to persist in the attempt to evaluate degrees of credibility, and to scrutinize beliefs critically according to some criteria of reliability, and that this is the proper business of an empiricist theory of knowledge, one troublesome question remains. By what criteria is this evaluation to be carried out, what principles guide the scrutiny, and what is meant by degrees of 'objective credibility'? The concept of the data depends upon there being some objective basis of evaluation; but they cannot themselves provide the criteria since they lack the indubitability which, for Descartes, would have been their guarantee. Failing indubitability, what are the criteria to be? The answer to this question brings us to a similar query resulting from the survey of the difficulties encountered in connecting realism with the empiricist analysis which we have been considering.

The consideration of the analysis of experience and its employment in Russell's epistemology showed the need of evaluating these in terms of the outcome of Russell's theory of knowledge, his concepts of knowledge and of truth. In tracing the analysis to data in which this concept of empiricism and the analytic method combined to fulfil the purpose of epistemological scrutiny and the ordering of 'degrees of credibility', we are brought again to the necessity of considering the concepts of knowledge and of truth. This necessity stems from the fact that the criteria of credibility are stated in terms of what is believed to be true, has no reasons against it, and has no reason to be accepted as true if it is not. Here again we are in the area of the definition of knowledge and of truth.

Russell had required of his account of knowledge that it conform to what common sense and science mean by knowledge, that it exclude false belief and accidentally true belief from its scope, and that it give a description of the 'sound evidence' on which beliefs may be accepted as knowledge. But here we come across as a fundamental difficulty, the disparity between the demands of truth and the empiricist limitations of evidence. As an empiricist, Russell strives to examine the basis of what we call 'knowledge' and to find this basis in experience. This is evident in his treatment of belief. But Russell also wishes to erect a standard for knowledge which will give us a goal for inquiry beyond inquiry. This motive is evident in the definition of truth as the correspondence of belief with fact where fact is understood to indicate what is beyond experience and may be beyond the existence of man and his knowledge. This same motive is evident in his demand that epistemology tell us not just how beliefs *are* formed and selected and criticized, but how this *ought* to be done. His desire is to erect criteria against which the actual course of experience and the actual building-up of knowledge can be evaluated. This same conflict of the empiricist and the logical motive is present in the conflicting concepts of data as epistemologically prior (what ought to be accepted) and as causally prior (what is in fact accepted).

The definition of knowledge itself reveals this conflict in Russell's thought; for knowledge is defined as a subclass of beliefs which are true and are believed on the basis of sound evidence. But these two requirements, of being true and of being believed on the basis of sound evidence, are essentially opposed to one another. Of course, if a belief is a true belief, it qualifies as knowledge; but if we had such beliefs, known to be true, the concept of knowledge would be unnecessary; true belief would suffice. The difficulty is that on Russell's realistic view a belief may be true in the absence of any evidence, or a belief may have mountains of evidence in its favour and yet be untrue. The second part of the definition of knowledge, accepted on the basis of sound evidence, discounts this inaccessible truth and comes to terms with the empiricist basis of the evaluation of belief. In the case of this requirement we may ask: Why bring truth into the definition of knowledge at all? Why not define knowledge on the basis of the standards of acceptance of belief worked out within the limits of inquiry? It would seem that the definition of knowledge in terms of truth points in one direction; the definition of knowledge in terms of evidence points in another. Russell himself recognizes a difficulty but never resolves the conflict implicit in this concept. In Russell's view it is necessary to save the law of excluded middle and to come to terms with the general view of nature which we have called 'scientific realism'; both objects entail the assertion of the independence of fact to belief, and the definition of truth as correspondence with fact. At the same time, as an empiricist, Russell is committed to finding the basis of knowledge in experience. This conflict is rendered even more severe by the adoption of the epistemological method of a scrutinizing analysis to which all beliefs must submit before they can be accepted as premises for knowledge. The same conflict between what ought to be believed and what is believed can be seen in the different meanings of data where the epistemologically prior is distinguished from the causally prior. What is believed is believed because of evidence and causes; what ought to be believed ought to be believed because it is true or logically inferred from what is true. But how does one ever know what *is* true? This is the gap between the realistic theory of truth and the empiricist theory of knowledge.

It was noted previously that Russell tried to close this gap by making perception and the 'pure datum' which is analysed from perceptual experience the key to the meaning of truth, the link between fact and knowledge. But in insisting that the fact and the perception can never be known to be completely the same and that the pure datum can be approached only 'asymptotically', he left the gap still there. Direct perceptual experience is the best clue to what is real and to which beliefs are true; but it is not itself the direct grasp of that truth, nor is the product of the analysis of the sensory core from the perceptual proposition the attainment of that truth.

Another aspect of the meaning of the realistic theory of truth is that it enables Russell to escape from the dangers of solipsism and phenomenalism. Perhaps it would be better to say that because he holds a realist position with respect to knowledge and truth, he does not follow the logic of his own empiricism into a sceptical, solipsistic, or phenomenalistic conclusion. It may be a prior assumption that gives this realistic status to knowledge, a kind of realist bias which might be called a 'prejudice' of his thinking. It is the same commitment that leads Russell to retain belief in the general reliability of common-sense and scientific knowledge. This scientific realism is an intrinsic part of Russell's theory of knowledge, and it prevents his taking the road which would lead by 'impeccable logic' to the 'solipsism of the moment'. But is this realism compatible with his empiricism? And does the method of analysis successfully mitigate the conflict between realism and empiricism?

The method of analysis, as we have discussed it, has several distinct aspects and more than one area of application. In the first place, the original intention of the logico-analytic method was to employ the techniques of mathematical logic to make a continuity of deductive inference with a minimum of assumptions between the empirical data and the common-sense and scientific knowledge which was aimed at. The method of construction accomplished this brilliantly, but left a gap in that it was necessary to assume the existence of other experiencers, the external world, the causal theory of perception, and unperceived particulars. These assumptions, justified only by the absence of disproof and the utility of their role, were a measure of the gap between what ought to be believed, the true, and what evidence justified, the known. But the gap became wider, as we have seen. In addition to *ad hoc* assumptions, it became necessary to use other kinds of analysis, physiological, psychological, and linguistic, in order to unravel all the built-in habits of inference from a complex perceptual experience which was neither pure nor known. This was an extension of the analytic method directed toward the distinguishing of different causal strands in the fused complex of perceptual experience, guided by a body of scientific knowledge with its own assumptions and using analytic techniques going much farther than those of deductive inference.

The conclusion of this analytic effort was the limited empiricism of *Human Knowledge*. This may be considered the delineation of the gap between the true and the known rather than the closing of the gap. It makes clear the degree to which Russell's tunnel between the data of sense perception and the beliefs of science is uncompleted. Russell uses two images of the effort of analysis and construction in bringing together the beliefs of common sense and science on the one hand, and the data derived from experience on the other; one is the image of the tunnel, the other the image of the bridge. If one chooses the latter image, one might describe the outcome of *Human Knowledge* in this way: One side of the bridge begins with perceptive experience and analyses from it by various techniques the most reliable elements; the other side of the bridge begins from the body of scientific and common-sense knowledge and argues back to that which must be assumed to justify this knowledge. In the middle is a small gap between the two spans, the gap of the data that are not quite 'pure' and of the postulates that are not entirely 'justified'. But the gap is narrow enough to jump across with a minimum of risk.

However, there is one respect in which the different uses of the analytic method which we have seen at work in Russell's theory of knowledge have succeeded in some measure in bringing what ought to be believed into accord with what is believed. The analysis of the method of construction showed reasons for preferring some kinds of deductive inferences to others, as involving fewer unsupported inferences. It was thus a successful application of Occam's razor. The analysis of the physiological and psychological aspects of the encrustation of memory, habit, and inference led to a more critical scrutiny of the beliefs based on perceptual experience. To this extent these methods of analysis contributed to the reasoned rejection of some plausible judgments and the more careful discrimination of different perceptual judgments as closer to or farther from the fact-perception-experience tie. Another kind of analysis, a lifelong concern of Russell's, the analysis of levels of language and of levels of propositions, added critical power to the distinction of levels of sentences and the selection of those closest to experience as most trustworthy. If all of the methods of analysis are taken together, we have the description of the multi-level critical approach necessary to epistemology if the beliefs most worthy of acceptance are to form the premises, and those least worthy of acceptance the questionable periphery of epistemology. This is an achievement of no small importance.

Some critics may say that Russell's task would have been easier if he had begun with a view of experience which was closer in accord with what experience is felt to be, and less atomistic. Other critics may say Russell could have avoided setting up an unbridgeable gap by abandoning the definition of truth in terms of fact and employing his analytic techniques in the ordering of degrees of knowledge measured only in terms of evidence. Other critics may say that Russell allowed himself to be led away from empiricism and the natural realism of common sense by an attachment to the artificialities of symbolic logic and the Cartesian demands of the indubitable premises, and that he would have done better to be guided by an analytic technique closer to empiricism, the analysis of the actual uses of language, and the linguistic discriminations of known and not known, true and false. A sympathetic tracing out of the themes of Russell's theory of knowledge would allow for any of these judgments. Yet, the achievement of his theory of knowledge is impressive enough in itself. No other contemporary has so thoroughly explored the resources of the traditions of Humean empiricism, and especially, using the method of analysis based on logic.

Whatever the final decision on whether Russell's kind of analytic philosophy of empiricism is or is not a viable alternative as a modern theory of knowledge, it is clear that we are greatly in his debt for the painstaking and honest analysis by which the limitations of the Humean tradition of empiricism are revealed. In this respect, one may place Russell as the foremost modern exemplar of British empiricism and find both its strengths and its weaknesses clearly revealed in his thought. As far as the method of analysis is concerned, no other contemporary thinker has as many logical and scientific resources as Russell and can convert, with such sureness, mathematically precise techniques to the analysis of experience and of belief. It is a great advantage, in this view, that he is able to use the products of modern scientific inquiry to help him, for surely a philosophy which proceeds in ignorance and irrelevance with respect to science can claim little and must run a large risk of error, as the history of western philosophy sufficiently illustrates. Whatever may prove to be the decisive direction of contemporary empiricism, Russell's thorough, detailed, explicit analysis is likely to contribute to the ongoing of both scientific and philosophical inquiry. It may be, as Whitehead is reported to have said, that Russell is a Platonic dialogue in himself. Whether this be censure or compliment, it has some important truth in it. In his writing, seen over a lifetime of work, there is a working out of a theory of knowledge, analytic, empiricist, realist, which promises to be fruitful for the searchers who follow after him.

NOTES TO CHAPTER VI

1. Russell, Preface to *Bertrand Russell's Dictionary of Mind, Matter and Morals*. See above, Chapter I, footnote 36 for the quotation.

CONCLUSION

2. Russell, *History of Western Philosophy*, p. 834.
3. See above, Chapter V, pp. 173 *f*.
4. See above, pp. 175 *f*.
5. See above, pp. 115 *f*.
6. See also a reference to his own earlier 'shaky inferences' in 'Reply to Criticisms', *The Philosophy of Bertrand Russell*, p. 707. See above, pp. 120 *f*.
7. See Chapter IV, pp. 129 *f*.
8. See Chapter V, pp. 165 *f*.
9. Russell, *My Philosophical Development*, p. 229.
10. For the references to the rejection of idealism, see *My Philosophical Development*, Chapter V, 'Revolt Into Pluralism'.
11. For the criticisms of Russell by Urmson, see J. O. Urmson, *Philosophical Analysis*, and for Russell's reply, see *My Philosophical Development*, pp. 215–30.
12. Fritz, *Bertrand Russell's Construction of the External World*, pp. 222 *f*.
13. See above footnote 11 of this chapter for criticism and response.
14. See above, Chapter V, pp. 178 *f*.
15. Warnock, *English Philosophy Since 1900*, p. 160.
16. Russell, *My Philosophical Development*, p. 217.
17. *Ibid.*, p. 230.
18. Warnock, *English Philosophy Since 1900*, p. 162.
19. A. J. Ayer, *et al.*, *The Revolution in Philosophy*, Macmillan, London, 1956. See specifically the Introduction by Gilbert Ryle, p. 5.
20. Russell, *Our Knowledge of the External World*, pp. 7–9.
21. John Passmore, *A Hundred Years of Philosophy*, pp. 215–16.
22. Ludwig Wittgenstein, *Philosophical Investigations*, translated by G. E. M. Anscombe, Basil Blackwell, Oxford, 1963, p. 51e.
23. For a statement of the critical and constructive tasks of philosophy as seen from the standpoint of contemporary analytic philosophy, see P. F. Strawson, 'Construction and Analysis', and G. J. Warnock, 'Analysis and Imagination', both in *The Revolution in Philosophy*.
24. Urmson, *Philosophical Analysis*, p. 25.
25. *Ibid.*, pp. 40–1.
26. *Ibid.*, p. 139.
27. *Ibid.*, p. 145.
28. Wittgenstein, *Philosophical Investigations*, p. 45e.
29. J. L. Austin, 'A Plea for Excuses', in J. L. Austin, *Philosophical Papers*, Oxford: at the Clarendon Press, 1961.
30. G. J. Warnock, 'Metaphysics in Logic', in *Essays in Conceptual Analysis*, ed. Antony Flew, Macmillan, London, 1956, pp. 90–93. This is only

part of a current dispute concerning the advisability of using an artificial language in philosophical discourse.

31. P. F. Strawson, *Introduction to Logical Theory*, Methuen, London, 1952; published in University Paperbacks series, 1963, p. 43.

32. *Ibid.*, pp. 211–13.

33. P. F. Strawson, 'On Referring', in *Essays in Conceptual Analysis*, Chapter II.

34. Strawson, *Introduction to Logical Theory*, Chapter 6.

35. Wittgenstein, *Philosophical Investigations*, p. 19e.

36. See, for example, E. Daitz, 'The Picture Theory of Meaning', in *Essays in Conceptual Analysis*, pp. 53–74.

37. For Russell's account of his thinking during the period of the influence of Wittgenstein and his later doubts and changing opinions, see *My Philosophical Development*, pp. 112–55.

38. Russell, 'Logic and Ontology', in *My Philosophical Development*, pp. 231–8.

39. Russell, 'Mr Strawson on Referring', *Ibid.*, pp. 238–45.

40. D. F. Pears, *Bertrand Russell and the British Tradition in Philosophy*, Collins, The Fontana Library, London and Glasgow, 1967.

41. Rudolf Carnap, 'Intellectual Autobiography', in *The Philosophy of Rudolf Carnap*, pp. 13 f.

42. A. J. Ayer, *Language, Truth and Logic*, Gollancz, London, 1936, Chapter III.

43. W. V. Quine, 'Russell's Ontological Development', *Journal of Philosophy*, Vol. LXIII, No. 20, Nov. 10, 1966, pp. 657–9.

44. *Ibid.*, p. 667. See also Carl G. Hempel, 'On Russell's Phenomenological Constructionism', in the same issue as above 668–70. This paper is a comment on Quine's paper, and in it Hempel agrees with Quine that the program of 'constructionism' has no hope of realization.

45. See, for example, G. D. Hicks, 'The Nature of Sense-data', *Mind*, XXI, No. 83, July 1912, pp. 399–409. D. Cory, 'Are Sense Data in the Brain?' *The Journal of Philosophy*, XLV, No. 20, Sept. 1948, pp. 533–48. E. P. Edwards, 'Are Percepts in the Brain?' *The Australasian Journal of Psychology and Philosophy*, XX, No. 1, June 1942, pp. 46–75.

46. John Dewey, *Essays in Experimental Logic*, The University of Chicago Press, 1916, pp. 403 f. For Russell's response to this criticism, see Bertrand Russell, 'Professor Dewey's "Essays in Experimental Logic" ', *The Journal of Philosophy, Psychology and Scientific Methods*, Vol. XVI, No. 1 (Jan. 2, 1919).

47. Russell, *My Philosophical Development*, pp. 139 f.

48. Russell, *Inquiry*, p. 329.

49. John Dewey, *Logic: The Theory of Inquiry*, Henry Holt, New York, 1938, pp. 154 *f.*
50. Bertrand Russell, *History of Western Philosophy*, p. 826.
51. In a letter to the author of September 30, 1967.
52. Elizabeth Ramsden Eames, 'A Discussion of the Issues in the Theory of Knowledge involved in the Controversy between John Dewey and Bertrand Russell', Unpublished doctoral dissertation, Bryn Mawr College, 1951.

SELECTED BIBLIOGRAPHY

Works by Bertrand Russell

RUSSELL, BERTRAND. *The Analysis of Matter*, George Allen and Unwin, London, 1927.

The Analysis of Mind, George Allen and Unwin, London, 1921.

Bertrand Russell's Dictionary of Mind, Matter and Morals. Ed. with introduction by Lester E. Dennon. Philosophical Library, New York, 1952.

A Critical Exposition of the Philosophy of Leibniz, Cambridge University Press, 1900.

'Definitions and Methodological Principles in Theory of Knowledge', *The Monist*, 24 October, 1914, pp. 582–93.

'Dewey's New Logic', in *The Philosophy of John Dewey*. Ed. Paul Arthur Schilpp. ('The Library of Living Philosophers,' V. 1.) Northwestern University Press, Evanston and Chicago, 1939, pp. 135–56.

History of Western Philosophy, George Allen and Unwin, London, 1945.

Human Knowledge: Its Scope and Limits, George Allen and Unwin, London, 1948.

Human Society in Ethics and Politics, George Allen and Unwin, London, 1954.

An Inquiry into Meaning and Truth, George Allen and Unwin, London, 1940.

Introduction to Mathematical Philosophy, George Allen and Unwin, London, 1919.

'Knowledge by Acquaintance and Knowledge by Description', *Proceedings of the Aristotelian Society*, 11, 1910–1911, pp. 108–28. Reprinted in *Mysticism and Logic*, 1918.

'The Limits of Empiricism,' *Proceedings of the Aristotelian Society*, 36, 1936, pp. 131–50.

'Logical Atomism', in *Contemporary British Philosophy: Personal Statements*, First Series. George Allen and Unwin, London, 1924. Reprinted in *Logic and Knowledge*.

'Logical Positivism', *Revue Internationale de Philosophie*, 4, 11, Janvier, 1950, pp. 3–19. Reprinted in *Logic and Knowledge*.

Logic and Knowledge: Essays 1901–1950. Ed. Robert Charles Marsh. George Allen and Unwin, London, 1956.

'Logic and Ontology', *Journal of Philosophy*, 54, April, 1956. Reprinted in *My Philosophical Development*.

'The Logic of Relations', in *Logic and Knowledge*. Translated from the French in Peano's *Revista di Matematica* [*Revue de Mathématiques*], 7, 1900–1901, pp. 115–48.

'Mathematical Logic as Based on the Theory of Types', *American Journal of Mathematics*, 30, 1908, pp. 222–62. Reprinted in *Logic and Knowledge*.

'Meinong's Theory of Complexes and Assumptions', *Mind*, 13, 1904, Vol. 1, pp. 204–19; Vol. 2, pp. 336–54; Vol. 3, pp. 509–24.

'Mr Strawson on Referring', in *My Philosophical Development*.

'My Mental Development', in *The Philosophy of Bertrand Russell*. Ed. Paul Arthur Schilpp. ('The Library of Living Philosophers', V. 5), Northwestern University Press, Evanston and Chicago, 1944.

My Philosophical Development, George Allen and Unwin, London, 1959.

'Mysticism and Logic', *Hibbert Journal*, 12, July, 1914, pp. 780–803. Reprinted in *Mysticism and Logic*.

Mysticism and Logic and Other Essays. Longmans, Green, New York, Bombay, Calcutta, Madras, 1918.

'The Nature of Truth', *Mind*, 15, 1906, pp. 528–33. Reprinted in *Philosophical Essays*.

'On Denoting', *Mind*, 14, 1905, pp. 479–93. Reprinted in *Logic and Knowledge*.

'On the Experience of Time', *The Monist*, 25, No. 2, April, 1915, pp. 212–33.

'On the Nature of Acquaintance', *The Monist*, 24, Nos. 1, 2, 3, 1914, pp. 1–16; 161–87; 435–53. Reprinted in *Logic and Knowledge*.

'On the Notion of Cause', *Proceedings of the Aristotelian Society*, 13, 1912–1913, pp. 1–26. Reprinted in *Mysticism and Logic*.

'On Order in Time', in *Logic and Knowledge*. Read to the Cambridge University Philosophical Society in March 1936.

'On Propositions: What They Are and How They Mean', *Proceedings of the Aristotelian Society*, Supplementary Vol. 2, 1919, pp. 1–43. Reprinted in *Logic and Knowledge*.

'On Vagueness', *The Australasian Journal of Psychology and Philosophy*, 1, 1923, pp. 84–92.

'On Scientific Method in Philosophy', in *Mysticism and Logic*. Herbert Spencer Lecture. First published, The Clarendon Press, Oxford, 1914.

'On Verification', *Proceedings of the Aristotelian Society*, 38, 1938, pp. 1–20.

Our Knowledge of the External World, Open Court Publishing Company, Lasalle, Illinois, 1914. Revised ed., George Allen and Unwin, London, 1917.

An Outline of Philosophy, George Allen and Unwin, London, 1927.

'Philosophical Analysis', *Hibbert Journal*, 54, July, 1956. Reprinted in *My Philosophical Development*.

Philosophical Essays, George Allen and Unwin, London, 1910. Revised ed., 1966.

'The Philosophical Importance of Mathematical Logic', *The Monist*, 23, No. 4, 1913, pp. 481–93.
'The Philosophy of Logical Atomism', *The Monist*, 28, October, 1918. Reprinted in *Logic and Knowledge*.
The Principles of Mathematics, Cambridge University Press, 1903. 2nd ed., 1938.
The Problems of Philosophy. (The Home University Library.) Williams and Norgate, London, 1912.
'Professor Dewey's "Essays in Experimental Logic"', *The Journal of Philosophy, Psychology, and Scientific Methods*, 16, January, 1919, pp. 5–26.
'The Relation of Sense-Data to Physics', *Scientia*, No. 4, 1914. Reprinted in *Mysticism and Logic*.
'Reply to Criticisms', in *The Philosophy of Bertrand Russell*. Ed. Paul Arthur Schilpp. ('The Library of Living Philosophers', V. 5), Northwestern University Press, Evanston and Chicago, 1944.
'Sensation and Imagination', *The Monist*, 25, January, 1915, pp. 28–44.
'The Ultimate Constituents of Matter', *The Monist*, 25, July, 1915. Reprinted in *Mysticism and Logic*.
Unpopular Essays, George Allen and Unwin, London, 1950.
'What Is Mind?', *Journal of Philosophy*, 55, January, 1958. Reprinted in *My Philosophical Development*.

Works by Other Authors

AUSTIN, J. L. 'A Plea for Excuses', *Proceedings of the Aristotelian Society*, 48, 1956–1957, pp. 1–29, Reprinted in J. L. Austin, *Philosophical Papers*. Ed. J. O. Urmson and G. J. Warnock. The Clarendon Press, Oxford, 1961.
AYER, A. J. 'Editor's Introduction', *Logical Positivism*. Ed. A. J. Ayer, The Free Press, Glencoe, Illinois, 1959.
Language, Truth and Logic, Gollancz, London, 1936.
AYER, A. J., et al. *The Revolution in Philosophy*, Macmillan, London, 1956.
BENJAMIN, A. C. 'The Logical Atomism of Bertrand Russell'. Unpublished Ph.D. dissertation, The University of Michigan, 1924.
BLACK, MAX. 'Russell's Philosophy of Language', in *The Philosophy of Bertrand Russell*. Ed. Paul Arthur Schilpp. ('The Library of Living Philosophers', V. 5.) Northwestern University Press, Evanston and Chicago, 1939.
BROAD, C. D. 'Critical and Speculative Philosophy', in *Contemporary British Philosophy: Personal Statements. First Series'* Ed. J. H. Muirhead. George Allen and Unwin, London, 1924.

CARNAP, RUDOLF. 'Die alte und die neue Logik', *Erkenntnis*, 1, 1930–1931. Trans. Isaac Levi in *Logical Positivism*, pp. 136–7.

'Intellectual Autobiography', *The Philosophy of Rudolf Carnap*. Ed. Paul Arthur Schilpp. ('The Library of Living Philosophers', V. 11), Open Court, Lasalle, Illinois, 1963.

CHISHOLM, RODERICK M. 'Russell on the Foundations of Empirical Knowledge', in *The Philosophy of Bertrand Russell*. Ed. Paul Arthur Schilpp. ('The Library of Living Philosophers', V. 5), Northwestern University Press, Evanston and Chicago, 1944.

CORY, D. 'Are Sense-Data in the Brain?', *The Journal of Philosophy*, 45, No. 20, September 23, 1948, pp. 533–48.

DAITZ, E. 'The Picture Theory of Meaning', in *Essays in Conceptual Analysis*. Ed. Antony Flew. Macmillan, London, 1956.

DEWEY, JOHN. *Essays in Experimental Logic*, The University of Chicago Press, 1916.

'Experience, Knowledge and Value: A Rejoinder', in *The Philosophy of John Dewey*. Ed. Paul Arthur Schilpp. ('The Library of Living Philosophers', V. 1), Northwestern University Press, Evanston and Chicago, 1939.

Logic: The Theory of Inquiry, Henry Holt, New York, 1938.

DORWARD, ALAN. *Bertrand Russell: A Short Guide to His Philosophy*. Published for the British Council. Longmans, Green, London, 1951.

EAMES, ELIZABETH G. RAMSDEN. 'The Consistency of Russell's Realism', *Philosophy and Phenomenological Research*, 27, No. 4, June, 1967.

'A Discussion of the Issues in the Theory of Knowledge Involved in the Controversy between John Dewey and Bertrand Russell.' Unpublished Ph.D. dissertation, Bryn Mawr College, 1951.

EDWARDS, E. P. 'Are Percepts in the Brain?', *The Australasian Journal of Philosophy and Psychology*, 20, No. 1, June, 1942, pp. 46–75.

EDWARDS, PAUL. 'Russell's Doubts about Induction', *Mind*, 48, No. 23, April, 1949. Reprinted in *Logic and Language*. First Series. Ed. Antony Flew, Basil Blackwell, Oxford, 1951.

FEIBLEMAN, JAMES. 'A Reply to Bertrand Russell's Introduction to the Second Edition of *The Principles of Mathematics*', in *The Philosophy of Bertrand Russell*. Ed. Paul Arthur Schilpp. ('The Library of Living Philosophers', V. 5), Northwestern University Press, Evanston and Chicago, 1944.

FRITZ, CHARLES A. *Bertrand Russell's Construction of the External World*, Routledge and Kegan Paul, London, 1952.

GÖTLIND, ERIK. *Bertrand Russell's Theories of Causation*, Almqvist Wiksells Boktryckeri AB, Uppsala, 1952.

GRÜNBAUM, ADOLF. *Philosophical Problems of Space and Time*, Alfred A. Knopf, New York, 1963.

HEMPEL, CARL G. 'On Russell's Phenomenological Constructionism', *The Journal of Philosophy*, 53, No. 20, November 10, 1966, pp. 668–70.

HICKS, G. D. 'The Nature of Sense-Data', *Mind*, 21, No. 83, July, 1912, pp. 399–409.

LAIRD, JOHN. 'On Certain of Russell's Views Concerning the Human Mind', in *The Philosophy of Bertrand Russell*. Ed. Paul Arthur Schilpp. ('The Library of Living Philosophers', V. 5), Northwestern University Press, Evanston and Chicago, 1944.

LEVI, ALBERT WILLIAM. *Philosophy and the Modern World*, The University of Indiana Press, 1953.

LOEWENBERG, J. 'Pre-Analytical and Post-Analytical Data', *Journal of Philosophy*, 24, January, 1927, pp. 5–14.

MOORE, G. E. 'Russell's "Theory of Descriptions" ', in *The Philosophy of Bertrand Russell*. Ed. Paul Arthur Schilpp. ('The Library of Living Philosophers', V. 5), Northwestern University Press, Evanston and Chicago, 1944.

NAGEL, ERNEST. 'Russell's Philosophy of Science', in *The Philosophy of Bertrand Russell*. Ed. Paul Arthur Schilpp. ('The Library of Living Philosophers', V. 5), Northwestern University Press, Evanston and Chicago, 1944.

PASSMORE, JOHN. *A Hundred Years of Philosophy*, Duckworth, London, 1957.

PEARS, D. F. *Bertrand Russell and the British Tradition in Philosophy*, Collins, London, 1967.

QUINE, W. V. 'On What There Is', *The Review of Metaphysics*, 2, September, 1948, pp. 21–8.
'Russell's Ontological Development', *The Journal of Philosophy*, 53, No. 20, November 10, 1966, pp. 657–69.

RIECHENBACH, HANS. 'Bertrand Russell's Logic', in *The Philosophy of Bertrand Russell*. Ed. Paul Arthur Schilpp. ('The Library of Living Philosophers', V 5), Northwestern University Press, Evanston and Chicago, 1944.

RIVERSO, EMMANUEL. *Il Pensiero di Bertrand Russell: Espozione Storico-critica*, Instituto Editoriale del Mezzogiorno, Naples, 1958.

RYLE, GILBERT. 'Theory of Meaning', in *British Philosophy in Mid-Century*. Ed. C. A. Mace. George Allen and Unwin, London.

SCHILPP, PAUL ARTHUR (ed.). *The Philosophy of Bertrand Russell*. ('The Library of Living Philosophers', V. 5), Northwestern University Press, Evanston and Chicago, 1944.

SCHOENMAN, RALPH. *Bertrand Russell: Philosopher of the Century, Essays in His Honour*, George Allen and Unwin, London, 1967.

STACE, W. J. 'Russell's Neutral Monism', in *The Philosophy of Bertrand Russell*. Ed. Paul Arthur Schilpp. ('The Library of Living Philosophers', V. 5), Northwestern University Press, Evanston and Chicago, 1944.

STEBBING, L. S. 'Constructions', *Proceedings of the Aristotelian Society*, 34, 1933–1934, pp. 1–30.

STRAWSON, P. F. *Introduction to Logical Theory*, Methuen, London, 1952.

'On Refining', *Mind*, 49, 1950, pp. 320–44. Reprinted in *Essays in Conceptual Analysis*.

THALHEIMER, R. *A Critical Exposition of the Epistemology and Psycho-Physical Doctrines of Bertrand Russell*, The Johns Hopkins Press, Baltimore, 1931.

URMSON, J. O. *Philosophical Analysis*, The Clarendon Press, Oxford, 1956.

'Some Questions Concerning Validity', in *Essays in Conceptual Analysis*.

USHENKO, ANDREW PAUL. 'Russell's Critique of Empiricism', in *The Philosophy of Bertrand Russell*. Ed. Paul Arthur Schilpp. ('The Library of Living Philosophers', V. 5), Northwestern University Press, Evanston and Chicago, 1944.

WARNOCK, G. J. *English Philosophy since 1900*, Oxford University Press, London, 1958.

'Metaphysics in Logic', in *Essays in Conceptual Analysis*.

WEITZ, MORRIS. 'Analysis and the Unity of Russell's Philosophy', in *The Philosophy of Bertrand Russell*. Ed. Paul Arthur Schilpp. ('The Library of Living Philosophers', V. 5), Northwestern University Press, Evanston and Chicago, 1944.

'The Method of Analysis in the Philosophy of Bertrand Russell.' Unpublished Ph.D. dissertation, The University of Michigan, 1943.

WHITEHEAD, A. N. *Process and Reality*, Macmillan, New York, 1929.

WHITEHEAD, A. N., and RUSSELL, BERTRAND. *Principia Mathematica*, Cambridge University Press, Vol. 1, 1910; Vol. 2, 1912; Vol. 3, 1913.

WITTGENSTEIN, LUDWIG. *Philosophical Investigations*. Trans. G. E. M. Anscombe, Basil Blackwell, Oxford, 1953.

Tractatus Logico-Philosophicus, Routledge and Kegan Paul, London, 1922.

WOOD, ALAN. *Bertrand Russell, The Passionate Sceptic: A Biography*, George Allen and Unwin, London, 1958.

INDEX

Acquaintance: with constituents of proposition, 67–8; and sensation, 92; and sense-data, 97; with simples, 98; with particulars, 132; with universals, 132; with self, 133; and analysis, 135

All, logical word, 116

Analogy, postulate of, 121

Analytic method: as 'prejudice', 48; levels of, 189; outcome of, 220–1; Chapter III *passim*

And, logical word, 116

Animal behaviour, and knowledge, 113. *See also* Behaviourism

Aristotelian logic: as opposed to symbolic logic, 64; weaknesses of, 64–6; existential inferences in, 64; subject and substance in, 64; predicates in, 64–5; relational propositions in, 65; metaphysical implications of, 66; and induction, 70

Artificial language: as logical technique 59–60; controversy concerning, 59–60; as opposed to ordinary language, 60; uses of, 61–3; assumptions concerning, 63; criticized by contemporary analysts, 204–5

Assumptions, necessary for analysis, 219–20

Atom, of experience, 90–1

Atomicity, and extensionality, Russell opposed to Wittgenstein, 120

Atomic propositions: and molecular propositions, 66–8, 87, 117; and fact, 67; components of name, 67; truth of, 147–8

Awareness, of self, 94

Ayer, A. J., on Russell, 15, 21, 209

Basic premises, and analysis, 112

Basic proposition: as problem, 108–9; and verification, 110; and analysis, 115; and fact, 118

Behavioural analysis: and basic premises, 112; and behaviourism, 112–13; and verbal knowledge, 114–15; and judgments of perception, 121

Behaviourism, and Russell's 'prejudice' 50

Behaviouristic psychology, influence on Russell, 102

Belief: definitions of, 140, 144–5; and judgment, 140–1; as organic state, 141–46; causal connections of 145–6;, as relation, 145; and behaviourism 146; correspondence with fact, 192

Benjamin, A. C., on Russell's logical atomism, 20

Black, Max, on Russell's theory of language, 13

Bloch, Werner, on Russell's concept of philosophy, 21

Bradley, F. H., internal relations in, 66

British Empiricism, and Russell, 190

Carnap, Rudolf: on levels of language, 72; influence of Russell on, 209

Cartesian scrutiny: of data, 99, 129; and objective credibility, 158–9

Cause: causal relations inferred, 95; causal theory of perception, 100, 106, 166, 192; 'causal' relation as 'seen', 109; causal connection of experience and proposition, 118; causal laws and induction, 160; and postulates of non-demonstrative inference, 121, 169–70; as observed uniform sequences of events, 160, 169; Humean concept of, 169; causal relation of fact and belief, 192

Certainty, subjective, *versus* objective credibility, 158–9

Changes in Russell's thought: as seen by Russell, 18–19; in analysis of experience, 101–22; summarized, 193–5

Chisholm, Roderick, on qualities, 13

Class: referent of class words, 171; as propositional function, 174

Coherence theory of truth, criticized, 152–4

Common sense beliefs, and sensation, 97

Complex described as complete, Russell and Wittgenstein differ, 120

Complex of compresence: and naming,

233

Logical contradictions: class which is member of itself, 70–1; and classes, 71; in *The Principles of Mathematics*, 71

Logical empiricism. *See* Logical positivism

Logical laws, status of, 161

Logically proper names: as basic epistemological problem, 67–9; and theory of descriptions, 75; and present experience, 117; non-relation terms, 176; and metaphysics, 178–180. *See also* Minimum vocabularies; Egocentric particulars

Logical method of analysis: 59; Chapter III *passim*

Logical positivism: Russell's relation to, 15; theory of truth of, 152–4; and pragmatism, Russell's response, 197; comment on Russell, 209

Logical symbolism, and Aristotelian logic, 64–6

Logical terms, referent of, 171

Logical truths: intuitive knowledge of 95; status of, 171; Wittgenstein on, 175; *a priori*, 175; changes in status summarized, 194

Logical words, and levels of language 116

Logic and the logical, in philosophical method, 45

Logic and philosophy: how related, 35, 40–3; change in view, 43–5

Logico-analytic method: in Russell, 189; Chapter III *passim*

Mabbott, J. D., specious present, 131. *See also* Specious present

Marsh, Robert Charles, early Russell in, 15

Materialism, Russell on, 51

Mathematical logic, relevance to philosophy, 61–3, 204–5

Meaning: analysed by components named, 73–4; expresses and indicates 143–44

Meinong, Alexius: incomplete symbols, 73; and sensation, 102; influence on theory of meaning, 174; mentioned, 191

Memory: given and inferred, 94; and data, 98

Metaphysical: theories of nature of world, 138; agnosticism rejected, 186; implications for universals, 186; assumptions, of analysis, 201–2

Method of analysis: as central theme, 56; defended, 57; produces knowledge, 57; levels of, 189; complexity of increases, 194–5; Chapter III *passim*

Method of construction: and analysis introduced, 72–8; and propositional functions, 76; and sense-data, 77; of 'thing', 77–8; in *The Analysis of Matter*, and *The Analysis of Mind*, 78; of scientific terms, 78–9; aim and use, 83–4; and Occam's razor, 84; survives in *Inquiry*, 120. *See also* Incomplete symbols; Theory of descriptions

Minimum vocabularies: and logical economy, 85; in *Inquiry*, 120; and metaphysics, 179–80; and science, 180; and method of construction, 180. *See also* Logically proper names

Mises-Reichenbach theory of probability, 163

Molecular propositions: distinguished from atomic, 66–8; as truth-functional, 68–9; non-truth-functional, 69. *See also* Atomic propositions

Monism: in metaphysics criticized, 199; in theory of truth criticized, 199

Moore, G. E., rejection of idealism, 172

Nagel, Ernest, on theory of matter, 14

Names: and simples, propositions and facts, 115–16. *See also* Logically proper names; Simples

Nature of philosophy, conflicting definitions, 34–5

Negative facts: accepted, 69; abandoned in *Inquiry*, 119

Neurath, Otto, and scope of philosophy, 51

Neutral nomism: described, 100; evaluated by Russell, 100–1; and immediate experience, 101; adopted by Russell, 101; Russell's emendation of, 102–3; effects of adopting, 108; changes in data because of, 127–8; William James and Russell, 211